ONE POINT SAFE

ANDREW and LESLIE COCKBURN

Anchor Books

DOUBLEDAY

NEW YORK   LONDON   TORONTO   SYDNEY   AUCKLAND

AN ANCHOR BOOK

PUBLISHED BY DOUBLEDAY

a division of Bantam Doubleday Dell Publishing Group, Inc.

1540 Broadway, New York, New York 10036

ANCHOR BOOKS, DOUBLEDAY, and the portrayal of an anchor are
trademarks of Doubleday, a division of Bantam Doubleday Dell
Publishing Group, Inc.

Book design by Stanley S. Drate/Folio Graphics Co. Inc.

Library of Congress Cataloging-in-Publication Data

Cockburn, Andrew, 1947–
One point safe / by Andrew and Leslie Cockburn.
p. cm.
Includes index.
1. Nuclear weapons—Russia (Federation) 2. Nuclear weapons
plants—Russia (Federation)—Security measures. 3. Nuclear weapons—
Government policy—Russia (Federation) 4. Smuggling—Russia
(Federation) I. Cockburn, Leslie. II. Title.
UA770.C628 1997
363.17′99′0947—dc21   97-23465
CIP

ISBN 0-385-48560-3

1   3   5   7   9   10   8   6   4   2

For Chloe, Olivia and Charlie

CONTENTS

BLACK JANUARY

The sabotage team crawled the last few yards through the snow, then rose cautiously to their feet. The first target loomed out of the darkness on top of the hill. As they expected, there were no guards, but before they set the first bomb they had to find the gauge. Risking a small light, one of them peered at the dial. It looked as if the huge tank was almost full. Hoisting the shaped-charge explosive, they carefully fastened it to the ice-cold metal and set the timer. It was designed to punch a hole clean through the skin, releasing tens of thousands of gallons of aviation fuel. Then they took the second bomb and put it on the ground directly beneath the first. There was enough dynamite to explode the JP-4 jet fuel gushing out of the hole and send a torrent of liquid fire down the hill and into the base. That would certainly keep the Americans busy.

Setting the second timer, they slid off down the hill. Now it was up to the others.

Down below, in the old Luftwaffe commandant's house, the telephone rang, at midnight, Central European time—the last breath of January 4, 1977. The colonel, his clothes folded away with habitual neatness, was just reaching to turn back the covers on his side of the bed when the ringing jerked him fully awake. Outside it was bitterly cold, with sheet ice covering most of the huge army base. Low clouds covered the moon and the glare of the lights of Frankfurt, thirty miles to the south.

"Burns."

"Duty officer here, sir. We have an incident. There's been an explosion. The jet-fuel tank up on the perimeter is burning."

The jet-fuel tank. Normally one hundred thousand gallons of JP-4 for the brigade helicopters. That stuff was hard to light. Someone had to have blown it deliberately.

"I'll be right over. Send my car and driver."

Ten years before, Bill Burns, graduate of Princeton and the Army War College, had been in combat in Vietnam. Now he commanded the 42nd Field Artillery Brigade at Giessen in the heart of Germany, and his base, peaceful ever since the last German commandant had surrendered in 1945, was under attack. The command post was a ten-minute drive away, and he still had to dress. Every second was precious. If he put on the ribbon-decked colonel's service uniform he had just hung in the closet, he could save the two minutes it would take to pull on and lace the calf-length combat boots that went with fatigues. But it looked like it was going to be a long night. If he was walking into a firefight on sheet ice, he needed the boots. He snatched his combat fatigues from the hanger.

The phone rang again. Ominous news from the duty officer.

"Sir, we have automatic weapons fire coming from the tactical area."

Burns tore out of the commander's house. His driver was nowhere to be seen. He fumbled for the keys of his own car, leapt into the driver's seat and raced to the headquarters. This was turning into something far more serious than any Vietcong attack. Giessen was not just another U.S. Army base. Burns commanded the Fort Knox of American tactical nuclear weapons.

No one without a need to know was meant to have the critical intelligence that his was the U.S. Army's main forward European depot for its nuclear arsenal. In the "tactical area," over on the far edge of the base, harsh floodlights glared down on unmarked storage bunkers. Behind the smooth steel doors was enough kilotonnage to wipe Germany off the map. Hundreds of eight-inch artillery shells and hundreds more warheads for the short-range Lance missile, each one a mini Hiroshima. Somebody was after them.

Roaring through the wide, empty streets of the sprawling military city, Burns had a good idea of who was doing the shooting. Six months before, he had driven down to Frankfurt to have a look at the bombed-out remains of the officers' club at V Corps headquarters in Frankfurt. Sixteen people were in the hospital. The next day the theater at the U.S. Air Force base at Wiesbaden had blown up—just two more bloody incidents in the vicious war being waged by the terrorist Baader-Meinhof gang. The string of murders, kidnappings and bombings they carried out across Germany had made them criminal celebrities. Ulrike Meinhof herself had recently hanged herself in a jail cell, but her bitter followers were fighting on, claiming credit as the "Ulrike Meinhof Brigade" for the havoc at the U.S. military targets. Their fierce, gaunt portraits stared out from wanted posters in airports and train stations all over Europe. They were fanatical, totally ruthless and very professional.

As he jumped out of the car at the command post, Burns could hear the sharp cracks of U.S. Army M-16s. He hoped they were following the orders he had laid down months before: anyone trying to get into the tactical area was to be shot on sight. That was the only way to guard nuclear weapons. He liked to remind his officers how, back when he was a junior officer in Germany in the 1950s, he literally lived with an arsenal of nuclear artillery shells. His battalion kept them stored in the cellar underneath the headquarters. A machine-gun team posted at the entrance had orders to kill anyone who didn't come up with the proper password very quickly. "The battalion lost more men that way than in combat in all of World War II," he told his officers at Giessen, without apology.

When he talked in this cold-blooded way, his lean frame taut and his narrow jaw set in intense concentration, none of his subordinates doubted that he meant it. Bill Burns was not a big man, but he had the straightedge spine and granite confidence that allows a commander of ordinary stature to fill a room. A keen student of military history and the Old Testament, he admired punctuality and intelligence and had little patience for those who fall short on either.

When this forty-four-year-old intellectual soldier took over Giessen he inherited a nuclear cache far too big to be hidden in a cellar. He was responsible not only for his own unit's warheads and shells but for those of other units in north-central Germany. The storage area lay a thousand yards from the outer fence of the base, isolated from the barracks by a no-man's-land of darkened warehouses. The site was set apart, lit like a Broadway stage and wrapped in a series of forbidding barriers—concertina wire, a chain-link fence and a thicket of barbed wire. A platoon of infantry was on twenty-four-hour guard. A company of armored infantry was on standby at all times, ready to rush to the rescue.

At headquarters the air was tense. The colonel was briefed on the run. The attackers had cut through the outer perimeter wire and were at the chain-link fence. German police had arrived and were blazing away outside the fence. The reserve guard company was racing to the scene in M-113 armored personnel carriers. The young lieutenant leading the platoon on the spot seemed to be keeping his head.

Down at the site, the platoon commander was firing steadily out through the wire and cursing the glare. The tactical area was always a blaze of floodlights, in case anyone sneaked in unobserved. But now he had the feeling he was onstage while out there people were shooting at him from the blackness. His orders were to hold and defend until the reserves arrived, but where were they? It had been nearly ten minutes since the first black-clad figure had appeared at the chain-link fence. He reassured his men that help was on the way and kept firing.

On the other side of the firefight, time was running out. The attackers had been counting on a massive diversion, but the twelve commandos of the Ulrike Meinhof Brigade could see that the plume of flame from their first bomb on the fuel tank was dying down. Why hadn't the second charge on the ground set off the conflagration that would distract the Americans?

Their plan had been ingenious—but with one fatal flaw. An American gauge reads differently from a German model. The diversion team thought the tank was nearly full—a hundred thousand gallons—and carefully placed the shaped charge well below what they thought was the surface level of the kerosene inside. But that night the tank really held only twenty thousand gallons, so the charge blew a hole eighteen inches *above* the surface of the fuel inside, igniting only fumes. There was no conflagration, no terrifying distraction for Burns and his men. The team assaulting the nuclear storage site were on their own.

The platoon at the site pumped bullets at the enemy struggling to hack their way through the chain-link fence. The minutes ticked by. Still no sign of the reserves, but the other side was taking casualties. Four of them went down, dragged away by their comrades.

Finally, after ten minutes, the reserve guard company arrived. By now the attackers were retreating back into the woods beyond the outer perimeter. That was territory that Bill Burns did not own. The German police arriving in full and noisy strength could take over now, though they seemed unnerved by the ferocity of the firefight they were joining. Back at the command post, Bill Burns slowly relaxed. It had been only twenty minutes since the first call to his bedroom, but in that short time, history had been made. No longer was it a question "if" terrorists wanted to steal a nuclear weapon. Tonight, they had actually *tried* to do it.

That history stayed secret. V Corps headquarters in Frankfurt knew, of course. But from there the news passed by only the most secure channels to the Pentagon, whence it disappeared into classified files. All that the outside world would learn was contained in a brief item, down-column on page 3, of the *International Herald Tribune* for January 6, 1977. It noted that "saboteurs" had cut through a fence at the U.S. Army base at Giessen and blown up a "gasoline" storage tank. There was no mention of nuclear weapons. After all, officially the warheads were not even there.

In Washington, President-elect Jimmy Carter was preparing his inaugural address and deploying his new administration. No one privy to the secret bothered to pass it on to the White House. An astonished Zbigniew Brzezinski, who became National Security Adviser just two weeks after the incident, learned of the attack only nineteen years later, when we told him what had happened.

There was only one visible clue that something strange had happened at Giessen. A sharp-eyed observer might have wondered why the officer of the guard and the midnight watch who defended the nuclear bunkers were suddenly sporting bright new medals on their dress uniforms.

Within five years Bill Burns was wearing a general's star, assigned to the powerful J5 Plans and Policy Directorate at the Pentagon. He was now in the upper reaches of nuclear warfighting policy as a representative of the Joint Chiefs of Staff for intermediate-range nuclear weapons—a long way from nighttime firefights at Giessen. This meant he was deeply involved in the intense diplomatic nuclear exchanges with the Soviets over their targeting new SS-20 missiles on Western Europe. With a break for a posting as deputy commandant of the

Army War College, Burns served the Joint Chiefs until 1986, when he was lofted to the State Department to run the powerful Bureau of Politico-Military Affairs. He had a front-row seat for the last campaigns of the cold war, a time when generals and their expert advisers still crafted intricate battle plans for the use of nuclear weapons in the heart of Europe.

There were several thousand such weapons in Germany alone. American nuclear land mines that fit in a backpack, artillery shells small enough to fit in a trunk, missiles two men could lift into a pickup. Batteries of longer-range Pershing missiles rumbled through the forests on mobile half-track launchers, their U.S. Army crews equipped with masks, respirators and protective suits that the war planners calculated regretfully as the fate of the infantry on both sides of the line.

The Russian troops behind the barbed wire, minefields and watchtowers that cut between East and West manned their short-range Frog nuclear missiles and longer-range nuclear Scuds. They tended their Soviet model land mines and cannons in their own version of the Giessen base, guarded by special troops of the General Staff and controlled by a mysterious unit called the Twelfth Department. Around the clock the miserable units dug in in the snow waited for the top secret codes that might arrive through the ether to unleash a nuclear war.

U.S. Army Field Manual 100-5, issued six months before the Baader-Meinhof gang breached the Giessen defenses, taught soldiers that nuclear firepower increased "lethality." A tactical nuclear weapon with a yield of one kiloton, or 2.2 million pounds of TNT, could kill as effectively as seven artillery battalions. A three-kiloton yield would burn troops to a crisp. But with the range of battlefield warheads the army had at its disposal, one to ten kilotons, the main killing agent was radiation. What the army called the "immediate incapacitation level" was estimated at 8,000–18,000 "rads." A soldier in a dugout exposed to 3,000 rads would collapse within three to five minutes. He might recover within an hour, but with bouts of

uncontrollable vomiting and diarrhea, he would be "only partially effective" until his death within a week. A soldier exposed
to 650 rads would show no symptoms. He would expire within
a month.

In conventional nuclear combat, advised the manual, the
prudent dose for assured death for the front-line enemy was
3,000–8,000 rads. That guaranteed the radiation would seep
into foxholes and revetments and penetrate the already oven-
like armored vehicles. The blast effects would knock out towns
as well as tanks and blow down the forests. It would cripple
helicopters, sending them to earth in flames. The thermal effects would burn anyone on the ground who was unprotected
and would explode supply dumps. Electromagnetic pulses
from the burst would sever communications. All telephones,
radios, televisions and computers would go dead.

The second stage would be sickness from what the army
called fallout, rainout and induced radiation. A nuclear
weapon detonated close to the earth's surface would suck dust
and debris into the air and deposit it as hot blankets of lethal
radiation. If it was raining, the cloud from a nuclear burst
would pass though the rain and fall back to earth in the drop-
lets as radioactive particles. Nuclear battlefield planners talked
about delivering a "pulse" of nuclear weapons, a package of
perhaps ten missiles, twenty artillery shells, five air-dropped
bombs, to wipe out enemy troops. Such plans, refined in secret
over decades, were the preserve of the high priests of nuclear
strategy and at the exclusive disposal of high-ranking generals
and heads of state.

Bill Burns spoke the language of the nuclear priesthood,
but, as he soared through the ranks, he also carried with him
the searing—and unique—memory of what the Baader-Meinhof gang had done. And when, on the crest of his career, the
Soviet Union began to buckle and heave, General Burns could
see all too clearly that a nightmare was unfolding.

As the Berlin Wall came down in November 1989, it exposed

a crumbling empire littered with some 45,000 nuclear weapons, up to half of them the kind of battlefield weapons he had grown up with as an artillery officer. He knew just how much assured death and immediate incapacitation could come from just one short-range missile warhead or artillery shell in the hands of a terrorist. Back at Giessen his guards had been well fed, properly paid and highly trained. There had been an efficient police force to back them up on the outside. Even so, the attackers had made it to the fence. In a dissolving Soviet Union, things might be very different.

•

"Holy shit!"

In windowless offices all over Washington, intelligence officers stared openmouthed at the classified cable that had come in from Moscow overnight. That morning in late January 1990, the world they knew was drawing to an end.

Rebels fighting Moscow's rule in Baku, the capital of the southern republic of Azerbaijan, the message announced, had stormed the perimeter of an army base and tried to steal the nuclear weapons stored there.

The news quickly spread around the huge subterranean network of the Washington intelligence community. "Did you see what happened in Baku?"

"Jesus Christ—do you think they got anything? What do they have down there anyway?"

"Baku, that's Fourth Army Headquarters. There's a bunch of tactical stuff for the southern TVD. Maybe they even have some torpedo warheads for the Caspian torpedo training school."

"Does NSA have any cuts on this?"

Nationalist rebellion had been festering in the outer reaches of the Soviet empire for some time. The Berlin Wall had come crashing down the previous month, and the Eastern European satellites were ready to fall like ripe fruit. The previous April,

Russian soldiers had run amok amidst a crowd of nationalist demonstrators in the Georgian capital, Tbilisi, hacking at women and children with sharpened shovels. Mikhail Gorbachev had just returned from a fruitless effort to steer the Lithuanians away from demanding independence. Now the rot had spread to Azerbaijan, a Shiite Muslim enclave on the Iranian border, where the Soviet occupation had always had shallow roots.

At roughly eight o'clock in the evening of January 19, with a frozen wind whipping off the Caspian Sea, a bomb blew apart the Baku television station. The sound of the explosion rumbled over the provincial capital, followed by four hours of uneasy silence. At midnight, the sky over the sprawling oil port that for centuries had attracted fire worshippers to the burning Surakhany fountains of natural gas lit up with brilliant arcs of tracer fire. Machine gun bursts ushered in tanks and armored personnel carriers erupting from the Soviet bases in and around the city and lumbering down the broad avenues, laid out at the turn of the century when Baku oil was controlled by great oil barons like Rothschild and Nobel. The Red Army was retaking the city from the rebel's Committees of National Defense.

Among these rebels was a group of "real crazies," as one U.S. intelligence official called them, "very close to the Gray Wolves." That was a sinister affiliation. The Gray Wolves were the right-wing Turkish zealots who had sent an assassin to shoot Pope John Paul II. The fledgling Wolves in Baku also had a covert relationship with Heidar Aliev—"Lizard Eyes"—a former KGB general who had once ruled as the undisputed boss of Azerbaijan. Displaced by Moscow a few years before, he was now intriguing with Machiavellian cunning to regain his power. It was these men who had recently torn down the fortified border fence with Iran, an act hailed by the Ayatollahs as an act of "Islamic zeal." In Baku itself they had commandeered trucks and buses for use as makeshift barricades outside the army and navy bases. Then, in the third week of January 1990, Nimet Panakhov, a fiery intriguer very much associated with the Gray Wolves, declared to a huge nationalist rally overflowing Lenin Square in the heart of the city that his men were ready to storm a Soviet base and seize a nuclear warhead.

Thousands of miles away in a Munich studio, Azerbaijani exile Mirza Michaeli was covering the events for the U.S. government-sponsored Radio Liberty. A fervent nationalist, he was exhorting his countrymen over the airwaves to rise up and "kill the giaour"—the infidels—but in between bloodthirsty broadcasts he stayed on the phone to Baku through an illegal hookup running twenty-four hours a day. He was among the few outsiders who knew of Panakhov's ominous threat. Nuclear storage sites were as big a secret in the U.S.S.R. as the Giessen dump was meant to have been in Germany, but Panakhov knew about the depot at the Bailov base as well as the nuclear torpedoes kept by the Caspian Sea flotilla at Zyh. "Maybe he knew about the sites from Heidar Aliev himself," said Michaeli later but "he definitely announced at a rally that January that he was going to take over the weapons. The whole place was sliding into anarchy."

In Washington, President George Bush pulled the Soviet ambassador aside at a private White House dinner and told him that he understood Soviet leader Mikhail Gorbachev's need to restore order. The Kremlin had a green light to send in the tanks before it was too late.

The barricades of buses, trucks and cars were no match for the massive T-72 tanks and BMP armored fighting vehicles that came crashing out of the military bases just after midnight. Behind them came squads of camouflaged infantry, firing automatic rifles indiscriminately at terrified civilians running through the streets. No one knows for sure how many died— but Baku natives later talked in hushed tones of thousands. Even to this day that time is still known as Black January in Azerbaijan.

The city dissolved in chaos. Anyone venturing out of doors was liable to be shot on sight. The rebel defenders were lightly armed with pistols, hunting rifles and a few machine guns. Some weapons had been smuggled across the border from Iran. But they did manage to put up some resistance and, at the Zyh naval base, someone did try to carry out Panakhov's threat. Fighting continued there for twenty-four hours after the military had crushed resistance elsewhere in the city. In the harbor, Panakhov's men commandeered a tanker and dragged a field gun onto the deck, from which they bombarded the enemy.

The city had been closed to foreigners weeks before the troops went in, but in distant Washington, D.C., intelligence officers and other government officials endowed with the indispensable "need to know" could assess the panic within the Russian nuclear bureaucracy from communications intercepts. The Twelfth Department headquarters in Moscow was getting signals that their men and their precious warheads were under siege. The same signals came via the circuits of the Third Directorate of the KGB, whose duties as secret policemen included monitoring the soldiers of the Twelfth. Faced with the threat to the nukes, the Soviet Fourth Army command in Baku sent urgently for reinforcements.

Ill-armed militias could stand out for only so long against tanks and thousands of heavily armed troops, and the Azerbaijanis never got their nuclear weapon. But a wall had been breached. The Soviet Union was visibly crumbling and now it was apparent that a vast nuclear arsenal could come adrift in the wreckage. The notion sent chills around the world.

It was a possibility that had been slow to dawn on both the White House and the Kremlin. The U.S. government had watched Mikhail Gorbachev's efforts to reform the Communist system with a wary and skeptical eye. Even when officials came to believe that the Russian leader really was serious about changing the U.S.S.R., they could barely grasp the incredible thought that this could lead to the breakup of the whole country and the downfall of Communism. Finally, someone at the top thought they'd better pay attention.

On July 18, 1989, Deputy National Security Adviser Robert Gates wrote an "eyes only" memo to President George Bush. Recent reports from the CIA, he noted, indicated that the situation inside the Soviet Union was beginning to deteriorate very quickly. "We must begin to think," he told the President, "about the possibility . . . [of] significant political instability. In terms of the future, we should very quietly begin some contingency planning as to possible U.S. responses, actions and policies in the event of leadership or internal policy changes or widespread ethnic violence."

As a result, Gates was authorized to set up a very small planning group of senior officials from the White House, State Department, Pentagon and CIA to think about the unthinkable—a fracture of the Soviet system. Known only as the "Rice group," because it met in the office of National Security Council Soviet specialist Condoleeza Rice, the team operated in total secrecy. Heading the list of their most urgent priorities was the safety of the Soviet nuclear arsenal. It was the tactical stockpile that concerned Gates most, particularly the fact that no one seemed to know just how big it was. CIA estimates ranged between fifteen and twenty-five thousand warheads. "Any time you have a spread of ten thousand," laughed Gates, "you know you don't have a very good grip."

More distressingly, no one was sure that the Soviets themselves had much of a grip. The books might be in order for newer systems like SS-20 missile warheads, but Gates and his officials had little faith in Soviet accounting on the older weapons, half-forgotten relics of a generation of nuclear build-up. "Land mines, artillery shells, torpedo warheads. The Russians didn't maintain good accounts on anything else, why should we assume they did on warheads?"

Black January in Baku confirmed every suspicion that had

caused Gates to set up his team in the first place: ethnic unrest, terrorist connections and old warheads at risk. A volatile cocktail indeed. The CIA's take was stark: armed dissidents had almost captured a nuclear warhead. They were getting near the edge of the precipice.

If it was impossible to count the number of Soviet warheads—how could a satellite look through the roof of a locked building?—then at least the United States needed to find out where they were. As part of the secret planning promoted by Gates, a five-person team in the CIA's Office of Soviet Affairs was detailed on a special assignment. Their job was to follow the Soviet nukes whenever they were taken out of the storage sites and moved.

It was not long before the CIA team began to report something extraordinary going on in the U.S.S.R. The bodies had hardly been buried in Baku when the satellites snapped long trains snaking through the Caucasus Mountains and into the Slavic heartland. To the uninitiated they looked liked ordinary freight trains. But an analyst who devoted his working life to the arcane study of Soviet nuclear transport systems concluded that the ventilation ducts on the roofs of nuclear weapons freight cars were shaped slightly differently from those on ordinary wagons. That meant only one thing: the cargo was warheads.

And the trains were not just coming out of Azerbaijan. Moscow had made the decision to pull all tactical nuclear weapons out of ethnic areas before they erupted. Trains rolled out of the Baltic States, where events were soon to take the same bloody turn as in Baku. Cars stacked with warheads pulled out of Uzbekistan, Tajikistan, Turkmenistan. So precipitous was the retreat of the Soviet forces from East Germany that the amazed CIA analysts detected weapons being moved in ordinary wagons so decrepit that the rain leaked in. U.S. intelligence received reports that one weapon waiting to be shipped from

Armenia had actually been stolen, only to be retrieved three days later.

It was a retreat from empire that the Soviet high command was soon to admit publicly. The chief of the General Staff himself, General Mikhail Moiseyev, declared in September 1990 that because of a "situation that doesn't fully correspond to the concept of national security, the warheads have been put in a more secure place." The following day the Ministry of Defense denied everything. Chaos was creeping into the heart of the beast. Mikhail Gorbachev, desperate to preserve his fraying inheritance, sought to capitalize the fact that his country was spinning out of control. If the West did not help preserve the Soviet Union, he told President Bush, the alternative would be nuclear anarchy, with the United States facing fifteen nuclear states amidst the ruins of the U.S.S.R. The threat was potent enough for Bush to make a desperate plea in July 1991 for Soviet ethnic minorities to stay away from "suicidal nationalism." But it was all too late. By the end of 1991 the Soviet Union was gone forever.

In Russia, there was little or no room for the weapons so hurriedly evacuated from the former colonies. They overflowed the existing bunkers. The head of the Russian nuclear weapons program loudly complained that they were "sticking out of warehouse windows." The White House had to have a firsthand assessment of just how bad things were on the ground, and the President appointed a Special Envoy to Russia for Nuclear Dismantlement. He turned to the man who had more practical experience than anyone of nuclear weapons at risk.

General Bill Burns took the call from the White House at home in Carlisle, Pennsylvania, and accepted the President's request. In March 1992 the new President's Special Envoy drove down Route 15 to the 270 spur and onto the Dulles Airport access road. At international departures General Burns flashed his passport with the VIP White House visa in Cyrillic script and boarded his flight to Moscow.

2

Z DIVISION

Every morning Jerry Dzakowic drives through the hills above the San Francisco Bay down Tesla Road to the valley floor, where he spends his days in a complex that has been described as the most feared laboratory on earth.

From the outside, there is little sign of what people do at Livermore Laboratory. The perimeter of the huge complex is bounded by a wire fence with yellow signs forbidding trespassing or loitering. The lab is a sprawling collection of temporary-looking buildings and trailers intermingled with massive concrete structures. Immediately inside the fence is a "white" area. Even members of the public can penetrate this far. When Jerry turns his baby-blue Mercedes 280 in through the main gate, he stops at the first guard post and shows them his ID badge. If the guard is following the rules he will examine it closely and touch it to make sure that it is not a fake.

Now Jerry is in the "red" area. This is as far as some of the lab workers go. They may be engaged in cancer research or

16

probing the greenhouse effect on the world's weather. There are many such projects at Livermore, but they have no military application. People who work here do not have high security clearances and they wear red identification badges. Even so, outsiders can enter the red area only if their visit has been cleared and they are escorted by an authorized person from the inside.

Jerry has to park his car before he can pass through the next barrier. Beyond this point only government cars are allowed. He steps into a booth and slides his ID badge into a slot in the wall. As he does so, he punches a series of numbers, a personal identification code, on the keypad next to it. It looks like a bank ATM machine, but this machine is judging him. The floor is actually a scale that silently measures his weight so that the security computer can compare it with the recorded weight on his personnel file. A few extra pounds are allowed in case he is wearing a winter coat or carrying an especially heavy briefcase that day. If the weight is way off, the doors of the CAIN-II booth lock shut until the guards come to investigate. The computer records the time he passed through.

This is the "green" area; only people with green ID cards can enter here. Sometimes people who are not "green" have permission to go farther, but they must pass through a special gate and be inspected by the security personnel. Then they wait for an escort, who will remain with them every minute they are inside the area. Should they go into one of the nondescript office buildings scattered across the concrete, signs flash in the corridor announcing "Uncleared visitor on premises. No classified discussions," reminding them that there are mysteries here from which they are excluded.

Jerry is going deeper. Once in the green area he collects an ID badge that is itself so secret that he is not allowed to take it home. This one is colored blue. Now he can pass through another ATM-type booth, the last barrier, into the "blue" area, and get on with the day's business.

There is no view of the hills from his office. In fact, there are no windows in the building where he works. The walls are lined with copper mesh as a protection against electronic eavesdroppers. In the language of security and classification that pervades the lab, this building is the SCIF, the *Sensitive Compartmented Information Facility*. In the layers of secrecy inside Livermore, each bounded by more rigorous security than the last, the SCIF is the most tightly guarded of all. It is the home of Z Division.

Ask the average person to name the various U.S. intelligence agencies and they will probably stop short at the CIA. More knowledgeable people will mention the DIA—Defense Intelligence Agency—and perhaps the intelligence "shops" of each military service or the military-run National Security Agency with its massive electronic eavesdropping capacity. Far down the list might come the State Department's INR, a lesser sibling of the giant agencies. Few will know that there is an intelligence division, the Office of Threat Assessment, devoted to nuclear matters at the Department of Energy. Only those with jobs in coded vaults in the White House and inside the community will add Z Division to the list.

Jerry first arrived at Livermore at a time when the superpowers were still spending untold billions to maintain their position in the global nuclear standoff. The lab was booming, a cornerstone of America's nuclear might. Just twenty-five years before he got there, Livermore had been a small, sleepy farm town on the road to Gilroy and the Central Valley. The townspeople lived off the cattle ranches that spread over the hills or the Wente Brothers and Concannon wineries on the valley floor. Apart from the small air base just east of the town belonging to the U.S. Navy, things hadn't changed much since the town was founded back in 1869.

In 1952, however, Washington decided to establish a new research laboratory. It was to have one function: the perfection of the thermonuclear "H" bomb, the ultimate weapon. The

United States already had one nuclear weapons design center, at Los Alamos in the mountains of New Mexico. The first atomic weapons had been designed and built there. These had been fission bombs, equivalent in destructive power to thousands of tons of TNT, and two of them had destroyed the cities of Hiroshima and Nagasaki. But in August 1949 the sky over a remote desert in Kazakhstan had lit up with the brilliant flash of the first Russian nuclear test. Now the race was on to build a weapon that would be thousands of times more powerful. The government decided that Livermore, convenient for the scientific powerhouse of the University of California at Berkeley, would be an ideal site for the new lab. The year it was born the first H-bomb test vaporized an entire island in the South Pacific.

Jerry was ten years old at the time, growing up on the South Side of Chicago, an easygoing boy from a staunch Catholic family. Like other children of that era, he learned in school about "duck and cover," how to hide under the classroom desks if the Russians should suddenly come and drop the Bomb. His main interests were already in the mechanical side of things. When he got to Michigan Tech, majoring in mechanical engineering, the writing requirements nearly caused him to flunk. By that time Livermore had grown to a workforce of 3,000. Behind the fences they had already refined the art of weapons design to the point where they could make a thermonuclear device small enough to fit on a missile launched from a submarine, the Polaris.

After getting his master's, Jerry went to work for the Westinghouse Corporation at their research center in Pittsburgh. Those were the days of the Apollo moon program and unlimited space budgets. Jerry was part of a team developing a nuclear-powered rocket for a mission to Mars. Then Neil Armstrong landed on the moon and America lost interest in further space exploration. Westinghouse folded the nuclear rocket effort and Jerry moved into research on the newly discovered technology of lasers. In 1974 he got the call to come to Livermore.

The lab wanted him to work on the futuristic technology of fusion power. The idea was that by "imploding"—crushing—a tiny pellet of hydrogen-deuterium fuel with enormously powerful lasers, it would be possible to release enough energy to provide a limitless supply of power. It was a benign side of the lab's work, even if the basic science was weapons-related, but Livermore's principal function was still the development and perfection of weapons of mass destruction. And before very long, Jerry found himself drawn into weapons work.

People who work with nuclear weapons form a distinct and sharply defined group, for they alone are "Q-cleared" and entitled to access the secrets of Restricted Data. The first Russian test had come as a great shock to the United States, and it was commonly believed that the Soviets could only have done it with the help of spies and traitors among the American nuclear community. Such a disaster was not to be allowed to happen again. In 1954 Congress passed the Atomic Energy Act, which classified as Restricted Data any information concerning the design, manufacture or use of nuclear weapons or the "special nuclear material"—plutonium and enriched uranium—that gives them their power. A new priesthood was created, its membership determined by their access to the mysteries of RD. Any ideas they had about the weapons or their components, any stray jottings or scrawls on a blackboard, were automatically secret, forever shielded from any and all outsiders.

No one can be initiated into this world without receiving a "Q clearance." Before this is granted the candidate's life must be examined in the most minute detail for any signs of disloyalty, instability, suspicious associations or habits, suspicious relatives (however distant), or anything else that might render him or her unworthy. Only when all reports are positive can a Livermore worker receive the coveted status of "Q-cleared" and the green identification badge that goes with it. That day is an important rite of passage. Livermore employees talk of "turning green."

Jerry does not look like a member of a priesthood. Genial but modest, an intelligence agency might want him for his looks alone, utterly ordinary and therefore invisible. His hair is receding. He wears eyeglasses that are often smudged and a zip-up windbreaker to hide a slight paunch. All in all he gives the impression of a middle manager with an errand to run at the hardware store, an impression that would be quite mistaken.

Most of his fellow commuters along Vasco Road to the main gate of the lab look similarly unassuming, remarkable only for the fact that for years the day's work for most of them has centered on ever more perfect ways of achieving mass destruction. They speak of it in unemotional, scientific terms, avoiding the more lurid aspects of nuclear weapons effects, such as the tendency of survivors' skin to slip off in large pieces. Jerry himself is far from a Strangelove, but his description of his first major weapons project is disarmingly low-key, especially in view of the emotional reaction it provoked in the world outside. In the mid-1970s the Livermore physicists came up with an elegant variation on the traditional thermonuclear weapon. The proper technical term for it was the "enhanced radiation" weapon, so called because it produced less destructive blast but vastly more lethal radiation than a traditional bomb. It became better known to the world as "the neutron bomb."

Sitting on the terrace of a winery near the lab on a sunny March day, with the hills still that vivid Irish green that had once helped lure him westward from a Pittsburgh winter, Jerry sums up the weapon's attributes as being to "essentially kill the enemy troops in place promptly and not destroy the city. The troops would be in their tanks, dead."

"The physics guys," as he calls them, the lofty Brahmins who came up with the concept, could prove that the principle worked. Jerry's challenge was to figure out how to package the device so that someone could actually use it, in this case as an eight-inch nuclear artillery shell. "The engineers come along and make it hold together. Shooting it out of a gun is a pretty interesting engineering problem, [given] its high acceleration as it's spun and launched," he explains as he picks at a chicken Caesar salad, one of the specials on the winery's restaurant menu that day. "It has to not go nuclear and explode in the gun, but at the other end when it's coming down."

Jerry solved the "interesting engineering problem" brilliantly. His eight-inch neutron shell went into the U.S. weapons stockpile, where it was officially known as the W79. But the problems had only just begun. The U.S. Army thought it would be ideal for use in Europe; Soviet invaders would die without Germany being blasted into rubble. The European public had a different reaction.

The new weapon was meant to be top secret, but its existence leaked out through a stray line item in the Pentagon budget. The notion of annihilating armies and—inevitably—civilians in the heart of Europe while leaving the architecture intact set off massive demonstrations and shouting matches in European parliaments. NATO was strained to the breaking point. People were afraid that such a "surgical" device made nuclear war fighting, the use of nuclear weapons by U.S. Army units like Bill Burns's 42nd Field Artillery Brigade in the middle of Germany, more palatable and therefore more probable. The Carter administration caved in under the storm of protest.

"We never did get the neutron [shell] into Europe," recalls Jerry with a good-natured laugh. "It was political. So from there, I went into underground testing." He gives another jolly laugh. "I've had a fun time. I've been to Nevada and felt the earth shake."

North of Las Vegas in the Nevada desert there lies a strange cratered landscape the size of Rhode Island, a monument to decades of U.S. underground nuclear tests. Once upon a time, before the superpowers agreed to stop testing aboveground, the U.S. Air Force had made a romantic film about the place, calling it "the valley where the giant mushrooms grow, the atomic clouds, the towering angry ghosts of the fireballs."

Nearby is a town called Mercury, almost deserted now. This was the base camp for the nuclear weapons teams while they prepared to blow radioactive holes in the earth. Mindful of how much of his life has been classified, Jerry will admit only that he made the journey to Mercury "more than twenty-five and less than a hundred and fifty" times.

Testing was where the work carried out at Livermore became real. Ever since 1961, all tests had been carried out underground. When a device went off, hundreds of feet down a twelve-foot-wide shaft drilled into the desert floor, some 5,000 intricately crafted components went through enormously complicated interactions that thousands of lab workers had spent a year designing. In the shaft, next to the device, an array of sensitive instruments enclosed in a huge canister weighing hundreds of tons monitored the process of the actual nuclear explosion. Sometimes, when they wanted to test the effect of a weapon on objects such as military vehicles, the necessary objects would be lowered into another huge horizontal tunnel deep in the earth to be blown up. For Jerry's neutron shell they took big howitzers down there and fired them.

Jerry was in charge of all the preparations for monitoring the test. If the instruments packed in the canister did not tell the scientists watching on the surface what was happening, the whole exercise would be a waste of time. Sometimes, after everything was in place deep below and thousands of tons of gravel had been poured down to seal the shaft, Jerry would find that one of the cables to the instruments had been broken. That meant he had to vacuum all the gravel out again so that the break could be repaired. When the countdown ticked toward zero hour for a test, the pressure was intense. By now, as Jerry's highly trained and specialized crews worked late into the night, the cost was running at $50,000 an hour. Finally, he and the scientists who had designed the bomb crowded into trailers carefully positioned a few miles from ground zero. Too far and they might lose some of the precious data. Too near and the shock could knock the trailers off the ten-foot-high blocks of white cushioning foam on which they sat.

The whole procedure was designed to track a series of events that passed in an infinitesimal fraction of a second before the searing blast of the nuclear explosion vaporized the test bomb and the canister, creating a huge cavern alive with molten rock and radioactivity. The watchers aboveground could see only a puff of dust rising above the point of the explosion. They waited and watched as minutes, sometimes hours went by. Finally, the surface at ground zero slowly sank into a saucer shape. Down below, the underground cavern was collapsing under the weight of earth and rock, adding another crater to the Nevada moonscape. "Each bomb had different characteristics, different experimental objectives," remarks Jerry matter-of-factly. "When they go off, they all feel the same, like an earthquake."

In the outside world, politicians and others sometimes talked about banning nuclear tests altogether. President Carter had made agreement on a Comprehensive Test Ban a priority of his administration, but opposition from the military—and the weapons scientists—ensured that nothing came of it. Instead, the 1980s brought the hawkish Ronald Reagan and his team to the White House. They talked of "winnable" nuclear war and a "Star Wars" missile defense. The Livermore budget soared to a billion dollars a year, and the desert shook to an accelerating tempo of test explosions. An elite team at the laboratory labored to develop a nuclear-driven X-ray laser for Star Wars, with money no object. This was to be part of what they called the third-generation nuclear weapons. For the Star Wars tests Jerry had to construct what amounted to an entire laboratory underground, ready to be obliterated in a fraction of a second.

But the world was changing. Reagan's rhetoric frightened people. Driving down Vasco Road to work in the mornings, Jerry got used to crowds of demonstrators outside the gates chanting antinuclear slogans. There were signs that the other side was tiring of the competition and ready to drop out of the race. In 1985, for example, the Soviet leader, Mikhail Gorbachev, announced that he was suspending testing. The United States paid no attention and after eighteen months the Russian explosions resumed. Gorbachev was talking about far-reaching reforms in the U.S.S.R. but meanwhile Livermore designers were hard at work on the X-ray laser as well as new and interesting warhead developments, including a new Cruise missile warhead, an "earth-penetrating" warhead and an underwater nuclear depth charge.

By now the fundamental principles of warheads and bombs were well established. The first bombs that had come out of Los Alamos seemed primitive and crude in comparison with the modern designs. Physicists and engineers like Jerry concentrated on ways to make the weapons "safer," to reduce the risk of an accidental explosion, or smaller and more "efficient" by using less plutonium, the deadly "fissile" heart of U.S. nuclear weapons. They explored interesting ways to produce explosions with extra radiation, as with Jerry's neutron shell, or the opposite, a heavy blast with very little radiation, or "dial a yield" weapons, in which the size of the explosion could be selected just before use, or "nuclear backpacks" that could be carried by just one soldier. It was subtle and challenging work, based on decades of experience. Only three other communities in the world could fully understand what they were doing. First and foremost there was Los Alamos, Livermore's deadly rival. "The Soviets are the competition," lab scientists used to joke, "Los Alamos is the enemy," At Los Alamos, high up on the mesa above Santa Fe in New Mexico, they returned the enmity, referring to their rivals as "Livermites."

The "competition" was more abstract. What little was

known about the Soviet labs remained shrouded in layers of classification and "need to know," but it was known that there were two design labs, just as in the United States. Arzamas 16, a few hundred miles from Moscow, where the first Soviet bomb had been designed and built, and Chelyabinsk 70, set amidst the forests of the Ural Mountains on the edge of Siberia. These were remote places, in thought as well as reality. The scientists who lived and worked there, crafting their own subtle variations on nuclear weapons designs, were on the other side of an unbridgeable gulf. They too might be working on their own versions of "dial a yield" or the nuclear backpack, but very little leaked out. Soviet security was very good, especially where nuclear weapons were concerned. Every so often the seismographs at Livermore would quiver as a test explosion deep under the desert of eastern Kazakhstan or the Arctic island of Novaya Zemlya sent shock waves pulsing through the earth's crust. A sign of life from the other side.

Then one day in December 1987, Jerry found Russians at Mercury. Not just any Russians, but an elite team of Soviet nuclear weapons scientists. Among them was an ebullient physicist with a penchant for hard liquor and attractive women named Victor Mikhailov. He had recently been put in charge of all nuclear weapons development in the U.S.S.R. Mikhailov and his group were at the closely guarded test site by official invitation because the two governments had agreed, after long haggling, to a joint experiment to check the "yield" of each other's tests. A group from the American labs had journeyed to Semipalatinsk, the Soviet testing ground in the desert of northeastern Kazakhstan. Senior officials, taking a sudden interest in the grunt work of testing, rushed to commandeer the spaces on the historic expedition. Jerry and his friends looked at a photograph from the "Semi" trip of some Americans hard at work. "Look at those four guys hauling on a cable," one of them remarked. "They all get $150,000 a year."

It was the first time Jerry had ever glimpsed the competition. It was exciting to meet what he called "the guys from the other team," but despite the enthusiasm of arms controllers hailing this token of cold-war thaw, he had strong doubts about the whole exercise. For one thing, they got in the way of any interesting testing. "What can you test when you have the Russians standing there, making measurements right there?" he complained. More important, the radioactive garbage littering the desert floor could yield secrets to an expert eye. The other team was under careful watch (an attractive female FBI agent decked one overly attentive Russian general), but the right handful of dirt could speak volumes about what was going on behind the high security fences at Livermore.

Whatever Jerry's suspicions about the visitors, the world that had nurtured Livermore was almost at an end. Gorbachev was contemplating unprecedented concessions on arms control even as he struggled to reform the sclerotic Soviet system. The cold war that fed the 8,000 Livermore employees and millions more around the world was winding down.

It took a while to sink in. Early in 1988, Bill Green, a Stanford University professor of Soviet studies who doubled as a reserve officer in Naval Intelligence, came and gave a lecture about events in the U.S.S.R. The Soviet Union, he bluntly told the bomb makers, was finished. Mikhail Gorbachev, he explained, was moving to allow relatively free elections for the first time in Soviet history. Green was certain that this would give nationalist minorities across the U.S.S.R. a platform and they would go on to press their demands for separation. At that point, he believed, the Soviet Union would begin to fall apart. He made one other point. Regions liable to split off from Moscow had a lot of nuclear weapons on their territory. What would happen to them?

This was all very interesting and the audience gave the professor a big hand, but for them, as for most people, the concept was far too staggering to be taken seriously. Green was politely thanked and sent on his way.

There was, however, one part of Livermore that had already given a lot of thought to the spread of nuclear weapons—Z Division. Back in 1983, for example, the United States had been trying to find a way to show the Pakistanis that, despite all the denials, the United States knew they were building a nuclear weapon. Z Division devised a convincing demonstration. Using the extensive and highly sensitive intelligence that had been collecting in the safes and secure computers of the windowless SCIF, the nuclear intelligence specialists built an exact model of what the secret Pakistani bomb was going to look like. The mock-up was flown to Islamabad and presented to the Pakistani government. Now the Pakistanis knew the United States knew they were developing a bomb.

At the end of 1987 Jerry was issued one of the rare blue ID cards that gave admittance to the SCIF, home of Z Division. "At least it keeps me off the street," he said, modest as usual. His weapons testings days were over.

Now he was in the intelligence business, with a ringside seat at the surrender of the Soviet Union after four decades of cold war. Arms control negotiations that had dragged on for years suddenly picked up speed as the Russians started caving in to American demands. Vexed issues, such as the stationing of nuclear weapons in Eastern Europe became moot as the Berlin Wall came down and the Russian armies abandoned barracks and bases, heading home at last.

But that was only the beginning. The professor who had predicted the breakup of the Soviet Union itself turned out to have been right. Obscure sites of tactical nuclear weapons in distant regions of the U.S.S.R. suddenly became of great interest to the men and women behind the windowless walls of the SCIF. Those long weapons trains snaking back across the Caucasus Mountains with their cargoes of warheads and bombs were reassuring. But what about other relics of the Soviet nuclear war machine? What would happen to them? From dealing with the sophistication of an "enhanced radiation" warhead blasted out of a gun, Jerry was going to have to think about weapons cruder than those that had wiped the two Japanese cities off the map in 1945, but perhaps more frightening than his neutron shell. These weapons might be used.

On the way into the fenced-off cocoon where he works, Jerry must pass another top security enclave, a two-story-high concrete structure with a distinctive blue collar around its roof. Next to it is a slightly taller square tower. The two buildings are ringed by a triple barbed-wire fence, an "exclusion area" under surveillance twenty-four hours a day by guards armed with automatic rifles and further protected by the most sophisticated electronic security technology available. Inside the blue-collar building is the lab's store of the most deadly substance on earth: plutonium.

Plutonium was first created in 1940 in the physics laboratory at Berkeley, an hour's drive or so away from Livermore. It does not exist in nature and for a time all the plutonium in the world was kept in a cigar box in a storeroom next to the office of one of its discoverers. The physicists, however, knew that this, along with uranium 235, was a "fissile material" suitable under the right conditions for producing the chain reaction that would lead to a nuclear explosion. It appears as a byproduct when uranium is fissioned in a reactor. The irradiated material must then be chemically treated, immersed in a powerful acid. Anyone in direct contact with the material during the acid treatment will die, due to intense levels of radiation. The process is manipulated by remote control as the plutonium is extracted from the spent fuel through a hazardous and expensive chemical process.

In total secrecy, on a remote plain at Hanford, Washington, the government built the production reactors that produced the plutonium for the world's first nuclear explosion, the Trinity test in July 1945. The amounts on hand were tiny; after Trinity only just enough remained, about six kilograms, to destroy the city of Nagasaki. (The Hiroshima bomb was made from uranium 235.) After the war more reactors were built and the stores of plutonium in the United States and other countries slowly but inexorably increased. The "restricted facility" a few yards from Jerry's office holds enough to make a hundred Nagasaki bombs.

In the decades after that first cigar box, world stocks of plutonium grew to hundreds of tons, but the amount needed to incinerate a city, at first about the size of a softball, got smaller. The designers in Livermore's B Division, responsible for the fission "primaries" that ignited thermonuclear fusion bombs, found ways to do it with amounts as small as a billiard ball. Even inert as a lump of metal, plutonium is dangerous. The silver-colored "pit" that goes into a bomb is hot to the touch from the radiation simmering within. Scratch it, and white sparks will fly out. The technicians who handle it know never to put too much of it together at one time, lest the radiation inside burst out in a chain reaction and consume them. That happened one day in 1946 at Los Alamos, when two spheres momentarily slipped together. There was a brief, brilliant blue flash and a young scientist named Louis Slotin died.

There are many competent scientists in the world who do not need a Q clearance to build a nuclear weapon, albeit a model infinitely cruder than the subtly elegant designs turned out at Livermore. The job becomes infinitely easier and cheaper if they can bypass the hard part—making the essential plutonium or uranium 235. Without one of these, there is no point in trying. Saddam Hussein spent eight billion dollars attempting to manufacture the nuclear materials essential for even just one weapon. That is why the little building next to Jerry's office is guarded day and night.

Jerry has always preferred to portray himself as an unsentimental technician with an offhand attitude toward his job. Creating earthquakes in Nevada was "a fun time" and his move into the secret intelligence facility kept him "off the street." But when he talks about Russia's nuclear legacy, he gets serious.

Sitting on the winery terrace on that windy March day, he muses about the spread of radioactive waste in Russia. Anyone breathing just a thousandth of a gram, he says, would die from massive fibrosis of the lungs within days, perhaps hours. A millionth of a gram in the lungs would be a death sentence from lung or bone cancer. He makes it sound alive. "It got into the rivers and people use the rivers downstream," he says quietly. "They use it for their drinking water. Little kids are the ones affected most. It accumulates in their bodies. They become radioactive themselves. It keeps migrating until it finds a host. Humans, like fish, are concentrators."

The Urals are still contaminated from one nuclear accident triggered in 1957. But it's a problem that could migrate closer to home, too. One could easily imagine someone mixing in some of the same material in ordinary high explosive. "Do it in a high-value real estate area," says Jerry Dzakowic, thinking of the World Trade Center, wrecked by a homemade fertilizer bomb in February 1992, "and change the way the United States lives." He gave one of his laughs, which might have been a little more uneasy than usual. "I hate to suggest how terrorists ought to do their work."

3

THE NEW RUSSIA

People were going hungry in Moscow in the winter of 1991. High-ranking dignitaries had usually escaped the hardships of ordinary citizens, so General Burns realized just how bad things had gotten when he saw his first breakfast. The best that his "first-class" hotel could provide was tea and half a slice of bread, the tea more like hot water infused with the faint sour taste of a sixth-hand tea bag. It was a telling introduction to a country in a state of collapse.

The Red Army that had menaced the West from the far side of the Wall in East Germany was now pouring into Russia on crowded troop trains, some so decrepit that the rain poured through the roof. But at the end of the line, there was nowhere for the soldiers or their officers to live. They were reduced to squatting in waterlogged tents in the dirty snow. Moscow sidewalks were crowded with hungry pensioners holding out a few pathetic belongings for sale—a candlestick, a picture frame—amidst mounting piles of garbage. "First-class" hotels for visitors like General Burns were thronged with prostitutes under the watchful eye of their heavily muscled pimps. One such hotel, the Ukraine, was serving as a battleground for a vicious war between Georgian and Chechen criminals, and guests on their way to breakfast found themselves skirting pools of blood from the previous night's shoot-out. Gangs of half-wild Gypsy children roamed the streets hunting down travelers to mob and loot. Everything was falling apart.

Mikhail Gorbachev had been evicted from office by former Moscow Party boss Boris Yeltsin, anointed as a democrat following the messy coup by former "hard-liners" the previous August. The red flag that had flown over the Kremlin since 1917 had come down on Christmas Day 1991. The Soviet Union itself had officially ceased to exist. To see the empire crumble, the nuclear power he had spent four decades preparing to fight, made the general queasy. Desperate people might do desperate things.

Anxious to find out what was happening outside the capital, Burns flew to Perm, a distant city in the Ural Mountains, which had been a hub for Soviet shipments of nuclear materials. He was taken to see what had become of a military production line that had once churned out millions of artillery shells. The scene was grim. The conveyor belt once laden with shells now carried bicycle parts for a model that looked like the one Burns had when he was eight years old, in 1940. The plant had a dirt floor and no heat in the bitter midwinter cold. The workers were covered with all the clothing they owned. They had not seen a pay packet from the factory, not one ruble, in six months.

Here, on the edge of Asia, it was dark by four in the afternoon. The lighting was dim, a shadowy glow from 25-watt bulbs. The only power came from a little donkey engine that ran the assembly line. The plant director was an air force colonel. How far, thought Burns, the Soviet military had fallen.

"You say you've made twenty thousand bicycles," he said. "How many have you sold?"

"None," answered the colonel.

"Who will you sell them to?"

"Africans?" The unsold bicycles were lying outside, buried under three feet of snow. There would be no sales.

The country was bleeding to death, stripped and robbed of its assets by their former guardians, like the Gypsy children roaming the streets. While the bikes rusted, the vast arsenal once built up regardless of cost—the guns, tanks, ammunition, fighter planes, ships, fuel oil—was waiting to be hauled away and sold in lots to black-market customers. The Russia that Burns found on that trip was about to turn into the greatest thieves' kitchen in history. The high command of the Russian military, custodian for tens of thousands of nuclear weapons, was in the front rank of the looters.

The old Soviet headquarters in what had been East Germany, at Wünsdorf outside Berlin, staffed by senior officers, the best and the brightest of the Soviet forces who had once planned battles against the armies of NATO and Burns himself, was now a cesspit of black-market operations. Personal gain took precedence over the army and the state. There was little attempt to conceal the wholesale robbery. Car ferries crossing the Baltic carried state-of-the-art MiG fighter jets, on their way to market for all the world to see.

No one in power was really interested in stopping the rot. While Burns was in Moscow, Boris Yeltsin dispatched a high-level investigator, Yuri Boldyrev, to ferret out military corruption. But State Inspector Boldyrev displayed unhealthy enthusiasm, charging commanders of the Western Group of Forces in Germany with corruption and illegal weapons sales. The findings were ignored. The investigator further overstepped his bounds and followed the money, digging up corruption in Yeltsin's inner circle. Within a year Yeltsin had fired the tenacious inspector. And the commanders in question were cleared. Later, Dimitri Kholodov, a courageous Moscow reporter who penetrated the dank world of military profiteering, was blown apart by a suitcase bomb. The Russian military was not only dirty; it was dangerous.

Burns's concern was the threat of the theft and sale of the nuclear stockpile. Military personnel were no longer honored or respected. Treated as dregs and constantly hungry, they acted as such. Deep in the Russian countryside that year, an SS-25 Mobile Intercontinental Ballistic Missile that belonged to the Strategic Rocket Forces, was discovered totally unmanned and unguarded, complete with its nuclear warhead. The crew, once elite and pampered, had abandoned their weapon. This missile targeted at the United States with a warhead that could pulverize half a state was deserted because the rations had stopped coming and the entire crew of missileers had left to search for food.

While the lower ranks suffered, the high command found imaginative ways to get rich. In 1992, Major General Vladimir Rodionov turned his top secret nuclear bomber unit into an international freight and charter service. The bomber pilots regarded their lucrative airline work as the top priority, while military duties got short shrift. How long would it be before the debased nuclear forces chose to auction off their warheads?

Burns started his White House mission with the unsettling knowledge that the Russians had a glut of nuclear warheads. Arms control treaties had reduced the number of missiles, thus generating huge numbers of excess warheads. These required storage. Tactical weapons pulled out of Eastern Europe, stockpiles being withdrawn from newly independent states like Kazakhstan and the nuclear battlefield weapons pulled back in a panic after the events in Baku were clogging the rail yards and bases. Thousands of weapons, most more powerful than the bomb that obliterated Hiroshima, had to travel by train. This was the same rail system that as of 1990, before the collapse, was losing track of a thousand railcars a day. Tracking weapons was critical. And if a railcar loaded with SS-20 warheads could be diverted by a corrupt general and his henchmen, the United States was in very serious trouble.

In March 1992, General Burns walked into the Ministry of Defense in Moscow, a complex of buildings spanning a city block, for his first meeting with the minister. The man who presided over hundreds of bases stacked with nuclear war- heads spread over six thousand miles was, thought Burns, overwhelmed. "Nobody really knew who they were working for. Or who was working for them," he reported later. The offi- cers at the ministry were still sporting cap badges with the hammer and sickle insignia of the Soviet Union, a state that no longer existed.

"Why don't you have new badges?" asked Burns.

"No money."

While the military was being stripped and pillaged by the senior commanders, the embittered lower ranks did what they could to get their share. The men were raiding depots, stealing weapons, ammunition and equipment. Sentries were handing out arms to civilian criminals willing to pay for access to stor- age sites. The plunder was especially widespread in the border regions. The miserable troops waiting to leave Germany for an uncertain future had sold everything from their uniforms to armored vehicles.

Surely, thought General Burns, the elite nuclear units, the Twelfth Department, based across the courtyard at the minis- try, the mysterious troops from the General Staff that Pentagon analysts had endlessly scrutinized to plot their movements and function, were still a cut above the rest. The department, called by those with a need to know the Twelfth GUMO (from the acronym of its Russian title), had always been staffed by men specially selected and trained to serve in its ranks—Russia's own nuclear priesthood. Confined to officers of Slavic origin, this was a lifetime calling and ethnic minorities were rigor- ously excluded. Once in the Twelfth, no one left.

These were the custodians, charged with tending the tens of

thousands of weapons in the stockpile, monitoring their delicate mechanisms, keeping careful count of their vast numbers. Official Washington fervently wanted to believe that while the rest of the military might be degenerating into a mob, the men in the most critical unit of all were paid handsomely and on time and were therefore resistant to temptation. Just one nuclear weapon under their charge was worth several hundred million dollars. Saddam Hussein had spent eight billion dollars trying to build one from scratch.

As it turned out, the custodians were granted a perquisite, a special gratuity to ensure their immunity from the criminal cynicism spreading through the Red Army. They each received an extra four pounds of sausages, once a month.

The system of weapons control was like a Russian Matrioshka doll, in which each doll contained a smaller version. Barbed wire, men with rifles, a restrictive pass system, circles within circles. The Twelfth Department had exclusive access to the bunkers where the warheads were stored. They passed through the steel doors in pairs, with each man opening the locks in proper sequence. In theory, an observer manning a remote monitor watched their every move. The moment either of the pair in the bunker behaved suspiciously, the third was to lock the doors. Between the bunkers and the perimeter fence, the grounds were patrolled by troops from the Russian Army, Air Force, Navy or Strategic Rocket Forces. Outside the fence, there were troops from the Ministry of the Interior, the MVD. The checks and balances were dependent on the natural suspicion and lack of camaraderie between the separate services and the Twelfth. The main line of defense was fear.

The system was perfectly adequate for a police state with sealed borders, when the enemy, the threat, had been American spies. No American agent ever got close. But in an anarchic post-Soviet world with an utterly porous border, there were serious problems. Three conspirators on the inside, no longer content with their sausages, could engineer a theft. If the ob-

server monitoring a pair inside the bunker was drunk or other-
wise inattentive or absent, it would take only two.

Such elite troops had every right to feel humiliated as they
watched the new class of speculators and black marketeers ordering buckets of vodka at the Metropole Hotel in Moscow
when an officer from the Twelfth could not afford the price of
a glass. There was immense pressure on every officer to crack,
to join the free-for-all of looting the military.

Even worse, Burns found that hundreds of weapons were
out of their bunkers, in transit, accessible not only to officers
of the Twelfth, but potentially to a host of organized criminal
groups—the burgeoning "Mafiya"—who controlled tens of
thousands of state and private organizations. Aleksandr Sol-
zhenitsyn called the new Russia through which the warheads
were moving an "amalgam of former Party functionaries,
quasi-democrats, KGB officers and black market dealers, a
dirty hybrid never before seen in world history."

It was not so much the tough-looking men in long overcoats
cutting a swath through Moscow who were the danger when it
came to the safe passage of weapons. It was a far more powerful mafia, the former Nomenklatura, the Soviet elite, who now
felt free to dispose of the assets of the second-largest economy
in the world and bank the millions. Where was the boundary
between vacuuming up government dachas, copper, silver and
titanium mines, oil wells, aluminum factories, auto plants, and
claiming ownership and cornering the missile market? If solid
citizens like some of the bosses of the Gazprom natural gas
monopoly could suddenly be worth hundreds of millions of
dollars when Gazprom was cut loose from government ownership, what Russian general didn't think twice about the market
value of his warheads? At the highest levels there was no one
to stop the thievery.

The KGB Sixth Directorate, the old "Big Brother" that
rooted out thefts of state property and scrutinized the daily
lives of weapons designers and engineers, had its own scams.

The dreaded "Chekisti" stashed $120 million in spanking new banks and businesses in 1990. A secret directive from the chief of the KGB to Military Counterintelligence in January 1991 instructed them to set up companies to sell military technology overseas, in case KGB leaders and operatives needed to flee the country. Money was flooding out of Russia to Austria, Cyprus, Switzerland.

At home in Moscow, anyone who wanted to stay alive needed criminal protection, a *krisha,* or roof. Tens of thousands of men were employed in private armies inside the city limits. What happened when one of the private armies, some filled with crack *spetznaz* assault units of the old KGB, robbed the weapons trains?

Warheads were being transported by train to new bases or to distant dismantlement sites. Like his fellow cold warriors, General Burns had always taken for granted that Soviet weapons security, even when the warheads were stacked in railcars moving thousands of miles across vast stretches of Soviet territory, was foolproof. He got a rude awakening.

The general asked the Minister of Defense for authorization to allow his team of American military and technical experts to inspect one specimen weapons transporter. Finally they were taken to see one, parked in a forest clearing "in the middle of nowhere." The weapons trains, guarded by soldiers from the General Staff in the front and rear cars, moved across Russia from missile bases along the Trans-Siberian Railroad to secret atomic cities known only by code names like Krasnoyarsk 26, Chelyabinsk 65 or Tomsk 7. The team of Americans arrived at the special weapons train to find a platoon of edgy infantry with fixed bayonets drawn up in front of the car. Someone had failed to alert the platoon that their old archenemy was to be allowed access to the train. Communications with Moscow were abysmal. There was an awkward standoff as the American team was kept at bay by armed and frightened provincial troops. Only after intense negotiations was the team allowed to cross the last fifteen yards of snowdrifts to the freight cars.

The soldiers had been guarding an empty car—no one in Moscow was prepared to show the Americans an actual warhead. But what they found still horrified them. There was no casing for the warheads. No coded locks on the cars. According to one technical expert, the loaders had been throwing the warheads up on the cars, spreading tarps over them and securing them with the equivalent of a bungee cord. The potential for nuclear train robbery was chillingly clear. One SS-20 warhead, one cruise missile, one modest ten-kiloton atomic bomb out of the rich bounty traveling the two thousand miles across the wild and open steppes, could vaporize midtown Manhattan. Detonated in Washington it would wipe out the White House, the Treasury, the Departments of Energy, Interior, Labor, Health, Education and Welfare, the Supreme Court, the Library of Congress, CNN, the National Press Building, the Smithsonian, the National Gallery, Union Station and both houses of Congress.

Burns, as the Special Envoy for the President, could afford to be generous. He swiftly arranged to ship a Russian nuclear railcar to the ultra-high-security Sandia National Laboratory in Albuquerque, New Mexico. At Sandia, part of America's network of powerful, tightly guarded defense laboratories, the Russian train would be overhauled and redesigned, free of charge. The warheads would no longer bounce around loosely in the car. There would be a system to alert the guards if one of the cars at the far end of the train was unhooked. The Russians were suitably grateful. But, even years later, no one in Washington could confirm with certainty that the Russians were using any of these fancy gadgets or whether they too had been sold on the black market. The problem was certainly still serious enough to worry the highest command. General Evgeni Maslin, the chief custodian of Russia's nuclear weapons, said openly, "What is theoretically possible and what we must always be prepared for is train robbery, attempts to seize nuclear weapons in transit."

The Burns team examining the loading train was alarmed by more than just the design of the cars. The warheads themselves could go nuclear if there was an accident. If the train derailed, for instance, Moscow would have on its hands a major nuclear explosion that would make Chernobyl look benign. In short, the weapons were not "One Point Safe." This precise term of weapons engineering refers to the standard that every U.S. weapon must meet, so that in case of an accident, the chance of its producing an explosion with a nuclear yield greater than four pounds of TNT is only one in a million.

The Russian warheads did not meet that standard. They could blow and go nuclear at the drop of a hat. Clearly the refitted trains would have to include weapons caskets and coded doors. The weapons would need to lie snug beneath Kevlar blankets. But even if the weapons survived their perilous journey, they could easily be lost at the station. The meticulous American accounting system for nuclear weapons used sophisticated computers and they were constantly tracked by means of bar codes on each warhead. By contrast, Burns found the Russian system was shockingly primitive. "The only record they had in each facility was great big thick ledger, the kind of thing a Victorian clerk in a Dickens novel would have used." And even if the warheads were successfully shipped and unloaded, the danger of theft at the other end was staggering. And it was a problem that would only get worse as more and more weapons were dismantled.

Inside every weapon there was a plutonium pit, the core of the atomic bomb. When squeezed by the tremendous pressures of the high explosives wrapped around it, the pit generates the nuclear explosion. Under normal circumstances, the pit would be removed every ten years. This had to be done because the plutonium produced a substance called americium, which eventually damaged the warhead. The pit would be extracted

and reconfigured for another weapon. This sphere of plutonium was the hardest and by far the most costly part of the
weapon to make. It required uranium, a nuclear reactor and a
reprocessing plant to produce even the smallest quantity. The
pit itself, wrapped in conventional explosives, without the trappings of the weapon casing, was a bomb within a bomb. Now
they were dismantled and left in sheds. The pits were piling up
by the thousands at Chelyabinsk and Tomsk.

The sheds at Tomsk 7 had odd bits of machinery, even broken refrigerators inside and metal siding whose sole function
was to keep the rain out. Inside a barbed-wire perimeter, two
of the sheds were stuffed to capacity with plutonium pits, each
one a potential atomic bomb. The number of pits had risen to
23,000, before the mayor of Tomsk called a halt to the shipments. Twenty-three thousand pits filled two sheds. One shed
door had a padlock, the other a simple code lock, as with a
Moscow apartment. Russian nuclear engineers knew there was
no technical control to prevent them from moving material.
You would have to sign out your container in the Tomsk book-
keeper's ledger—unless you planned to simply blow a hole in
the metal siding with a rocket-propelled grenade . . .

The barbed wire around the sheds marked the border of
the closed zone. The woods beyond were accessible to anyone,
including an armed terrorist. And once the wire had been cut
and the metal siding blown out, stealing a bomb meant simply
carrying a sixty-pound two-foot-high container the size of a
small suitcase. A tank guarding the entrance to the sheds was
on the wrong side, away from the clear escape route to the
forest.

Just down the road from the sheds, there were literally tons
of bomb-grade plutonium and uranium, materials that were
used to fashion nuclear weapons. Burns's directive from the
President was both to find out what needed to be done to keep
Russian warheads intact and unmolested and to sort out the
problem of the enormous stocks of bomb-grade materials scat-

tered the length and breath of the former Soviet Union. No one knew precisely how much bomb-grade uranium there was in Russia. The CIA spent years counting the barrels of nuclear waste outside weapons plants that showed up in satellite pictures but could never come up with a satisfactory answer.

Not long before Burns took off for Moscow, a brilliant MIT physicist named Tom Neff imaginatively suggested that the White House pick a round number like 500 tons, buy it, and use it for U.S. nuclear power stations. The President's Special Envoy was looking at the option. That amount alone would be enough to build 20,000 Hiroshima bombs.

Only a very special material—an unstable isotope—can be used to produce nuclear fission. Uranium 235 and plutonium are the stuff of atomic bombs. The first American tests in the Nevada desert and the skies over Japan demonstrated just how small a quantity is required to unleash unmatched destructive power. The bomb dropped on Hiroshima by the *Enola Gay*, with a yield of 13,000 tons of TNT, required just sixty kilos of uranium 235 to leave 100,000 dead. The Nagasaki bomb, equivalent to 20,000 tons of TNT, required a mere six kilos of plutonium to kill 60,000 people. Burns knew the figures. He also knew that the American intelligence estimates placed not only over a hundred tons of plutonium but even more highly enriched uranium in the former Soviet Union.

The overflowing stores of bomb-grade uranium and plutonium were inside the inner sanctum of the Russian state. Stretching across the vast country, deep in the forests east of Moscow, in the foothills of the Ural Mountains, in the endless plains of central Siberia, there were ten "secret cities," whose existence was not recorded on any map. This is where physicists and nuclear engineers had labored around the clock to make the Soviet Union a nuclear superpower. These were the enclaves of the elite, "the chocolate eaters," as ordinary Russians called them. Now they were the decaying repositories of a commodity incomparably valuable to any country anxious to join the nuclear club.

The secret cities had names like Arzamas 16 and Sverdlovsk 45. Visitors required a special visa. They were entering what Russians called a "country within a country," a conglomerate of the cities, their mines and construction firms controlled by a giant ministry called Minatom. It was a ministry that fed two and a half million Russians, that was, in spite of the chaos devouring the country, a functioning state. It was described by one of Boris Yeltsin's men as being no less powerful and secretive than the KGB.

The man in control of this huge and powerful complex liked to call himself the Hawk. Victor Mikhailov was nearing sixty and at the apex of his career. Powerfully built with jet-black hair, he walked with a conscious swagger. His eyes held you as though you might be something edible. He was the hunter. Everyone else was his prey. He was a man the White House and Pentagon would come to hate.

Mikhailov had the one friend who counted. In February 1992, Boris Yeltsin, still celebrating his takeover of Mikhail Gorbachev's Kremlin office, boarded his presidential jet for the forty-minute flight to the secret city where the first Russian bomb had been created, Arzamas 16. He treated the bomb makers now working for him with all due deference, but he bonded most closely with one of his escorts, the chief of the nuclear weapons program. Mikhailov not only had obvious management talent but an awesome capacity for vodka. This was fortunate, since the weapons boss was hardly a longtime Yeltsin partisan. When the Communist old guard mounted their ill-fated coup in August 1991, Mikhailov, in Geneva for a conference, greeted the news with approval. It was good, he said, to get rid of all that democratic nonsense. Within a day of the collapse of the coup, as a CIA report noted sourly, Mikhailov had become an ardent democrat.

Yeltsin liked the dynamism of the man. Mikhailov was a

force. With Yeltsin's blessing, the former weapons designer moved into the minister's office, the size of a ballroom, in the huge black building fronted with Greek columns on Ordynka Avenue in downtown Moscow. He was now a driven, chain-smoking CEO with a bank of telephones at his elbow who wanted to do business. On the wall, to the right of the massive deck, he hung a photograph of the Mercury nuclear test site in Nevada, a memento of the day he had been in the first party of Russians to watch an American underground test shake the Nevada desert. Mikhailov loved nuclear explosions. Overshadowing the photo was a portrait of his patron, Boris Yeltsin, the only man who could, perhaps, control him. The ministry might be strapped for cash, but Mikhailov was ready to deal himself into the novel game of free enterprise. Western visitors soon spotted his new $30,000 Rolex watch.

When the American general was ushered into the cavernous office of the minister, Victor Mikhailov lit another Marlboro. He could not resist toying with the White House Special Envoy. Burns was unruffled.

The general got right to business. He had come to make a deal. The White House envoy, with the support of President Bush, wanted to buy Russia's enriched uranium. He had dispatched a sketchy outline of the terms to the Hawk's office before the meeting. The general did not waste time. The United States would pay $12 billion for five hundred tons of bomb-grade enriched uranium to get it out of Russian territory. Deliveries of the dangerous cargo would continue until the year 2014. Twelve billion was a fair price. The White House wanted the stuff out of the madhouse that Russia was becoming.

Mikhailov preened. He had ostentatiously scrawled all over the papers with a big green pen. He was short of time. He had a meeting with President Yeltsin at four. Either Burns accepted his changes or Mikhailov would inform the President the agreement was dead.

General Burns loved to play chicken.

"Mr. Minister," he said crisply, "one does not threaten the United States."

Burns stood up and unceremoniously walked out. The gambit worked. An hour later there was an urgent call to the American embassy from the office of the Minister of Atomic Energy. The minister had reconsidered. The Hawk wanted an appointment that afternoon. Burns asked what time.

"Whatever time would suit you."

Burns was prepared to be cruel.

"Four o'clock," just when Mikhailov had claimed he would be closeted with the President. The Minatom aide replied nervously that the minister might be engaged.

"I am only available," said Burns firmly, "at four o'clock."

General Burns had his way. Back at the ministry, the copy of the agreement to buy the uranium mountain was clean save for just two inconsequential green marks.

"I've reconsidered," said Mikhailov inhaling another cigarette. "We can do this agreement."

"Fine," said Burns drily. He had called the atomic tyrant's bluff.

Even had the deal gone ahead smoothly, the general's massive purchase left a whopping seven hundred tons—50,000 Hiroshimas—littered around the ruins of the Soviet empire. Most Russians were never gong to see any of that $12 billion. Most of them no longer saw their monthly paycheck. But enough of them knew exactly where to find the uranium that bombs are made of to keep American intelligence officers awake at night.

JESSICA STERN

Jessica started running. Bolting down the stairs and across the hundred yards between the Sensitive Compartmented Information Facility and her office, she shoved her green ID badge into the slot beside the door. Urgently, she punched her personal identification code on the keypad. The moment it accepted her right to entry with a soft click, she shoved it open and dashed to her room. She had only been gone twenty minutes. Too late. On her door a freshly posted notice broadcast the words "SECURITY INFRACTION."

The rules were clear. No classified material was ever to be left unsecured. Doors of unoccupied offices containing classified materials were to be shut and locked at all times. She had been flipping through a file marked "confidential," the lowest level of classification, when she remembered an errand over at Z Division and ran out, leaving her door open. Now this lapse would stay on her record forever.

Jessica Stern had grown up with national security secrecy.

She had been molded in the elite, cerebral world of defense research at MIT, the Massachusetts Institute of Technology, where her father was a senior electronics scientist at the Lincoln Laboratory. But the security paranoia she experienced at Livermore was something new. This was a place where they guarded the secrets of weapons that could tear the world apart, secrets that no outsider could ever be allowed to glimpse.

Jessica had arrived at the laboratory a year before, in the fall of 1991, hired as a specialist in chemical weapons. Behind the security barriers at Livermore she found a strange, introverted society of highly educated men fascinated by massively destructive weapons, who by and large had a problem with women.

Short and pretty, the thirty-three-year-old scientist with dark unruly hair and brown inquisitive eyes obscured behind small round eyeglasses sometimes joked that she herself was a classic nerd. She majored in chemistry and her master's in the intense academic pressure cooker of MIT focused on the Soviet military, while the dissertation she wrote for her Harvard doctorate concerned chemical weapons. But Cambridge, home of MIT and Harvard, was a cosmopolitan center where people talked easily about politics, books or the theater. At the Livermore lab, just forty miles from the Bay Area, the big cultural attraction was the town rodeo.

Jessica drove in and out of this strange world twice a day. Every morning she woke up looking out over San Francisco Bay from her house on Panoramic Heights above the Berkeley campus of the University of California. Berkeley, she thought, was the epitome of a liberal town, where the city council was as likely to spend its time discussing support for Nicaragua as it did repairing potholes. This was not a community where nuclear weapons and the people that built them enjoyed much support. Out at the lab they called it "Berserkley." The sociology professor Bob Bellah, who lived right next door, was a leading member of the campaign to sever all links between the university and Livermore. Whenever they got together he would challenge Jessica: "How can you work at that death factory?" But those long arguments in the comfortable houses on Mosswood Road always stayed friendly. Civilized people in academic society could agree to disagree.

She had moved to Berkeley because her second husband, Jeff, whom she had married in the summer of 1990, was on the faculty. He had an easy commute, down the hill past the football stadium to the economics department, where he was a rising star. Jessica meanwhile made her bag lunch, always a peanut butter sandwich, collected the books and papers that seemed to need more than two arms to carry and set off on the drive down Interstate 580, past Oakland and Pleasanton. It took fifty minutes from her front door to the armed guard at the first security checkpoint at the Livermore lab. Sometimes she had to wait there while the guards brought up the sniffer dog for one of their random searches of her car. At the end of the day they might search again.

When Jessica first started working at Livermore as a postdoctoral fellow hired to help advise the lab directory on chemical arms control issues, her office, an unprepossessing trailer, was in the red area. If she needed to talk to someone "green," they had to come out to meet her. The system worked on her the same way it did on everyone else—leaving her feeling left out, excluded from the secret knowledge on the other side of the CAIN booth. The precious green badge would come only after "they" had finished the exhaustive check into her background and pronounced her "Q-cleared."

That took a long time. One day a friend called. "An FBI agent has just been round to my house asking about you. He said he felt sorry for you, your clearance is being held up because they can't find your ex-husband."

"It's taken the FBI four months not to find him," said Jessica to herself. "I'm going to find him today." She had not seen or heard from Steve since their divorce years before. An hour later she had tracked him down. Jessica liked to get the job done, fast.

Now that she was green she could call up secrets on her computer terminal. Much of the jealously guarded information was highly technical, impenetrable to anyone but a weapons specialist. The classified internal E-mail gossip was more dramatic. Judging by what came up on the screen, her fellow workers were far more worried about their own future than the state of the world. The nuclear arms race was over. The START treaty signed by George Bush actually cut the number of strategic missiles on each side. Bush had pulled most U.S. tactical nuclear weapons out of Europe. The defense budget was going down. Nevada shook to its last test in 1991.

Not surprisingly, Livermore felt under the gun. There were ominous rumors that the lab would get the ax. Later, when Energy Secretary Hazel O'Leary announced wholesale declassification of decades-old U.S. nuclear secrets, including horrifying accounts of radiation experiments carried out on unwitting human guinea pigs, the electronic gossip grew vituperative. Releasing secrets made people nervous. Jessica got used to messages that began, "Did you see what O'Leary said now?" The world was changing and they felt threatened.

There were some places she still could not go. One of them was the "exclusion area" with its own triple barbed-wire fences that housed the lab's store of deadly plutonium. Another, not far from her trailer, was the windowless Sensitive Compartmented Information Facility that housed Z Division, Livermore's own intelligence agency. It was the only part of the lab that was getting busier. On her rare visits to the canteen Jessica would see Z Division people huddled at their own exclusive tables.

Very occasionally she bumped into a middle-aged Z Division analyst named Jerry Dzakowic. Mild and self-effacing, he rarely joined the canteen get-togethers. She liked him, another loner. What she didn't know, however, was that Jerry had been watching her for some time himself.

It did not bother Jerry that Jessica lived in Berkeley and liked to talk to people in the outside world. In fact, he thought it a definite plus. No one like her had ever been brought in to work on a Z Division project, but for Jerry, seasoned in circumventing bureaucratic barriers, this made Jessica all the more attractive. When he hired someone, the accountants factored in a percentage of the total lab overhead on top of their actual salary and benefits. That meant that someone like him went on the division budget as costing $300,000 a year. But because of a quirk in the bookkeeping temporary people did not get the overhead tagged on, so they looked inexpensive. Jessica was officially a postdoctoral fellow, not part of the permanent lab staff. Jerry looked at her and thought, "A highly qualified, inexpensive head. That's a good investment." After a while, he started dropping by her trailer and talking to her about what was happening in the ruins of the old U.S.S.R., trying to get her interested in the subject.

Jessica hated the idea. She certainly knew a great deal about Russia, spoke fluent Russian. It was just that the thought of that country brought back a lot of memories from the time she had lived there, most of them bad. She had moved to Moscow in 1982 with her first husband because her grandmother had used family connections to get him a job with a secretive international trading company called the Chilowich Corporation, which had been doing business with Russia since before the revolution. At the time she arrived the cold war was settling into its last bitter freezing spell, Ronald Reagan was making speeches about the "evil empire" and telling jokes about bombing Russia in five minutes. And in Moscow the KGB were doing what they could to make life unpleasant for any Americans within reach.

She remembered the times she had unlocked the door of her apartment on Kalanchevskaya Street, near the Kazan station and found everything seemingly the way she left it. Then, nervously, she checked the bathroom. There they were again; the cardboard ends of Russian cigarettes floating in the toilet, a *znak*, a sign, to let her know that the KGB's Second Directorate (charged with monitoring foreigners) had been making themselves comfortable in her home.

Once, she and the rest of the American community in Moscow were summoned to the yellow building on the Garden Ring Road that housed the U.S. embassy to hear a dire warning: the KGB was monitoring their movements by covertly sprinkling them with a fluorescent "spy dust" that stuck to everything they touched. The object was to monitor people's movements, but the dust was potentially lethal—mutagenic, explained the embassy helpfully—and could give them cancer.

It had been seven years since she finally put Moscow and a failing marriage behind her. Now Jerry, from the mysterious Z Division, was insisting that she start thinking about Russia again. He needed her help in answering a vital question. What was happening to the Russian nuclear weapons and materials stockpile? It took her a month to run out of excuses before she reluctantly agreed to consider it.

Just to make sure, the nuclear weapons maker turned intelligence analyst gave his prospective recruit a test. "What's going to happen in the Ukraine?" he asked. "Is it going to split apart? I've got to give a presentation about it. You've got three days."

"Okay," she said, happy to be faced with a challenge.

Usually, this sort of study at Livermore was carried out with reference to the in-house files and databases, all classified. Jessica went about it a different way. Using her own Rolodex and network of contacts, she worked late into the night, calling up every academic specialist on the Ukraine around the country. Three days later, on the deadline, she had it done. Jerry was impressed. She was hired.

Jerry was at home with technical intelligence. He knew just

how to analyze the data that flowed in from the vast collection systems of U.S. intelligence, all of which were at the disposal of Z Division. In the 1980s, for example, the CIA devised a "Geiger counter bug," code-named Absorb, that could count the number of individual warheads hidden under the nose cones of Soviet missiles. The CIA aimed to plant the bug on a freight train so that it could carry out its silent tabulation whenever it rolled past the huge missiles on their special trains. It was a brilliant piece of technical espionage, except that CIA traitor Aldrich Ames sold the secret to the KGB. But by 1992 Jerry was faced with technical questions that needed political answers. It was Jessica's role to supply them.

For forty years U.S. intelligence had the straightforward mission of penetrating the intentions and capabilities of the Soviet Union. How many nuclear missiles were they building? How powerful were they? What did the Kremlin plan to do with them? Intelligence on the Soviet threat had never been easy to come by, but at least analysts like Jerry had been dealing with a well-organized machine, centrally directed from Moscow. Now there was chaos. Four nuclear states emerged from the wreckage of the U.S.S.R.—Ukraine, Belarus, Kazakhstan and Russia itself. The United States was pressuring the first three to send all their weapons back to Russia, but there was no guarantee that the situation there was any more stable.

The pair started with the warheads. The official word from Moscow was that all the tactical warheads were safely back in Russia and under lock and key. Jerry was skeptical. The United States, he thought to himself, didn't even know how many of these warheads the Soviets had turned out in the first place, and no one on the Russian side seemed in a hurry to supply the answer. He vividly recalled the case of the wayward SS-23, a short-range tactical nuclear missile. Under a previous arms control treaty, all the SS-23s were supposed to have been moved back well out of range of the borders, yet some turned up in the wrong place. The Russians simply said it was a mistake—the "oops" factor, he called it. He just could not believe that an "oops" nuclear weapon would not turn up somewhere in the former Soviet Union where it was not supposed to be. To take the matter further, suppose that the territory on which the nukes were sitting suddenly shifted—split off from Russia in the same way the Soviet Union has just fissioned into more than a dozen separate countries? It was a difficult and intriguing question, the kind that Jerry liked.

The first stage was to look for weapons. That was his job. Tracking nuclear weapons, especially if they are as small as an artillery shell or a short-range missile warhead, is a very specialized art. Practitioners have to have at their fingertips such arcane knowledge as the shape of that telltale ventilator on the roof of nuclear railcars that distinguishes them from ordinary freight wagons; the frequencies employed by the Twelfth Department when they are preparing to move a weapon; the bridges in a given area strong enough to bear the weight of a mobile missile and its launcher. There are not many people who can do this and they keep in touch. Jerry had his contacts around the far-flung U.S. intelligence community, informal liaisons carried on over secure phone lines linking agencies like CIA, DIA, NSA, NPIC, in which information and ideas could be traded back and forth, favors earned and repaid.

Jessica had a different task. At her desk in the trailer office she was building a network of her own. The outer provinces of the newborn Russian Federation were in a state of swirling political chaos. Enclaves like Tatarstan or Chechnya or far eastern Siberia were barely above the intelligence agencies' horizon; no one apart from a few dedicated specialists had ever thought they were worth bothering about. She worked the phones, calling on people she remembered from her time in Moscow, academics who had been pursuing a lonely obsession with corners of the world that most people could not find on a map, travelers who had found their way to places she was interested in. She devoured the daily transcripts published by the CIA's Foreign Broadcast Information Service, begged or borrowed precious copies of obscure provincial Russian newspapers from anyone who could lay their hands on them.

The last time Jessica had been in the foothills of the Caucasus Mountains, north of Baku, she was riding Chechen-bred Arabian horses. She and her then husband had been sent by the trading company to check out the local bloodstock. After a day of galloping through the lush green foothills of the Caucasus their hosts would build a fire and roast *dikii kaban,* the meat of black boar. Now Chechnya had declared its independence, led by a former Soviet nuclear bomber general, Dzokar Dudayev. In the summer of 1992, he paraded tactical missile launchers through the streets of Grozny, the Chechen capital. They had simply been left behind by the Russians when they pulled out. No one in Washington seemed to care. Out at Z Division, Stern and Dzakowic were convinced their subject was vitally important.

They were an odd couple. Jessica, looking younger than her age, was driven with enthusiasm for the job and ready to work day and night to get it done. Jerry, the meticulous engineer who had spent most of his working life at Livermore, seemed much more conventional. After all, he came out of the system. But he wasn't satisfied to go through the motions, stay out of trouble and wait for his pension. Intensely patriotic, he used the system for his own ends. If there was an element of beauty and the beast in their relationship, neither of them noticed. Jessica worshipped Jerry Dzakowic, and the feeling was mutual.

There were still things she was not allowed to know, lacking the precious blue card that would give her unimpeded access to the SCIF. In her early days at the lab she had felt like a lesser person because she was excluded from the green area. Now it grated on her that she was not blue. Some things Jerry didn't bother her with—the political situation inside Z Division, for example. There was a division inside the organization, both physical and cultural. Jerry and the physicists were on the sec-

ond floor of the SCIF. The first floor was given over to the political scientists. "Hard" sciences had more prestige, and those
down below resented Jessica, who seemed to be dealing with
political questions, continually skipping up and down the
stairs. And on Jerry's floor there were those who felt the same
way. Jessica, however, remained blissfully unaware of these
undercurrents. Jerry protected her.

There were other things he did have to teach his new partner. One of them was the way people in his world communi-
cated ideas and information. Up until this point, Jessica's
professional product had consisted of densely written research
papers, complete with copious footnotes. Now Jerry had to ed-
ucate her in the national security community's preferred
means of communication: the oral briefing with Vu-graph
slides. He was an acknowledged master of the art. Patiently he
explained to her how complicated arguments could be explained in simple statements flashed up on the screen, backed
up by a fluent and confident commentary. "Remember," he
said, "no more than four lines to a slide."

"The dog and pony show," they called it. It was a presentation on the tension between the center and the periphery in
Russia and how nuclear weapons might pop out of the cracks.
Jessica developed a list labeled "Indicators" to identify potential problems in a given region. Were they producing their own
money? Did their local constitution contradict the constitution
of the Federation? Tatarstan duly came up on the radar screen,
deep in the Russian heartland. Secession there would slice
Russia in half, like a rebellion in Omaha. They spend long
hours poring over other indicators in the Volga region, the Far
East, the Caucasus. Their presentation was called "Russian Fission."

Finally it was time to take the show on the road. Their Vu-
graphs (with maps in full vivid color) were refined for maximum punch. The out-of-town tryout was before colleagues
down the corridor in Z Division. The response was enthusias-

tic. From there, they moved on to other divisions at the lab. Whatever its other rigid customs, there was no dress code at Livermore and Jessica usually wore whatever felt comfortable, which normally meant jeans. But for these sessions she started putting on formal suits. Presentation was all-important.

The lab management reviewed their performance with satisfaction and gave clearance for the pair to go national, starting at the Department of Energy's Office of Foreign Intelligence in Washington. From there they would move on to the other national security departments in the capital—State, Defense, the CIA.

One afternoon in late October 1993, they were at DOE headquarters on Independence Avenue talking to a roomful of intelligence analysts. The next stop would be the CIA. That afternoon, however, Stern and Dzakowic got a peremptory order to be back at 8:30 A.M. sharp the following day.

The next morning, when Jerry and Jessica arrived in the secure briefing room on the fourth floor of the DOE building, they found some heavy firepower in the room. Waiting impatiently were John "Jay" Stewart, the chief of Foreign Intelligence at the department, and his deputy, a former inmate of Los Alamos named Notra Trulock. Sitting next to them was Jim Ford, the deputy director of the Energy Department's Office of Nonproliferation and National Security. The atmosphere was tense.

Jerry talked first, giving a technical description of precisely where the Russian arsenal was located and how vulnerable the weapons were to a takeover or accident. Then it was his partner's turn. Jessica did not know it, but she was stepping into a vicious high-level battle being fought behind closed doors in Washington. The facts and arguments on which she had been toiling late into the night out at Livermore had already cost one man in the room his career.

Jay Stewart had been thinking about nuclear security ever since he got out of air force counterintelligence after the Vietnam War. He spent years studying threats to U.S. nuclear reactors and materials on the part of terrorists or treacherous insiders. Security of weapons and stockpiles in the cold war Soviet police state never seemed to be a problem.

By 1990 Stewart had risen to the top of the DOE's Foreign Intelligence Service. Almost immediately, he found himself working full-time on the crisis of Saddam Hussein's invasion of Kuwait and the planning for the war to drive him out. On the day the Gulf War started, as Stewart was trying to persuade the Pentagon to do something about Saddam's plans to blow up the Kuwaiti oil fields, a weapons scientist on his staff snared his attention with a dire prediction about the Soviet nuclear stockpile. "We need to think about Surety," he said. In the coded language of nuclear intelligence, that meant the Safety, Security, Command and Control of nuclear weapons. The scientist suspected Surety was failing in the crumbling U.S.S.R. The harassed intelligence chief told him to go away and find out more. Six months later, the man reported back with the conclusions of a careful technical study. The warheads were not safe. That got Stewart's attention. From that moment on he began a campaign to make the security of Russian nuclear weapons the number one priority for U.S. intelligence.

By the fall of 1992 it was becoming clear to the nuclear intelligence chief that the Russian Federation that had emerged from the wreckage of the U.S.S.R. could itself fall apart. Stewart put in a call to Z Division and asked Jerry Dzakowic, whom he knew and admired, to start looking at the nuclear implications of a breakup.

From around the community, raw intelligence on the state of Russian nuclear weapons was beginning to flow in, most of it frightening. The CIA got wind of a hair-raising security breach in which a group of armed rebels in western Russia attacked a Russian Strategic Rocket Forces base that housed SS-25s—huge mobile ICBMs that could incinerate New York or Washington. Special troops from the Ministry of the Interior had to be called in to save the weapons. A senior official from the Agency's Intelligence Directorate confronted the Russians with details of the incident at a high-level meeting at the Foreign Ministry in Moscow early in 1992. They all vehemently denied that anything of the kind could have occurred. The intelligence veteran thought that, while the civilians' shock and horror at the idea was genuine, a senior general representing the General Staff at the meeting seemed to know exactly what he was talking about. There were things that the military were keeping secret from the civilians.

The implications of such intelligence were beginning to dawn on the U.S. military. In April 1992, a select group of officers gathered at the Marine Corps' Wargaming and Assessment Center at Quantico, Virginia. They were there to play a deadly "game": A small country had negotiated to buy a nuclear weapon from someone in the former Soviet Union. The players had to try to prevent the device from being smuggled out or, if they failed, to prevent the buyer from using the weapon. The results of the exercise were classified at a high level, but plans for follow-up games at Quantico were abruptly canceled. Asked why, a senior Pentagon official said guardedly, "Maybe because we lose the war, even if we retaliate."

A few months later however, a super-secret "black" Pentagon program called COG, for Continuity of Government, wargamed a variation of the same nightmare. The premise was that President Qaddafi of Libya purchases six nuclear artillery shells from a corrupt Russian general. The Libyan leader arranges to ship them surreptitiously to the United States with the aim of incinerating Washington, D.C. In the unfolding exercise, U.S. forces were unable to detect and intercept the shells as they wended their way to the United States. Nor was the plot foiled when the cargo reached Washington. The U.S. government was decapitated.

These bad dreams were classified. In the outside world people were euphoric that the cold war and the threat of nuclear annihilation, of cites vaporized within minutes of an enemy "first strike," was gone. The generation that could remember growing up to drills of leaping under school desks at the sound of a nuclear alert, that dreamed of being entombed in an airless bomb shelter, no longer had to ask themselves why they had brought children into a world stockpiled with nearly 100,000 nuclear weapons. Ten years before, in 1982, half a million people had rallied in New York's Central Park in a despairing protest against the looming threat of nuclear extinction. Now, suddenly, the Russians were our friends and thermonuclear war was an anachronism, part of history along with duck and cover jingles and Dr. Strangelove. As Jerry and Jessica were soon to find out, the U.S. government had no intention of puncturing the euphoria.

In October 1992 Stewart invited a very select group of specialists on Russia and nuclear weapons experts to a conference in Washington that December. "Classification," the invitation stated, "will be SECRET/NSI with the potential for up to SCI working group discussions." The agenda was the "implications . . . of potential further disintegration of Russia or other nuclear equipped republics." Jerry and Jessica's findings were about to reach a wider audience.

Everything to do with that gathering in December 1992 was secret. Those attending were for the most part unknown to the general public, but their names were potent in the world of defense and intelligence, men like Larry Gershwin, National Intelligence Officer for Strategic Affairs at the CIA, Andrew Marshall, director of the Office of Net Assessment at the Pentagon, and Bert Weinstein, head of Z Division. They presented their credentials to the guards at Marshall Hall, an imposing building on the well-manicured grounds of the military's Fort McNair on the banks of the Potomac in southeastern Washington. No one without a clearance was admitted. James R. Schlesinger, known for the fierce authority with which he had run the CIA, the Pentagon and the Department of Energy in the

1970s, set the mood in an introductory speech: "The wide-spread belief in the United States that the possibility of a sub-stantial nuclear exchange has now disappeared is a misapprehension."

Detailed presentations from the fifty conferees, some based on the work of Jerry and Jessica, were no less sobering. The prevailing mood was that Russia could easily disintegrate. Behind the closed and guarded doors the experts talked about the powder keg of dozens of minorities in the Russian Federation. Intelligence officials warned that the potential for Mafiya groups "to access nuclear weapons is high and getting higher, and the potential political and economic payback from such access is growing." Most ominous of all was the common view that the Russian strategic nuclear arsenal—thousands of intercontinental nuclear missiles—might be slipping out of President Yeltsin's control. As one speaker stated, the Russian leader "cannot block the use of nuclear weapons if that decision should be taken elsewhere." It could no longer be assumed that the trappings of the nuclear standoff, red phones on the President's desk and the "football" with the launch codes that followed him everywhere, meant anything in Russia.

Early in the new year, amidst a power vacuum in Washington as the Bush administration packed up to go home, Jay Stewart moved on to the next stage of his plan to concentrate official minds on the Russian nuclear threat. With Notra Trulock in tow, he set off for Europe.

In Brussels, the intelligence officials had an important audience of one: Manfred Wörner, Secretary-General of NATO. At the alliance headquarters Wörner sat openmouthed as they bluntly laid out what a secret State Department cable reporting on the meeting described as "an extremely bleak assessment, emphasizing the fragmentation of the Russian Federation, the breakdown of civilian control of the military and erosion of the military's own cohesion as the material welfare of the officer corps deteriorates in tandem with the general collapse of Russian society."

Wörner was most shaken by their statement that Yeltsin "lacked the technical ability to prevent a launch of ICBMs" and their conviction that the " 'unthinkable' scenarios involving the unauthorized launch of nuclear arms could no longer be ruled out." The Secretary-General was galvanized. "I found the possibility for further chaos and its potential impact on nuclear security most disturbing," he wrote in a grateful letter to the incoming Secretary of Energy, Hazel O'Leary. "I feel this information should be brought to the attention of our member nations."

The freshly installed Clinton administration was aghast at the news from Brussels. This was not at all what the new team had in mind. Their policy, as propelled by the President's old college classmate and former *Time* magazine correspondent Strobe Talbott, was to speak and hear no evil about Boris Yeltsin and his government. "Russian Fission" gave absolutely the wrong message. Five days after Stewart had met with Wörner, James Collins, deputy chief of mission at the U.S. embassy in Moscow, fired off a bureaucratic counter-salvo. "Things are admittedly tough in Russia right now," he cabled with breathtaking understatement, "with a deteriorating economy and a degree of political fragmentation evident." However, there was no need to worry about the Russian military and their nuclear weapons. "We continue to see nuclear weapons safety as one area where things still work and excellence is still taken seriously."

Back in Brussels, the Secretary-General of NATO waited in vain for further briefings.

In late March 1993, Jim Ford and Jay Stewart walked into the office of John Keliher. Keliher had just been parachuted in as a Clinton political appointee to the key post of Assistant Secretary and director of the Office of Nonproliferation and National Security, which made him their boss. He was sitting at his desk looking disgustedly at the manuscript of "Russian Fission," the report on the Marshall Hall conference. The report could not be distributed without his clearance.

The Assistant Secretary, who liked to be called "Jack," was a former army colonel who later served as staff director of the House Intelligence Committee, a post that calls for a politically sensitive nose. He gestured at the report, on which he had already scribbled furious objections.

"I'm not going to publish this," he said.

"Why not?"

"Well, for one thing the title is too catchy." More substantively, he mentioned that Vice President Al Gore was about to meet with Yeltsin's Prime Minister, Victor Chernomyrdin. The policy of the new administration was to be friendly with the Russians. Releasing "Russian Fission: The Nuclear Consequences of Political Disintegration" would send quite the wrong message. The matter was closed. Stewart suspected that he was acting under orders from someone higher up. This was evidently no time for a U.S. government agency to be raising questions about Yeltsin's control of the military and nuclear anarchy in Russia—especially under a title like "Russian Fission."

"If this ever sees the light of day, somebody will be fired," said Keliher finally, gesturing at the report. "This program is over."

For a time there remained an actual record of the conference itself. The proceedings had been videotaped throughout and there were also a lot of papers and notes contributed by the high-powered attendees. Then even these all vanished. Despite a later denial by Secretary O'Leary, unimpeachable sources at the department insist that the tape was burned and classified documents shredded. Keliher did his best to seize and destroy all copies of the report. The policymakers were determined to wipe all memory of "Russian Fission" from the face of the earth.

Ford had agreed with Keliher on one concession. Work on the issue could proceed very quietly, without openly bucking the administration line, deep in the classified vaults of Z Division. Now, ten months after the Marshall Hall conference, Jerry and Jessica were stepping onto the battlefield.

As soon as Jessica finished speaking that October morning, Trulock launched a full-scale attack. He left Jerry alone—no one would want to challenge him on technical data. But Jessica and her pessimistic political analyses drew the intelligence official's acerbic contempt. "Your conclusions are just all wrong," he barked.

"Aw, come on, Note," interjected Stewart. "She's right."

Jessica stood her ground. For every detailed criticism launched by Trulock, she had an equally detailed rebuttal. Ford was polite, but his questions were hostile. Stewart not only backed her up but encouraged her to expand on her arguments. For the eager young analyst who had worked so hard to get the job done, the confrontation was a shattering experience. A few days later, back at Livermore, she sent a grateful note to Stewart. "I want to thank you again for all your support last week," she wrote. "It meant a lot to me."

Stewart appreciated the letter, but he knew that his days were numbered. As far as the outside world was concerned, he was still the chief of Foreign Intelligence at the DOE, but in the corridors of power he now had the pariah status bestowed on those who fight and lose a bureaucratic war. The previous week's argument showed that even Trulock was no longer his ally. A few months later, he was out of the government.

Jessica was beginning to learn how the world worked. "There is politically correct intelligence and politically incorrect intelligence," she said later. "This was politically incorrect intelligence."

Home again and far from the political judgments of Washington, Jerry and Jessica went back to work. Neither of them shared the standard official view that nuclear weapons safety was "one area where things still work and excellence is still taken seriously." Jessica was not at all sure that the system had been excellent to begin with. She knew that they took inventory of the warheads—as Russians put it, *"nap' tsakh"*—with the fingers. After talking to Russians who had experience with the system from the inside, she reported, "Basically the weapons are just counted. It's an amateurish process." It would be easy, because of the way the inventory is conducted, to replace a warhead with an "imitator," a dummy that no one would notice for a long time. The Russian military in fact had a supply of test warheads for exercises, replicas of the real thing without the pit, the heart of the bomb. A test warhead would make an ideal imitator.

"The seals," to guard the warhead against theft, "are not tamper-proof," she pointed out. "They remove them in the process of inventory. They're not checking for the presence or absence of the essential part of the bomb, but checking the electronic components. That's why nobody would notice."

Jerry had no problem with the idea that someone would substitute a fake for a real bomb. "There's no way we can go in and check all of them"—he laughed—"because they're not even willing to tell us how many they have."

Just before the last Russian nuclear weapons in East Germany were piled onto leaky railcars and shipped home, anti-nuclear activists from the Greenpeace organization had negotiated with a twenty-eight-year-old senior lieutenant from a unit of special General Staff troops guarding a warhead storage site not far from Berlin to steal (or at least borrow—they were going to hand it back after a press conference) a nuclear weapon in exchange for resettlement in the West. In addition he wanted $320,000 for the operation, but agreed to settle for the movie rights to his story. The details had all been worked out and agreed to when the officer abruptly vanished in the turmoil that swept the Red Army at the time of the August 1991 hard-liners' coup against Mikhail Gorbachev. He had, however, convinced the antinuclear activists that he could personally, with the help of only two men, remove a 1,500-pound nuclear warhead for a Scud missile from its bunker, load it on a truck and hand it over. Greenpeace had checked his story carefully and found it entirely credible. The lieutenant planned to make the heist during the changing of the guard on the perimeter fence. There was no other security, apart from locks on the bunkers for which the officer had the codes. It would have been that simple.

In the two years since then, the Russian military had plunged ever deeper into the abyss. Once honored, respected and pampered, the officer corps were now being reduced to poverty and desperation. It was only a matter of time before some of them sought the same way out as that lieutenant in Germany.

In the Arctic city of Murmansk, exactly one month after Jessica's angry meeting in Washington, three men took that fatal step.

THE ICEBERG CLUB

On November 27, 1993, at one o'clock in the morning, a Russian navy captain stood waiting in the darkness outside 9 Ushakov Street in the far northern city of Murmansk. Alexei Tikhomirov was thirty-five years old and the navy had been his life. In fifteen years with the Northern Fleet he had earned a reputation with his commanders for being an "efficient and disciplined officer." Only a few years before, his future would have been as assured as that of the military machine he had been raised to serve. In those days, the Soviet Navy was reaching out around the world, challenging the cold war enemy on every ocean. The nuclear submarines he was trained to repair, miracles of technology, outnumbered their American counterparts. His father, retired Captain First Class Yuri Tikhomirov, now asleep in the house behind him, had once commanded a ballistic missile submarine with enough nuclear firepower in its firing tubes to obliterate half the United States.

All that had meant something in the vanished era of the Soviet Union. Everything was different now. Tonight Alexei Tikhomirov was turning into a thief.

In his pockets were burglar's tools: flashlight, hacksaw, pliers, a pair of rubber gloves and a padlock. He knew from the American movies he had seen that the gloves were necessary to mask his fingerprints. The new padlock was to replace the one he would have to break on the door of the storage shed. He knew exactly where to go and what to do, thanks to his brother Dmitry.

Dmitry was nine years younger. He too had followed the family tradition and joined the navy. Now he was a senior lieutenant assigned to warship PM-78 moored in Murmansk harbor. A PM, a *plavuchaya masterskaya,* is a floating nuclear refueling maintenance ship and Dmitry was a specialist in the nuclear fuel rods that powered the ships and submarines of the Northern Fleet. He knew exactly where they were stored, how they were guarded, how to take them apart and how to handle them. With his inside knowledge, the robbery would be easy.

A pair of headlights lit up Ushakov street as a car stopped in front of number 9. The third conspirator had arrived. Oleg Baranov was one of Alexei's closest companions. They were neighbors in Polyarny, one of the "closed" military cities surrounding Murmansk. He too was a naval man, a graduate of the Popov Naval Higher Radio-Electronics School. But after he had climbed the ranks to captain (third class) his career had come to an end. The Navy, strapped for cash, was getting rid of surplus officers. Now in his mid-forties and married—like Alexei—he was out of a job.

In the long twilight of the 1993 Arctic summer, Oleg had made a proposal. There was, he confided, an "opportunity" to sell the fresh nuclear fuel for the submarine reactors on the black market. Alexei did not rush to embrace the scheme. He wanted his brother Dmitry's assessment of whether it was possible. Dmitry knew the landscape of nuclear fuels storage on the Murmansk docks intimately. Every shed was familiar ground. He knew the guards, their habits and shortcomings. He knew the system, the alarms, the defenses, and how to separate fuel rods. When the two captains boarded Dmitry's ship and spilled their scheme to steal 20-percent-enriched uranium and sell it illegally, the senior lieutenant told them where to look.

Tonight, things were already going wrong. The plan had been for Baranov to pick up Dmitry in Polyarny before driving on into Murmansk, but he was alone. Dmitry had missed the rendezvous.

Unlike his sobersided brother, Dmitry had been accumulating black marks ever since he graduated from the Naval Higher Engineering School in Leningrad. His commanders rated him as "inefficient and undisciplined." Although he had spent hours with Alexei and Oleg explaining the layout of the fuel storage depot he never really believed they were going to go ahead with it. And right now he was locked in his cabin on the ship getting drunk with his white rat.

Everybody knew Dmitry, the nuclear fuel specialist who oversaw the recharging of the reactors, thanks to his pet, Alexander Alexandrovitch—"San Sanich" for short. The rat was a favorite of the entire ship, famous for his love of vodka. He even had his own tiny naval uniform. Tonight as his fellow conspirators waited in vain, Dmitry slopped more vodka into his friend's bowl and took another swig himself.

Meanwhile the naval captain, embarking on the first criminal act of his life, chose to go ahead. He got into the car. And with Oleg at the wheel, the pair drove off through the silent streets of the military port to steal enriched uranium, the stuff of nuclear weapons. They were Washington's worst nightmare coming true.

Murmansk sits at the hub of the Kola Peninsula that juts into the Arctic Circle. The architecture of the city is Soviet concrete slabs, assembled in haste, a forest of drab apartment blocks. Statues of Lenin stand proudly in public squares and vacant lots, braced against the frigid wind blowing off the Barents Sea. The icons of the revolution, toppled in Moscow and St. Petersburg, here in the north gaze steadfastly over the industrial terrain of the once vital strategic port, to Finland and Norway to the west, the White Sea to the south and the radiation-rich tundra, the detritus of the cold war, to the east.

The great nuclear-powered Northern Fleet—the nuclear subs, nuclear battleships and nuclear icebreakers based here—that inspired awe in the warrens of U.S. Naval Intelligence, that consumed thousands of hours of military appropriations hearings on Capitol Hill and occupied top secret NSA satellites around the clock, was turning into a collection of corroding, listing hulks. For decades these vessels were fed with enriched uranium shipped from the Machine Building Plant at Elektrostal near Moscow and the Ulbinsky Metallurgical Plant far away at Ust-Kamenogorsk in Kazakhstan. Now seventy of the Northern Fleet's 150 submarines were out of operation, laid up at local bases, with 135 nuclear reactors on board. One member of Boris Yeltsin's national security staff called them floating Chernobyls.

This strip of Arctic coastline with a dozen naval bases is Russia's largest nuclear zone, a jungle of hot fuel rods, leaky waste drums and aging ballistic missiles that could still vaporize New York. Nuclear bases at Zapadnaya Litsa, Pechenga, Motovsky Gult, Olenyaguba, Litsa Guba, Iokanga, Gremikha, Polyarny and Severomorsk crowd the coast like one long military metroplex. The Kola Peninsula has been called the most dangerous concentration of radioactive military hardware in the world. Nuclear cruise missiles, anti-ship missiles, nuclear depth bombs, nuclear artillery, nuclear torpedoes and nuclear antisubmarine missiles and rockets litter the Arctic storehouses. The Soviet Navy had a favorite joke. "How can you tell an officer of the Northern Fleet? He glows in the dark."

The propulsion reactors in Soviet submarines and surface

ships run on enriched uranium. The level of enrichment varies from 20 percent to 90 percent U-235, weapons-grade uranium, suitable for bombs. The latest generations of submarine reactors use highly enriched fuel. The Alfa Class sub, powered by liquid metal reactors to make it the fastest submarine ever built, was designed to run on weapons-grade uranium. Eight Russian icebreakers are powered with bomb-grade fuel. An aspiring weapons builder would pay dearly for such raw material. Even uranium enriched to a lower level could be precious. Purifying it to a higher level is far easier than starting from scratch. In enough quantity it could theoretically be used to make a bomb just as it is. The submarine fuel that Tikhomirov and his friend were planning to steal was enriched to 20 percent. Nuclear scientists call that "weapons-usable." The nuclear storehouses of the Northern Fleet were a lethal treasure trove for desperate men.

Four months before the night on which Tikhomirov set out to commit the first crime of his life, two navy servicemen broke into a fleet depot at Andreeva Guba, thirty miles from the Norwegian border. They stole three pounds of 30-percent-enriched U-235. Arrested, they claimed they had been ordered to purloin the uranium by two naval officers. Military investigators suspected a possible connection with a Murmansk-St. Petersburg criminal ring. The thieves' motive was apparent: money.

By 1993, two years after the Soviet collapse, Northern Fleet paychecks were running two to four months late. Even when they were paid they often got only a third of their salary, just enough to buy bread. Even at the top, the system was hand-to-mouth. Once a month, a plane flew up from Moscow carrying ruble notes. The commander in chief of the navy's sprawling Severomorsk closed zone counted it himself. He always found the amount was short. Cash had been siphoned off in Moscow. The admiral had to parcel out what was left to his subordinate commanders. The first priority was the admiral's own headquarters staff. Equally important were the ballistic missile submarines, symbol of Russia's credentials as a great power. At the very bottom of the list were the crumbling facilities for storing nuclear fuel and the lethal cesspits of nuclear waste. The salvage teams trained to handle the waste had in any case been dispatched to Vietnam to earn hard currency by clearing mines. Sometimes, there was not enough food for the sailors. In 1993 in the Pacific Fleet four enlisted men actually starved to death.

Looting the system that failed to feed them was a natural recourse for the officers and men. It was an attitude that predated the collapse of Communism. There had long been an attitude among naval officers that stealing from the state was not stealing. Stealing, selling, swapping—anything went so long as it didn't sink the ship. Now the controls that had kept vital and dangerous materials like weapons-usable uranium safely locked up was breaking down. For Tikhomirov, whose salary—when he got it—amounted to $210 a month, the lure of instant riches was irresistible.

The two men drove through the poorly lit industrial zone to a deserted building site on Nakhimovskaya Street. Alexei, who once had high hopes of a brilliant naval career, left his accomplice behind the wheel in the getaway car. The novice thief walked gingerly along the railroad tracks that led to the nuclear site.

A rustic wooden house with yellow-and-blue trim bore a sign reading Military Unit 31326. It was surrounded by decaying apartment blocks. Neighborhood children liked to climb the packed snow wedged against the fence and play king of the mountain, yards away from Quonset huts stuffed with enriched uranium. Alexei did not have to climb the half-rotten boards; there was a hole large enough to walk through. No one stopped him. The place was deserted. He darted through the snow toward the emergency door at the back of storage shed 3–30. The only barrier was a padlock.

Alexei attacked the hasp of the lock with his hacksaw. After ten minutes of hard sawing it gave way. Ripping it off, he flung it away. Now he looked for the panel of firefighting equipment near the entrance. Snatching down a red metal hook, he levered open the door and ducked inside, throwing the hook aside. No armed guards appeared, no alarm blasted as he switched on his pocket flashlight.

There was indeed an alarm on the door. As soon as the thief forced it open a bell should have gone off in the guard post not far away. But the bell stayed silent. The ancient system had been corroded by the salt sea air. It was permanently stuck.

There were guards on duty: three old ladies armed with pistols, which they were afraid to touch. They had no intention of making the rounds of the uranium storage sheds. The area was littered with scrap metal and very dark. "How can I go there?" one of them later told an investigator. "I'm going to get raped."

Inside the shed, on the left, Tikhomirov looked for radiation package 23, stored under a tarp. By the light of his flashlight, he inspected the fuel rods inside and found the spot where he would have to break the assembly. Alexei vigorously sawed. After ten minutes he had made a dent in the hard metal. With a vigorous twist, he was able to break the assembly in two. He carefully packed the enriched uranium in his bag and wrenched two more assemblies apart.

Forty-three minutes later Alexei stole back across the dark lot with his precious cargo and through the porous fence to Baranov's car. In his nervous haste the captain forgot to shut the door and put on the new padlock he had carefully brought to replace the one broken on the way in. The old lock was still lying where he had thrown it. He and Oleg shifted the bag into the trunk and sped off down the Murmansk-Severomorsk highway. They stopped once to dispose of the pliers and the rubber gloves. Oleg dropped Alexei off at his parents' house and went on home to Polyarny, where he hid the booty in his garage. They had stolen nine pounds of enriched uranium.

Twelve hours later the daytime duty officer of the guard,

another lady, decided to inspect the storage sheds. On the ground outside storage shed 3–30 she found the broken pad-lock. The red fire hook Tikhomirov had grabbed to open the door was lying nearby. By the end of the day the navy knew that someone had stolen the enriched uranium from three fuel rods. But no one had any idea where to look for the thieves or their loot, let alone in a garage in the closed military zone in Polyarny.

The conspirators went to ground. It was Baranov's job to find a buyer. At the time he had first approached the Tikhomi-rov brothers he had been in touch with a Mafiya group. No deal to buy the uranium resulted, but it may have been then that the conspirators fixed on their asking price: $50,000.

The months rolled by. The uranium stayed safe and undis-turbed in its hiding place. Dmitry, who had stayed away the night of the robbery getting drunk with his rat, was in bad odor with his co-conspirators. Now his recklessness sank all three of them. When the buyer promised by Baranov failed to material-ize, it was Dmitry who took the initiative to broadcast the fact that stolen nuclear materials were hidden in Oleg's garage.

Reeling over to his friend Lieutenant Parolov at the cap-tain's June drinks party, he asked him to help "sell some met-als." Parolov didn't take him seriously. Four days later, Dmitry was back, using every art of persuasion to enlist Parolov as a fourth conspirator. It took Parolov another four days before he decided to turn in his friend. On June 28, Parolov knocked on the cabin door of Captain Kalinkin on board ship PM-12 and told his senior officer the unpleasant truth. The criminals were military men. It was a stain on the Northern Fleet. Nonetheless, Kalinkin alerted the high command. The Tikhomirov brothers and Baranov were arrested. They confessed and said that they had been driven to crime by "despair and poverty."

When Yuri Tikhomirov heard that his two sons had been arrested for serious crimes against the Russian Navy and the state, the old captain first class had a stroke.

Alexei drew a sentence of three to five years in prison. Oleg got three years. Dmitry, because he had stayed home with the rat, was granted amnesty and discharged.

The investigation was headed by the tough young "Investigator of Particularly Important Cases at the military office of the public prosecutor of the Northern Fleet in Severomorsk." His name was Mikhail Kulik and he liked to refer to himself as a "Russian tiger." This was his second nuclear case; he had already dealt with the sailors who had robbed the storage depot at Andreeva Guba. "There are only two other investigators like me in this country," he said. "And they're both drunkards."

Kulik was a fourth-generation naval officer and, amidst the general corruption and decay of the system, he still projected a sense of pride and honor. He was outraged by the case and openly contemptuous of the conspirators. For one thing, in aiming to score a $50,000 payoff, they hadn't set their sights high enough. "In St. Petersburg, that's one three-room apartment, not three bedrooms. They wanted a new car, maybe a TV, videos. For $50,000, what else can you get?" Nor did he think much of Alexei's efforts at criminal professionalism. Tikhomirov "was a great watcher of American movies. So he was wearing rubber gloves. They are not safe. A professional wears leather gloves."

For Kulik, the real outrage was that these amateur thieves had almost gotten away with it. If the panicked Alexei had not forgotten the padlock, no one might have noticed that the fuel rods were gone for another ten years. "Let's call it a walk-in. My daughter's five. She could do it. He went in, opened the container, took out the rods of uranium, got the pieces he wanted, and took them away."

After reviewing the broken alarm system, the old ladies afraid to touch their guns or go out in the dark, the hole in the fence, the investigator thought seriously of bringing charges against the site commander. "But how could I? For ages the

commander was screaming and shouting about a new alarm
system. The answer was: 'No money.' "

If Baranov's original discussions with the mysterious criminal group had panned out, the materials might never have been
recovered at all. Kulik's private theory was that the gangsters
wanted it as a murder weapon. He had data on assassinations
done with uranium dust, a subtle tool that killed its victim
slowly. "In the analysis after the death," he explained, "they find
only the leukemia. You need only a very small amount of dust.
You can put it in a fur hat and they die."

There were plenty of criminals on view in Murmansk itself.
While the once mighty Northern Fleet rusted at its moorings
and the admiral waited desperately for the cash from Moscow,
the Mafiya were packing out the cavernous dining room of the
Arktika Hotel every night. More prosperous mafiosi made their
way in their Lada Samaras with smoked-glass windows to the
Iceberg Club, tucked behind a nondescript office block not far
from the city center. Inside there was blond wood, nouvelle
cuisine and Courvoisier. This was the haunt of the Murmansk
new rich, the black marketeers and import-export merchants
bringing their molls for caviar blinis—businessmen who could
see an opportunity. The club sat in the midst of a vast reservoir
of enriched uranium, the legacy of the cold war navy. To what
extent some of the customers might have dabbled in the nuclear export trade was their own closely guarded secret. Kulik
had enough evidence to state that the Northern Fleet was in
the Mafiya's sights.

"According to my data," he reported, "organized crime
groups have become more active in trying to obtain large con-
signments of radioactive material from the Northern Fleet.
They contact the staff, study weak points of the system and the
possibilities of large-scale thefts."

In the wake of the Tikhomirovs' arrest, the Russian Navy
hastened to claim that the nuclear storage site was now secure.
But nine months later it was still possible to drive up to the site

and, in broad daylight, climb up a mound of dirty snow and over the fence. Close by, a nuclear icebreaker with bomb-grade fuel in its reactor lay moored at the dockside, apparently deserted.

Out of the eighty-eight Northern Fleet nuclear submarines that had been taken out of service, only thirty-two had been dismantled. The others were floating stores of nuclear fuel. Each sub held two nuclear reactors. The reactor cores held 200 to 300 fuel assemblies. If the fuel was 90 percent enriched, ten fuel assemblies had the requisite uranium to build a bomb. The only facility in all of Russia where they could be dismantled and rendered harmless was at Chelyabinsk 65, a closed city of the nuclear complex thousands of miles away in the Ural Mountains. Once, four closely guarded trains a year had made the long journey. In a hundred and fifty years all the fuel from the obsolete subs would have been moved. But now the navy owed Chelyabinsk five billion rubles, money it did not have. No more trains were running. The fuel had to stay where it was, or so the authorities hoped.

Thanks to the broken padlock abandoned by Alexei in his frantic hurry to get away, the navy knew within hours that the uranium was missing. Had the captain been a more professional criminal (and his brother less reckless) the robbery might never have been discovered. Even after the navy was aware of the break-in, the news was kept secret for eight months. No one in the outside world knew that enriched fuel had disappeared without a trace that November night in 1993. The Yeltsin government preferred that the world believe that the military officers responsible for nuclear materials and nuclear weapons were an incorruptible force, high priests guarding Russia's greatest treasure. But the system was breaking down. The same month that Captain Tikhomirov carried the uranium through an unguarded fence, an infinitely more ominous event occurred in a secret city in the heart of Russia.

There were ten secret cities in the Russian nuclear weapons

complex, so secret that they never appeared on any map. Even in the classified directories in Moscow they were given misleading names linked to towns many miles away. They had been built years before by prisoners of the Gulag for the sole purpose of designing and building the Soviet nuclear arsenal. The 700,000 people who lived in them were privileged prisoners, hemmed in by barbed wire and layers of security but at the same time granted a standard of living far above that of the average Soviet citizen. Outsiders envied the "chocolate eaters," even though they needed special permission to leave their gilded cages or even make a long-distance phone call.

By the middle of 1993 the good times were gone. Moscow, which had once lavished the best of everything on the nuclear workers, no longer cared. Paychecks stopped arriving in April. There was no medicine in the clinics, once so well stocked. Soon there might be no food. The guards who had patrolled the perimeter were beginning to desert. The cries of desperation inside were growing louder. "We are desperate," the chocolate eaters said to anyone who would listen. "We have got to have money."

As Russian warheads were taken out of the silos because of the START arms reduction treaty, they were shipped back intact to the plants where they had been made. The numbers mounted steadily.

Zlatoust 36, deep in the Urals, is one such city. Thirty thousand people live there. On a Friday evening in November 1993, two Zlatoust workers from the seventh section of the Priborostroitelny Zavod—Equipment Building Plant—drove out of the plant in a truck. In theory, any nuclear weapon not in a bunker was specially guarded. Even when weapons were locked behind multiple steel doors, access was restricted to carefully selected two-man teams, independently monitored by a third—in theory. In theory, all vehicles leaving the site had to be rigorously checked and searched. That day, no one bothered about the rules. In the back of the truck were two nuclear warheads.

These were the most fearsome weapons of all, because Zlatoust 36 was the designated assembly center for ballistic missile reentry vehicles, the multimegaton strategic warheads normally trained on American targets. Tikhomirov had been after bomb-making materials that could be used to assemble a crude bomb. The nationalists in Baku, years before, had threatened a cache of small tactical weapons—torpedo warheads. This was something different.

From the plant, the workmen drove into the town. Their cargo would normally travel only in a heavily guarded convoy to a special train with its own detachment of troops. These men had enough firepower bouncing around in the back of the truck to wipe out half the eastern seaboard. Turning down a side street, they stopped outside a private garage. With difficulty, they manhandled the warheads, each weighing several hundred pounds, off the truck and inside. Then they went home.

Three days later, sometime early on Monday morning, someone at the plant did a count and realized that two nuclear warheads were missing. A rapid check revealed that they had been loaded into the workers' truck. Soon after, they were retrieved from the workers' garage. The men were arrested and jailed.

This terrifying incident was so embarrassing to the military custodians of the warheads that they kept it a closely held secret. Even the military prosecutors who handled the men's secret trial were given only the barest details. They could only speculate why the men had done it. One benign speculation was that the men handling weapons powerful enough to evaporate a city were simply blind drunk and made off with the lethal cargo for a bet. Having successfully gotten away with it, they opted to hide them in the garage while they thought about getting them back. Others who got wind of the affair thought that they had seized an opportunity in the hope of finding a market. The most sinister explanation was that a buyer was waiting to take delivery.

Officially, the incident never happened. General Evgeni Maslin, the head of the Russian Defense Ministry's Twelfth Directorate, the man in charge of all the military's nuclear weapons, continued to proclaim, "There have never been diversions of nuclear weapons. There are no grounds for concern." Fortunately for Maslin, there were people in Washington who took him at his word. They still believed in the Surety of Russian nuclear weapons and materials.

Then, in June 1994, just as Dmitry Tikhomirov was pressing a fellow officer to help him unload the enriched uranium stored in a closed-zone garage, an incident in the quaint Bavarian town of Landshut, Germany, caught the attention of the White House. A Czech, four Slovaks and a German woman were arrested for smuggling nuclear materials. German authorities sent a sample of the material to the Karlsruhe Institute, where nuclear scientist-detectives search for "fingerprints" to determine the life history of a sample of uranium. They can tell which country it came from and whether it was used in a reactor, a weapons plant or naval fuel. Russian material, say the detectives, has a distinctive signature.

After analysis of the 0.8 gram of uranium 235 seized in Landshut, it was clear that the chaotic state of Russian nuclear security was no longer just a problem for a Russian tiger.

MIRAGE GOLD

The rising tide of intelligence flowing into the White House on theft of nuclear materials landed in a vaultlike office studded with locks. The vault was attached to one of the White House situation rooms, where access was denied to anyone without the entry codes. This fortress in the recesses of the White House complex was the home of the Nuclear Smuggling Working Group. The roster of members included specialists from the CIA and the Defense Intelligence Agency, from the Department of Energy, the State Department and the FBI. This elite corps of scientists, terrorism advisers and intelligence analysts reported to the National Security Council, the branch of the White House responsible for both Russian policy and nuclear security, which was headquartered in the Old Executive Office Building just to the left of the main White House gates. The OEOB was a massive Victorian gray elephant. Most Washington visitors stared at it blankly and asked, "What's in there?"

Inside the cool, wide halls with towering ceilings and pol-

ished wood floors led to the warren of offices where White
House staffers toiled late into the night drafting Presidential
Decision Directives, poring over legislation, liaising with government agencies and assembling "the book" for presidential
summits. It was where much of the White House business got
done. It also housed the secure area where embassy cables, Interpol reports, CIA assessments and NSA code-word intercepts
were read and coordinated by the White House Nuclear Smuggling Working Group. In September 1994, the Working Group
got a new recruit, Jessica Stern.

The woman who feasted on black boar in the Caucasus and
made her mark at Z Division moved into the White House vault
only two months after the Tikhomirov brothers were exposed
by their fellow officers in Murmansk. Jessica landed at the
White House gate as a prestigious Council on Foreign Relations Fellow, once again an outsider moving into an entrenched
and hostile bureaucracy. This time, the Z Division alumna and
protégée of Jerry Dzakowic was in the "shark pool," as the
White House was known to staffers. The minute she put her
decaf cappuccino on the vault desk, Jessica had more enemies
than friends. But there was a small endangered group sounding the alarm on nuclear security. From the first day on the job,
Jessica's new colleagues warned her that the threat of Russian
nuclear materials or a tactical weapon entering the United
States was a low priority. The allies she found she could trust
were deep inside the national security fiefdoms of the State Department, Pentagon, CIA and Department of Energy. They told
her the issue was falling through the cracks.

In the White House pecking order Stern was very junior.
Three layers of officialdom separated her from the President.
At the Nuclear Smuggling Working Group, she answered to the
Directorate for Russian, Ukrainian and Eurasian Affairs under
Nicholas Burns. In that chain of command, she carried the title
of director. In nuclear matters, she also was reporting to Dan
Poneman, at the Nonproliferation Directorate, a skilled in-

fighter who had weathered the Bush and Clinton administrations. He in turn answered to Anthony Lake, the President's National Security Adviser, who only considered an issue or a request if it was urgent, which meant a crisis to defuse or a rush briefing that had to be on the President's desk within twenty-four hours. In the charged air of the National Security Adviser's office, bomb-grade uranium turning up in Landshut, Germany, had to compete with massacres in Bosnia, the tumultuous China trade issue, the specter of Vladimir Zhirinovsky, the Russian nationalist who would sweep up parliamentary seats in the December 1994 elections, grabbing votes with his pledge to clear the wreckage of the Soviet breakup and restore the Czarist empire.

Lake was like a surgeon treating gunshot wounds. Problems were bandaged up and wheeled out of his office to make room for the next one. The handful of senior advisers beneath him were clamoring for his attention. Jessica in her vault rarely occupied his thoughts. He would make time for her when a terrorist group detonated a nuclear weapon or Saddam Hussein got the bomb.

The White House job gave Jessica stratospheric clearances. She knew as much as anyone else in the government about the crumbling state of Russian nuclear stockpiles and fuel depots. She escaped the vault most afternoons, striding across Pennsylvania Avenue to the Au Bon Pain coffee shop. There she mulled over the list of "nuclear incidents" of missing materials in 1994. She was looking at five cases a week.

Uranium and plutonium were seeping through the porous borders of Russia on trains, in the baggage holds of airplanes, in private cars. Some smugglers were ignorant about their cargo. One placed a pellet of radioactive cesium in his pocket and before finding a buyer expired from radiation poisoning. Others who had entered the obscure and tentative trade made her catch her breath. Their methods seemed dangerously professional. The list reflected both.

Hungarian border guards had seized uranium bound for Austria concealed in a fruit jar. Bulgarian police found capsules of radioactive material on a bus bound for Turkey. The Turkish police arrested an Azeri national, from somewhere near Baku, selling 750 grams of enriched uranium. Four Indian villagers were arrested in the act of selling 2.5 kilograms of yellowcake, uranium extracted from ore. Estonian police had arrested a man with three kilograms of uranium 238 buried under his garage. Jessica skimmed most of the incidents. The uranium was the wrong kind to make a bomb. There were others that bore investigating, including the capture of three Russians with nearly nine pounds of highly enriched uranium in St. Petersburg on June 6 and the seizure of U-235 in Russia on October 17 along with "twelve members of a criminal gang." On July 19 the Turkish national police arrested seven Turks and claimed to have seized twelve kilograms, thirty pounds, of "weapons-grade uranium." Jessica now had the entire intelligence apparatus of the U.S. government to probe details of anything startling in the reports. She was looking for patterns, for any evidence of systematic smuggling and polished skills. Her worry was any sign of the Russian Mafiya.

Jessica was coming to appreciate how badly prepared the legions of government agencies dealing with nuclear matters were for battling that kind of enemy. The Nuclear Smuggling Working Group, the White House attempt to face the problem, was little more than a Band-Aid. It was an "interagency group," with members from rival bureaucracies. Jessica quickly discovered that skirmishes and the occasional bloody battle over turf were the order of the day. Agencies were going off on their own when there was a smuggling incident. That was causing havoc. There was no communication, only bitter competition between the FBI and CIA over who "owned" the issue.

If smugglers did manage to insert a nuclear device into an American city and threatened to evaporate several city blocks, making that city uninhabitable, the U.S. government could not

stop it. Bungling, arrogance, logistical chaos and the unwilling-
ness of agencies to communicate were paralyzing their ability
to defuse the worst nightmare of the post-cold-war age. The
problems became abundantly clear that October, a month after
Jessica entered the vault, in the streets of New Orleans.

●

There had been heavy rains that fall pounding the rising Mississippi and filling the levees. The air was muggy and uncertain
under a gray metal sky. The sound of the foghorn seemed to
echo through the massive grain silos along the shore that stood
like a battery of missiles. Sometimes the silos blew up from the
combustible dust swirling inside.

On Sunday, October 16, at 7:55 in the morning, most of the
city's inhabitants were asleep. The only sound was the river-
front streetcar bell and the engines of the tankers gliding down-
river to the Gulf. The early-morning trade was drinking chicory
coffee and eating beignets, New Orleans doughnuts. The musi-
cians in the Vieux Carré had put their instruments to bed. The
praline and perfume shops, the po'boy and snowball stands,
were closed. The rows of shotgun houses, weathered down to
the cypress boards, showed little signs of life behind the jalou-
sie shutters. Café Brazil and Café Istanbul, the House of Blues,
Snug Harbor, were recovering from another Saturday night.
And there were only smudges of blood on the waterfront left
over from the midnight cockfights.

That morning New Orleans was invaded. Eight hundred
and fifty "players" in a full-scale nuclear exercise converged on
an empty industrial complex on the Intracoastal Waterway.
The participants from the Department of Defense, the Department of Energy, the FBI and the Federal Emergency Management Agency were operating under the strictest secrecy. Their
mission was to save New Orleans from a catastrophic detonation of a nuclear bomb. Mirage Gold was the code name for
this deadly game. Two and a half years of planning had gone

into the details. A "no notice" Emergency Deployment Readiness Evaluation had already been conducted in June to test the precise number of hours and minutes it took to get the Nuclear Emergency Search Teams (NEST) airborne from Travis, Nellis, Andrews and Kirtland air force bases.

Searchers and the equipment packs had been called up at the Department of Energy Nevada Operations Office at Las Vegas, the Livermore and Sandia nuclear labs, the Atlanta office of the Department of Defense Joint Nuclear Accidents Coordinating Committee, and WAMO, the Washington Aerial Measurements Office. There were careful guidelines drawn up nearly a year before at the MICA DIG "tabletop" exercise in Washington for the Pentagon, the Department of Energy, the FBI and the Federal Emergency Management Agency to pool their vast resources to find the bomb in New Orleans, what they called the malevolent nuclear threat.

At the New Orleans Naval Air Station, Alvin Callender Field, one hundred and twenty controllers, evaluators, players in the game, had spent four days in September setting up communications equipment. Code-named Mild Cover, the secret pregame test checked the "secure" voice and data transmission systems, the radios of each agency, the microwave links, the telephone systems, the compressed video displays, the TAC SAT tactical satellite installation at the Forrestal Operations Center. With so much planning and rehearsing, Mirage Gold should have run like clockwork. The only complaint might have been that everything was too staged. But on the first gray morning in October, things were already falling apart.

The Mirage Gold crisis itself, dreamed up by a Scenario Working Group, was prophetic, coming six months before the bombing at Oklahoma City. The Patriots for National Unity, a fictitious homegrown terrorist group, was plotting to overthrow the U.S. government. The FBI knew from an informant that the PNU terrorists were planning a bombing campaign, conventional bombs packed with high explosives, or so the FBI thought. The FBI's special agent in charge got word that their informant was now a hostage of the Patriots, at a New Orleans safe house.

In the first hours of Mirage Gold, the FBI's hostage in the safe-house drama dominated play. The other agencies, massed in the various buildings of the Brown and Root warehouse complex on Engineer Road in Gretna, just across the Mississippi from Moon Walk and Bourbon Street, sat tight. The organizational chart for this exercise looked like a maze: there was the ECP, the Exercise Command Post, the JOC, the Joint Operations Center, the CM Cell, the Consequence Management Cell, the TOC, the Technical Operations Center. There was also the DOD/DOE CP, command post for the Defense Department and the Department of Energy. There was the FBI Command Post and the FEMA Command Post. When the players from one agency entered the sanctuary of another, everyone shielded their computer screens.

Early Monday morning, the FBI's Hostage Rescue Team and the New Orleans SWAT team stormed the safe house in an "assault," killing six terrorists and rescuing their hostage informer. Inside the safe house there was evidence, planted for the game, that the Patriots had a stash of nuclear materials. The rescued hostage said the surviving Patriots were scouting for a bomb site. One of the terrorists had leased a boat, moored on Lake Michaud. With the introduction of a nuclear threat, the FBI called in the Pentagon and the Department of Energy. No one bothered to call in the New Orleans police, then under investigation for corruption by the FBI.

The task now was to comb New Orleans for an atomic bomb. The "real world" intruded almost immediately when a Nuclear Emergency Search Team member stepped off a plane and had a heart attack. Then there were the problems with the badges. Seven different security badges were issued to Mirage Gold players. Anyone who wanted access to an exercise site at the New Orleans International Airport, the Superdome, the

Inner Harbor Navigation Canal, the A. B. Patterson Power Plant, needed to be cleared. The FBI were temporarily "Q-cleared." Other government agencies, to their rage, were "red-badged," with the same designation as vendors selling lucky dogs. FEMA, the Federal Emergency Management Agency, whose job it is to cope with the evacuation of New Orleans, the prevention of uncontrolled panic, the protection of millions of people from lethal radiation, was red-badged. The other agencies would not tell FEMA people what was going on. In fact, every agency whose job it was to look after the safety of the people of New Orleans was kept in the dark, including the state and city police and the governor of Louisiana. The governor was so enraged that the FBI would not talk to him that on Tuesday he called the President of the United States.

"The protection and safety of the population" if the bomb went off "was not considered by the FBI," wrote FEMA in its after-action report.

The Department of Energy balked at the FBI's treatment of the state of Louisiana. The FBI was required by law to alert state authorities about a potential hazard to the public. "It is a drastic mistake," said the DOE report, "to assume that NEST technology and procedures will always succeed, resulting in zero nuclear yield." New Orleans had to be ready for a dose of lethal radiation.

Even those players who were "Q-cleared" for nuclear secrets found Mirage Gold artificial to the point of absurdity. Critical information that warped the game was leaked to players. And the NEST teams were even told where to find the bomb.

On Tuesday morning, the Nuclear Energy Search Teams were tipped off to drive by a small flying service at an airstrip off Magazine Road in Belle Chasse. Team members got a "hit" of radiation on their detectors and tracked down the nuclear device in a "hot" airport shed. Three terrorists from the Patriots for National Unity were camped at the airport. At the FBI's orders, players waited patiently until noon the following day

until the Patriots sped off in a van. The FBI "secured" the airport and everyone concentrated on the storage garage with the
atomic bomb inside. It was armed and set to detonate at noon
on Thursday.

The NEST team erected a forty-foot cone over the shed that
housed the bomb. They pumped in thick foam to check the
blast effects and catch radioactive particles. Unfortunately the
exercises planners, after two and a half years of preparation,
had not secured permission to detonate the simulated bomb.
The shed was on Belle Chasse Naval Air Station property. Still,
permission was never obtained. Without a detonation, the
dense watery foam would not turn into a manageable pool of
slurry. No one could battle the foam to see if the bomb was
properly disabled. No forensic specialists could search the
drenched crime scene. Worst of all, no one knew how to get rid
of the foam. There was nothing in the OPLAN, the Operations
Plan, the Technical Support Plan, the Communications Plan,
the Evaluation Plan, the Controller Plan, the Safety Plan, the
Security Plan, the Opposition Force Plan, or the Real World
Plan, for disposing of a forty-foot-high cone of foam. There was
no technology for foam dispersal. No one had worked the foam
problem into the $10 million budget. The disheartened search
teams were left with a stubborn mountain of foam and no hard
data on dismantling an atomic bomb.

In the end, in the black comedy unfolding in New Orleans,
the Department of Energy concluded that the teams did not
stop the release of radioactive fallout. Had this been real, the
city of New Orleans would not have been protected.

Mirage Gold, from top to bottom, was an exercise in confusion. The nuclear search teams had no local drivers. The FBI
escorts, who were supposed to guide them, were often late and
regularly got lost. The escorts did not know New Orleans. Batteries for the hand held radios ran low. There were no spares.
The players' phone directory, essential for contacting various

agencies using fake numbers, were not ready until two days after play began.

With all of the elaborate planning, there were not enough computers for the players. In any case, many did not know how to use the program or the electronic message board. Some of the computers did not have the correct software. Information was wiped out during a power cut. The result was that many of the eight hundred and some participants were out of touch for much of the week until the "hot wash" on Friday morning. Those who showed up at the TOC, the command center in the warehouse district, could not find enough chairs to sit on.

Other players at the bomb site were so overworked they suffered from heat exhaustion in their nuclear suits. Bad briefings, poor intelligence, and the "unrealistic" events left most players thoroughly depressed. Mirage Gold was not a pleasant experience. "We were operating," said one weary NEST player, "in a vacuum."

In the White House, Jessica knew that if they could not prevent the catastrophic detonation of a nuclear weapon on American soil, she and her colleagues would have to stop the leakage of nuclear materials outside the United States, preferably inside Russia. Soon after the fiasco of Mirage Gold, Jessica was made chairman of the Nuclear Smuggling Working Group.

Like Cassandra, she sat in the vault, too preoccupied with doomsday scenarios to think about dinner at Café Milano or dancing at the Nine Thirty Club. She stayed after hours trying to detect any signs that organized crime was moving nuclear materials. And when two caches of highly enriched uranium turned up on the black market with the same signature, meaning it was uranium from the same Russian source, Jessica knew she was no longer dealing with the lone amateur thief.

•

The Bavarian town of Landshut is something out of *Grimm's Fairy Tales*. The crooked medieval streets lie in the shadow of an early-thirteenth-century castle on the prow of the ridge above. The Renaissance capital of lower Bavaria lies on the banks of the Isar River. Step-gabled fifteenth-century houses line the Altstadt. The people of Landshut are not accustomed to seizures of highly enriched uranium.

It was not the quantity of uranium 235 seized in July 1994 along the Isar that was intriguing but the high quality. Alarm bells started to go off in Jessica's vault and across the river at CIA headquarters at Langley, Virginia, when a uranium sample from Landshut had exactly the same "fingerprints" as another, much larger batch seized six months later in the Czech Republic. On December 14, Czech police confiscated 2.72 kilograms of highly enriched U-235, 87.7 percent enriched, from the back seat of a car in Prague. It was the largest confirmed seizure of near-bomb-grade nuclear material to date. When police rounded up the smugglers, a Czech nuclear physicist was among them.

Stern concentrated on the connection between Prague and Landshut. The White House was convinced the Russian material was now seeping out of the once impervious secret cities, closed to the public and absent from any map. Identical nuclear fingerprints from two smuggling operations uncovered in different countries meant organization, criminal conspiracy. Stern had been bracing herself for this.

When Dan Wagner, a seasoned analyst from the CIA, disclosed the Agency assessment of the Prague and Landshut cases to the Working Group in the White House vault everyone knew they had a problem. Nearly seven pounds of highly enriched uranium, so potent that it could easily be converted into a bomb, was far more ominous than even the Tikhomirovs' fuel rods in Murmansk. The Czech authorities were reporting that the shipments were part of a larger cache of ten kilos, twenty-two pounds, enough to obliterate downtown Washington.

The highly enriched uranium had been smuggled out of Obninsk, a secret city eighty miles southwest of Moscow. Obninsk was home to research reactors, bomb assembly plants and Russian naval training facilities. The Institute of Physics and Power Engineering there was the guardian of a vast stockpile of weapons-grade uranium. On site there were zero power research reactors and a mountain of small disks that looked like smooth tin pillboxes. Some were stuffed with fifty grams of plutonium. Others were filled with bomb-grade uranium. A dozen disks slid effortlessly into a jacket pocket.

The smuggling ring looked like a *Mission Impossible* team—a truck driver, a mechanic, a bus driver, a metals trader and a nuclear physicist. As a group, their expertise ran from the rudiments of transport, essential knowledge for navigating the territory between Moscow and Europe, to the subtleties of esoteric nuclear materials and inside connections to the nuclear world. The physicist was Jaroslav Vagner, who quit his job in a Czech nuclear research institute because of the poor wages. Vagner had then made the unlikely career choice of opening a bakery. The physicist-baker developed interesting ties to an import-export trucking firm called Autotransport.

Autotransport's drivers were hired in Russia and Belarus. One Russian smuggler caught in Prague was Alexandr Scerbinin, a former nuclear worker employed by Autotransport. Scerbinin was jailed along with another former nuclear worker on the Autotransport payroll. Valera Kunicky was from newly independent Belarus, an impoverished wasteland badly irradiated by the Chernobyl accident. Whole regions of Belarus were condemned. No-entry zones, where the abandoned villages were too "hot" for human habitation, were now a thieves' den for Belarussian criminals. The post-nuclear world of mutants and criminals was reality in Belarus.

The Russian nuclear worker Alexandr Scerbinin was a foot soldier in the nuclear smuggling ring. A senior Czech official who interrogated him found the Russian was paralyzed with fear. It was not Czech justice that terrified him but his masters back in Russia. Scerbinin said that his family in Russia would be murdered if he talked. His fellow smuggler Kunicky had the same apprehensions. "We caught the couriers," said the senior intelligence official to his colleagues.

The couriers and the physicist had packed the sample of the highly enriched uranium in metal containers and boarded the train in Moscow for the long journey to Prague. Czech investigators reported that at one point a sleeping-car conductor was enlisted to store the material in a secure car, restricted to train personnel. The journey through Belarus and Poland included a change of trains in Warsaw. No one noticed the metal containers. Once in Prague, the uranium was deposited in a bank safe. Again, no one asked questions. The smugglers were free to begin their search for a buyer, armed with a certificate from Obninsk with photographs of the available stock and a price from the Russians. They were charging $800 per gram.

The Czech physicist and the Russian from Autotransport then managed to contact German middlemen prepared to move their deadly goods. The middlemen were well versed enough in nuclear matters to gauge a market price, double what the Russian sellers were asking. Vagner and Scerbinin sat tight in Prague, waiting for the middlemen to find clients and a deal. At first, there were snags. North Korean nuclear shoppers allegedly pulled out of negotiations because they found what they needed elsewhere. Spanish buyers wanted to use counterfeit dollars. A potential Nigerian sale was canceled when the men from Lagos, according to the Czech authorities, wanted to pay in drugs.

The German middlemen then found their buyer. The terms were shipments of five kilograms of highly enriched uranium per month. According to the Czech police, the Russian suppliers informed their couriers, Vagner and Scerbinin, that the requisite materials were available, ninety pounds of uranium so highly enriched it was easily converted to bomb grade. Over the long term, the Russian sellers were offering a ton.

The physicist, the Russian and the Belarussian were arrested as they sat in a late-model Saab in front of a Prague restaurant. The goods, seven pounds' worth, were in the back seat. They were waiting to meet their buyer. Five others were later rounded up, including a Prague policeman.

Soon after the exceptionally high-quality Prague uranium had been analyzed, the Czech Republic's top spymaster was summoned to CIA headquarters in Langley. The Czech official was younger than his counterparts. He was slight and soft-spoken. He had been in the intelligence business only since Václav Havel and his coterie of intellectuals and artists took power. The intelligence man learned his craft as a dissident in the Czech underground, taking enormous risks, leading a double life under the watchful gaze of the Czech secret police. Now, after three days of secret talks at Langley, the spy agency's sprawling complex across the Potomac from Washington, he moved with his closest associate to a private apartment on Central Park West in New York. Looking out over the reservoir, he chain-smoked.

"It could easily be converted to weapons grade," he said, puffing thoughtfully. Material enough for several hundred atomic bombs might have been sold on the Prague pipeline. The fears were justified about the new Russia. You could buy anything. He had hoped the gloomy predictions were wrong because the Czech Republic was wide open as a transit country. In fact, it was ideal, like America at the beginning of the twentieth century.

He lit another cigarette and joked that the thieves' Saab had been impounded in his personal parking place for three weeks after the capture. "They stole my parking place."

The spy chief returned to Prague with the unsettling knowledge that, for the first time, an expert in the business, a physicist, was involved and the U-235 was so close to bomb grade that in the hands of a nuclear physicist, it could be a devastating weapon. The relief of having the physicist and friends behind bars was short-lived.

What happened after the defendants were in jail was more hair-raising for him than a potential sale to foreign buyers. One of the Czech investigators on the case received a letter. The sender offered him substantial sums in a Swiss bank account to release Scerbinin, the Russian. If the carrot was appealing, the stick was very unnerving. The sender threatened to explode a small nuclear device in downtown Prague.

In the narrow streets of the baroque old town, paved with rough cobblestones, the cafés every few yards in Staromestske were always jammed. It was a popular gathering place for American students, equipped with the *Rough Guide* and laden with backpacks. Any backpack in the square, the Czech spymaster knew, could be a tactical nuclear bomb. The maze of alleyways led to the six-hundred-year-old Charles Bridge, where puppeteers and street vendors trolled for business in the crowd. The crowd funneling under the bridge towers joined by a castellated arch moved in a viscous mass uphill through the artists' quarter of Malo Starna. A small nuclear device here in the medieval streets would kill thousands.

The men in jail had said very little. They would talk only if the spymaster could get their families out of Russia. That, he knew, was impossible for the time being. It required the cooperation of the Russian authorities, who had steadfastly denied that the uranium was Russian. Victor Mikhailov, Russia's nuclear Czar, accused the Czech spymaster of fabricating the theft, of running a sting. Why should the families be given protection to be spirited out of Russia if there was no Russian involvement? This was Mikhailov's cruel Catch-22. What did he care about these smugglers or their families?

The Czech intelligence man did not know who in Moscow was clean or dirty. He was wary of the new KGB. He was wary of Minatom. He had determined that Russian organized crime was indeed involved in this case and that it was not the only one. A theft uncovered across the border in Slovakia was not the work of amateurs. "That was organized crime, like the case here in Prague," he told the CIA. This was sensitive intelligence. Not even Congress in its subsequent investigation of nuclear materials trafficking was given the disturbing assessment of Czech intelligence.

The question the Czech spymaster had been asking, since concluding that the Prague case involved one of the shadowy criminal rings dedicated to looting Russia's resources, was what complicity there was with such enterprises at the highest levels of the Russian government. To what extent had the KGB's successor agency, the FSB, been penetrated by criminals? To what extent was the government itself organized crime? "That's what everyone wants to know. That's what we want to know. That's what the CIA wants to know." In the meantime, he and his agents had the unenviable task of ensuring that no one entered the country with a tactical nuclear weapon and detonated the bomb in Prague.

Weapons like SADMs, Special Atomic Demolition Munitions, could easily slip into the city. These were Russian nuclear confetti. A SADM was a suitcase bomb. Who would spot it on the Charles Bridge? Like his colleague in Prague, a twenty-year veteran of Pentagon intelligence was taking a close look at the murky world of Russian officialdom. The bear of a man with his booming voice was regarded in Washington as one of the best and brightest of the Russia analysts. He liked to say that Russia would be the supply house. The victims would be someplace else, someplace like New Orleans or Prague. He glanced at stacks of files in Cyrillic in a northern Virginia think tank with more security than the White House. He was in constant touch with the chairman of the Nuclear Smuggling Working Group. He and Jessica Stern traded information. "We have indications that the Russian military has sold off SADMs," he told the Working Group chairman. Jessica respected him because he spoke fluent Russian, knew the Russian system and had very well-placed Russian friends in the military. There was nothing like first-rate "humint," human intelligence. The Russians told him there were demolition munitions, small portable tactical nuclear weapons, on the loose. Outside his window, leaf blowers patrolled the immaculate northern Virginia streets. "Russia's just a goddamn Third World country with nukes."

The former denizen of Pentagon intelligence had established close contact with a Russian colonel who quit the MVD, Russia's Interior Ministry troops, in 1993. The colonel quit with three nuclear smuggling cases on his plate. He was pursuing them vigorously. Things went badly wrong when he laid a trap for a Hungarian in Moscow who had incriminating evidence of how one nuclear deal was financed and who in Russia was involved. When the colonel was ready to move in, he entrusted the information to one Interior Ministry officer, two KGB men and one Interpol detective. "We were the only ones who knew," the colonel told the Defense Intelligence Agency veteran. Three hours after the colonel informed his associates of the details of the operation, the Hungarian vanished. His Moscow apartment was stripped. There was not a shred of evidence left. "It looked like the moving men had been there."

The colonel was scared. His fear was compounded when he was summoned by his "boss's boss" and abruptly removed from the case. "I didn't know who I was working for," the colonel told his American friend. "I don't think it was MVD." The Russian colonel thought his own Interior Ministry had been "bought and sold."

The twenty-year veteran of Pentagon intelligence scowled. "He got the hell out. This is a lot more serious than the cold war. In the cold war, I was up to my eyeballs in all this Soviet intelligence stuff. I was reading generals' mail. We got into a couple of high-risk situations. [Aldrich] Ames got a few people killed. *This is going to kill a lot of people. The cold war was a game. Now it's real.*"

It was Jessica's job to separate what was real from the stings and scams polluting the black market. The zeal of the German

authorities was such that the ground was thick with undercover agents looking for a deal. Jessica could see that few of
the smuggling cases that erupted all over Germany in 1993 and
1994 were free from the taint of law enforcement. That is just
the way the CIA and no doubt their German counterparts
wanted it.

"Stings and scams," in the view of the CIA, inhibited sales.
The Agency was actively promoting the notion that at the end
of every smuggling route Western intelligence was poised for
the kill. A recently retired senior CIA official admitted that the
common assumption that the only market for materials was
the canny agent was partly his doing. "We advertised all these
stings. Because we wanted people to think it was impossible to
sell a nuclear weapon or nuclear materials without running
into U.S. or Western intelligence. I'm not sure that's so," said
the senior CIA veteran, "but it's a good idea to advertise it as a
fact."

One such sting caused a titanic battle in the German government and in the press over the use of entrapment, commonly employed for cocaine and heroin busts, for something
as dangerous as nuclear materials. When the evening Lufthansa flight from Moscow touched down in Munich on August
10, 1994, German authorities knew that 363 grams of weapons-
usable plutonium were on board. Inhaling a speck of plutonium is deadly.

Had the traveling case been opened and checked by an unwitting Russian customs official or a Lufthansa security agent
and handled carelessly, the customs hall, the agent, whoever
the agent shook hands with, would be "hot." The paperwork he
passed to accounting, the men's room sink he used to wash his
hands, the trousers he wiped his hands on, the fork in the airport cafeteria, would be contaminated. Wherever the plutonium happened to flow in the dishwasher's drainpipe would be
contaminated. Plutonium dust kills for at least 24,000 years.
Wherever and however the dust might be ingested, breathed

in, licked by mistake, it was the world's most potent killer. Plutonium was looking, as Jerry Dzakowic of Z Division saw it, for a host.

The plutonium in the cargo bay of the Lufthansa flight was absolutely safe so long as no one tampered with the box. It belonged to a Colombian doctor, Justiniano Torres Benítez, who had studied medicine in Moscow in the 1980s and had returned to make his fortune after the collapse selling helicopters and military supplies. The business was foundering when Torres received a call from a Spanish business contact who was in the "import-export" business between Spain and Russia. Julio Oroz Eguia was in the market for plutonium. Torres had contacts. His wide circle of friends happened to include a Russian scientist, Genadi Nikiforev. On Torres's behalf, the scientist contacted another Russian, Ivan Ivanovich Obukhov, who investigators believed had contacts in the closed city of Obninsk. Through a second friend in Kazan, Nikiforev found a source in another closed nuclear city, Tomsk. Through friends of friends, the harvest of the cold war years of nuclear production was ripe for picking by a failed Colombian entrepreneur. The secret cities could not be more porous.

To move the material, Torres simply called a fellow countryman, Pérez Ramírez César Adolfo, living in Moscow. Ramírez recommended Lufthansa as the most relaxed airline. Aeroflot, he advised, was too strict on searches. But anything could be arranged with a thousand-dollar payoff to a Peruvian in town with very good friends in customs. The way of doing business in the new Russia was very familiar to the South Americans. This was certainly the way things got done in Bogotá.

The Russians who joined Torres in his nuclear smuggling deal had hoped for large profits from an eventual eleven kilos of plutonium. They were stiffed by the buyers, German undercover agents. The unwitting Torres, with his 363 grams of plutonium, was arrested at the Munich airport. The fact that the Spaniards and Colombians had no prior experience in shipping plutonium out of Russia implicated the German authorities as engineers of the deal. The Munich defense lawyer, Werner Leitner, fumed, "The artificially created demand for plutonium has produced a market for suppliers but not for buyers. On this suppliers' market there are undercover agents, policemen, intelligence service agents and, not least, journalists" eager to make hidden camera buys. "The millions that are offered in this business are waking sleeping dogs and are attracting innumerable imitators. This is no way to fight crime; this is a way to create crime."

Leaving aside the complicity of the German government, the Munich case demonstrated all too clearly that even a Colombian helicopter salesman could find enough plutonium in Russia to paralyze Munich or Manhattan. Had he befriended Egyptian fundamentalists with a mission to blow up targets in New York, his suitcase on board the Lufthansa flight could have added a very ugly ingredient.

"The Munich case," said Jerry Dzakowic at Z Division. "If that was exploded, it would have caused a lot of radioactive contamination. And that's just putting that suitcase into the truckload of explosives" driven into the World Trade Center garage. Just dumping the plutonium into the van without the headache of fashioning a bomb was a terrible weapon. "It's making a radioactive contamination threat in a highly populated area. You would have to evacuate everyone from the area and scoop it all up, like we did in some of our early days with nuclear weapons where we had accidents. We took part of Spain and brought it back to the United States," after nuclear weapons were disgorged from the cargo bay of an American bomber by mistake. "So this would be high-value real estate that became difficult to live in. Suddenly, low-value real estate." The star of Z Division pondered the effects. "A lot of unhappy people," Jerry said quietly.

Jerry out at Z Division and Jessica in her vault talked often that fall and winter of 1994 about the nightmares haunting the

White House. They were both cleared "blue" to talk about the darkest nuclear secrets.

One secret facing officials at the highest level of the CIA and the State Department stood out as more dangerous than any "incident" on the Working Group list. It played into Jerry and Jessica's worst fears going back to their dog and pony days of sounding the alert on the breakup of Russia. Dzokar Dudayev, the former Soviet nuclear bomber general who had seized control of Chechnya, claimed he had two Russian tactical nuclear warheads, stolen when Moscow pulled out its forces two years before. General Dudayev was in an uneasy standoff with the Kremlin. No country had yet recognized Chechnya as a sovereign state since Dudayev declared independence in 1991. Now, as Russian forces massed just across his border and Moscow desperately intrigued to solve the problem, Dudayev was threatening nuclear blackmail.

The White House sat up in bed. The Chechen warlord contacted Washington. His discreet conduit was a retired American official who had spent much of his career in the Caucasus, where Jessica had chased wild horses and Dudayev now ran his mountain kingdom. General Dudayev's claim that he had the warheads was credible. The Soviets had deployed warheads of that type in the Caucasus before the collapse. The details that Dudayev passed along made the CIA and the National Security Council take him very seriously. His blackmail threat sent a chill through the corridors of the Old Executive Office Building. Unless the United States recognized Chechnya as an independent country, the Chechen general said, he would offer his nuclear booty to Muammar Qaddafi. There was no doubt in the White House and the intelligence agencies that he would find a ready buyer. The Chechen nuclear blackmail carried the highest classification. This was classified Top Secret/Compartmented/No Forn.

The price of diplomatic recognition of President Dudayev's government was far too high. American acceptance of an independent Chechnya would poison the Clinton administration's prized relationship with Moscow. Ever since Jay Stewart's "Russian Fission" initiative had been stopped dead the year before, any discussion of the breakup of the Russian Federation had been struck off the U.S. agenda. On the other hand, no one wanted to entertain the idea of the Libyan leader getting his hands on tactical nuclear weapons. Stalling for time, in the deepest secrecy, Washington asked Dudayev for more details. The Chechen warlord was delighted to have evoked a response. He raised the ante. The Americans, he said, were welcome to send a technical team to Chechnya to inspect the weapons personally. He made one stipulation. The Russians were not to be informed.

The offer set off a frenzied debate in the executive corridors of national security in Washington. If it leaked out that a team of U.S. government agents was in Chechnya behind the Kremlin's back, Boris Yeltsin would be outraged. On the other hand, there was the terrible possibility that Dudayev was telling the truth. No one was prepared to take that risk. After weeks of stormy meetings at the White House, the State Department and the CIA, there was a compromise decision. The U.S. government would take Dudayev up on his invitation and agreed to send a secret intelligence team that would slip into Chechnya without the Russians being told.

The promise to the Chechens was instantly broken. The Kremlin was secretly informed. In a telling confirmation that the vaunted Twelfth Department, Russia's nuclear guardians, did not know where all of its warheads had ended up, the Russians agreed to an American mission. They were just as anxious to find out whether the rebellious Chechens really had the ultimate weapon. The CIA assembled a team of undercover operatives and one technical weapons specialist to make the hazardous journey.

They would infiltrate through Turkey, making their way north through the anarchic new states of what had been the southern Soviet Union. Washington liaised with the CIA stations in Moscow and Ankara before the expedition got the green light. By late summer of 1994, after a treacherous journey, they arrived in Chechnya. Their rebel hosts greeted the team warmly and promised there were tactical nuclear weapons for them to see. "We will show them to you tomorrow," the CIA men were told. "There is no problem." The following morning there was a problem. No transport. They would have to wait. The next day, the regretful officials had another excuse why they could not inspect the weapons—they had been moved to a different location. The commander who now controlled them had to be contacted. Days wore into weeks. By October, frustrated and exhausted, the team gave up. They contacted Washington on their secure satellite link to report that there was no evidence of nuclear weapons in Chechnya. They were ready to come home.

At the CIA and the White House, particularly in Jessica's vault, there were sighs of relief. Jerry's intelligence shop at Z Division could breathe more easily. There was relief too in Moscow. Chechnya did not have nuclear arms. Boris Yeltsin was convinced that it would now be easy to subdue the upstart province.

On December 18, 1994, as the Russian armored columns were massing on the Chechen border, Victor Mikhailov, master of the Russian nuclear complex as head of Minatom, got a call on the special secure phone that links the men who rule Russia. He recognized the voice at the other end. It was Prime Minister Victor Chernomyrdin, the man who actually ran the government from day to day.

"Victor Stepanovich, how are you?" he boomed warmly.

Chernomyrdin wasted no time on pleasantries.

"Victor Nikolayevich, are there any dangerous nuclear materials in Chechnya?"

"Absolutely not," said the Minatom boss confidently.

"Are you sure? We have reports that there might be."

"Absolutely sure."

Two days later, the Russian Army stormed into Grozny, the Chechen capital. The Chechens might not have nuclear weapons, but their ferocity and firepower astonished the overconfident Russian generals as ill-trained conscript units were shot to pieces in the city streets. The Chechen war, which was to last for two terrible years and kill 100,000 people, had begun. There was also shock in the White House, where the very idea of a fissioning Russia, with a warring state like Chechnya wrenching free, had been a taboo subject too sensitive to discuss.

Acts of nuclear terrorism were well within the range of the Chechen Mafiya in Moscow, one of the capital's most vicious criminal organizations. The KGB's successor organization had quietly called the Chechen mob's bosses into Lubyanka to encourage them not to bring the war to Moscow. But the Chechens were not the only Mafiya in Russia.

Ultra-secret National Security Agency intercepts were convincing top officials in Washington that one or more criminal organizations with ties to the old KGB had entered the nuclear trade. The officials left their offices to discuss it, for fear of bugs. Ian Fleming had been right, one said. The KGB and the Mafiya would join forces, move offshore, wreak havoc around the world. Those who were cleared to know had furtive conversations about an organization they called SPECTRE, because it so closely resembled Ian Fleming's fantasy of a criminal enterprise using all the assets and talents of Russian intelligence. The new SPECTRE described in closely held intelligence reports in Washington and Germany was worthy of James Bond.

THE VIENNA CONNECTION

I n February 1995, the overseer of German intelligence operations, received a strange request. General Rozhkov, deputy director of Russian Foreign Intelligence, had arrived in
Bonn and wanted to see him, unofficially, on an urgent matter.
Rozhkov's organization, known by its Russian initials SVRR, is
the successor agency to the former First Directorate for foreign
operations of the KGB. Only a few years before, the two men
had been cold war antagonists. Bonn, the sleepy German capital on the Rhine, had been one of the KGB's most successful
fields of operations. The government had been regularly
wracked by scandals when high-level moles were uncovered in
sensitive positions, even in the office of the Chancellor himself.
Those days had ended with the fall of the Berlin Wall. Now the
Russian spymaster had come with a plea for help.

In the last years of the Soviet Union, the general explained,
the KGB had poured billions of dollars into front companies
around the world. Now, he lamented, the whole system had

spun out of control. The SVRR did not understand what was going on and wanted the help of German intelligence to find out. The businesses had become independent, and some of them had turned into completely criminal enterprises. One of the former front companies with which the SVRR had "a very big problem," Rozhkov confided, was called Nordex.

Bernd Schmidbauer, the silver-haired confidant of Chancellor Kohl, was noncommittal. His visitor was not telling him anything he did not know. Out at Pullach, the headquarters of the German intelligence service, BND, there were already burgeoning files on the KGB's corporate spawn. Among the fullest was the one on Nordex—a name that evoked a frantic reaction among intelligence services not only across Europe but in Washington.

The Prague and Landshut cases that exploded in the headlines in 1994 had raised the specter of organized criminal groups becoming interested in nuclear materials smuggling. Only a very few people in the intelligence agencies and the White House knew of the reports, classified beyond top secret, that a Mafiya group, risen from the ashes of the KGB, was moving into the business. As Jessica scanned the growing number of smuggling cases in her secure vault in the White House basement, shaken officials were facing the possibility that a worst-case scenario might be coming true. The name they barely dared mention was Nordex.

"It's one of the fallouts of the cold war," one senior administration official whispered to a trusted visitor. "They're involved in arms, drugs, the whole nine yards. They deal in strategic materials," including plutonium and uranium.

Uttering an urgent warning against tangling with what he termed "vicious killers," the official explained that U.S. intelligence had discovered that the "ex-KGB front company in Vienna" was shipping nuclear-bomb-making materials to Saddam Hussein. The transaction between the company and the Iraqis was being done through a "cutout" company in the middle. The

United States knew this because "we've got the cutout penetrated." In other words, there was an agent in place.

This tightly held intelligence was even more shattering because it touched on the President of the United States himself. On October 21, 1993, President Clinton had taken a few hours off from the affairs of state to attend an important political dinner at a museum a few blocks from the White House. The event was thronged with party heavyweights, including Vice President Gore and twenty Democratic senators. As Clinton moved through the crowd shaking hands, a politically well-connected New York real estate executive named Sam Domb stepped forward. At his elbow was a balding, heavily jowled man who looked like he was not yet quite used to the Armani suit draped around his massive frame. Domb introduced his friend, Grigori Loutchansky, an entrepreneur from the former Soviet Union who had built up a flourishing business from the ruins of the Communist economy. A photographer raised his camera. Clinton and Loutchansky smiled. The amiable meeting was captured for posterity.

What happened next is a matter of dispute. Loutchansky claimed later that the President asked him to carry a private message to the President of Ukraine offering U.S. support in exchange for Ukraine speeding the removal of Soviet nuclear missiles from its soil. The White House denied using the thickset Latvian as an intermediary. Still, in the following twelve months Mr. Domb donated $160,000 to the Democrats at the national level, $153,000 more than he gave in any other year, before or since.

The meeting, and Domb's sudden generosity, might have passed unnoticed had it not been for strange bursts of electronic chatter that began to flow into the great antennas of the National Security Agency the following month. Messages plucked out of the ether indicated that the Nordex Corporation was exporting nuclear weapons components and materials to pariah states such as Iran and North Korea. At some point the

CIA inserted its agent into the cutout in the chain linking supplier and nuclear customer and the picture became even darker. As intelligence officials scrambled to find out more about the history of the mysterious Nordex and its president, their alarm mounted at the possibility that the man who had shaken hands with the President of the United States was running a Mafiya group founded with the help of the KGB.

The growing files on Grigori Loutchansky in the archives of U.S. and Western European intelligence agencies read like a history of the end of the Soviet Union and the birth of the new Russia. He was born in Tbilisi, Georgia, in 1945 to a poor family of Ukrainian Jews and grew up in Latvia, where he eventually graduated in economics from Riga University. He was active in the Komsomol, the Communist youth organization, which was itself a vast and powerful institution. His membership in the Community Party was sponsored by none other than Boris Pugo, the boss of the KGB in Latvia.

By the early 1980s Loutchansky had risen to be a professor of economics and vice-rector of Riga University, but his interests already evidently extended beyond higher education to the world of commerce, an illegal activity under the Communist system. In 1982 he was arrested by the KGB and sentenced to nine years in prison. Accounts varied as to the reason for his incarceration. One report stated that it was in connection with a large sum of money missing from a government organization. Another cited his involvement in a complicated scheme to barter furniture for cars. He himself claimed it was because of his political opposition to the regime. In any event, it was a bad time to be in business. The Soviet economy was already groaning at the seams and secret police chief Yuri Andropov had decided that the problem lay with "speculators"—businessmen. The German BND intelligence service noted in its file that while behind bars he was recruited by the KGB.

Within three years Loutchansky was a free man again, just in time to take advantage of Mikhail Gorbachev's efforts to energize the economy by using free enterprise rather than the Gulag. Despite his jail term, the portly vice-rector had an important connection to power through his position in the Latvian Komsomol, where he was now second secretary. In looking around for trustworthy men who could be granted the dangerous privilege of independent trading, the regime often found recruits in the Komsomol hierarchy. They were talented and young by comparison with the old men dominating the Communist Party itself. They also tended to enjoy a close relationship with the KGB, which moved swiftly to control the privatization program for the Soviet economy. The secret policemen, who had once ruthlessly persecuted "speculators," were now heavily involved in commerce themselves. Officially, they were the spearhead of Gorbachev's *perestroika*—restructuring—but Western intelligence organizations eventually realized that the KGB had another objective. Under the cover of foreign partnerships, vast sums of money controlled by the Communist Party and the KGB itself were moved out of the Soviet Union and into safe havens in Switzerland and elsewhere.

In 1989 Loutchansky was given official license to go into business, exporting mineral fertilizer for a big government agency called Adazhi. With official backing, this was a license to print money. In the controlled Communist system, commodities like fertilizer were assigned an artificially low price, far below the world market. Loutchansky was able to buy cheaply in rubles and sell dearly for dollars. The hard currency revenues soared.

Shortly afterward, on December 14, 1989, Loutchansky set up a new company in Vienna with two Yugoslav partners. Although he was the president of the new corporation, he was not acting on his own but as the representative of the Soviet-owned fertilizer firm. The new company was called Nordex. A classified German intelligence report drawn up a month before General Rozhkov's visit to Bonn stated that the corporation was set up to "generate hard currency for the KGB." Since then, the Germans noted, "there is much evidence to suggest that Nordex has subsequently evolved into at least a partially criminal organization."

Vienna was a natural haven for such an entity. Ever since the days of *The Third Man*, Graham Greene's classic novel about the postwar days of military occupation, the city had been a center of shadowy East-West deals, neutral ground where intelligence agents from both sides could meet, barter and intrigue in the quiet cafés of the gray stone capital on the Danube. Part and parcel of this legacy was the ironclad secrecy of Austrian bank accounts that had facilitated many discreet transactions across the Iron Curtain. Professional money launderers considered the system far superior to that of Switzerland as a haven for questionable money. The game changed when the Iron Curtain came down and vast sums of money began to flow out of Russia, but Vienna retained its attractions.

Installed in an elegant mustard-colored town house on a tree-lined street close to the U.S. ambassador's residence and the Schönbrunn Palace, Loutchansky soon began to cut a social dash, giving freely to local charities and, more discreetly, to influential figures in his new hometown. He also spent lavishly on streams of visitors from around the world. In 1993 alone, he is reported to have spent no less than $50 million on "entertainment." For the headquarters of the new concern, he settled on a location dripping with gilt-edged respectability.

Prinz-Eugen-Strasse, opposite the serene Belvedere Gardens, is one of the most fashionable streets in Vienna. Nordex moved into number 32, where a graceful gated arch leads to a cobblestone courtyard (that rapidly filled up with serried ranks of Mercedes) fronting an exquisite white baroque mansion. On one side of the gates a discreet blue sign read NORDEX, with a lightning bolt piercing the o. The sun-filled lobby was occupied by polished multilingual receptionists and monosyllabic but well-muscled individuals with bulges under their jackets. Visitors were conducted upstairs to the high-tech conference room, by secretaries in size-two leather pants and quantities of eye shadow, via a glass-backed elevator with a fine view of the lush block-wide Nordex woodland gardens.

The bulging jackets in reception were the only visible sign at headquarters that Nordex could be anything other than "your partner of choice and expert advisers for doing business in the former Soviet Union," as its glossy full-color brochure pro-claimed. Other, more anonymous Nordex properties were sprinkled around Vienna on quiet side streets and back alleys, with no outward advertisement of what went on within. U.S. intelligence agencies were especially interested in one property in the little town of Lilienfeld, several hours west of the Aus-trian capital. The town lies deep in a picturesque mountain valley, with steep red shingle roofs, stone turrets, apple blos-soms and birch forests winding up the mountainside. The lo-cals did not like to talk about the massive complex behind multiple barriers at the end of a narrow road high above the town. Beyond the checkpoint, paved roads led to buildings, greenhouses and ultimately an immense villa with an arcade of arches.

This, according to Nordex, was the campus of the "GUS [the German acronym for Former Soviet Union] Management Cen-ter . . . dedicated to educating bright young people in modern management, marketing and general business practices." Fit young men could be seen driving past the barriers, which al-ways shut promptly behind them. U.S. military intelligence of-ficers in Washington seriously speculated whether the complex was defended by air defense missile systems.

In the few short years since the Kremlin authorized Lout-chansky to go into business, the operation he headed had spread out around the world, with offices from New York to Hong Kong. The records to be found in the Austrian govern-ment's corporate registry conveyed the impression of a vast and growing octopus: "Nordex Chemische Produktions, 100 percent export from the Former Soviet Union . . . chemicals,

metals, oil, fertilizers, coal." At the touch of a computer key-
board, extensions of the corporate web spooled out of the
printer. Nordex Shipping and Transport, IFS Freight Services,
Kazakhstan Trading House, GUS Management Center, Nord-
sen, Nomo. Interesting Moscow partnerships emerged, including Glavsnab, a Moscow city government enterprise, as well as
two transport firms, Intourtrans and Intourservice—the latter
having managed to open its doors in 1987, at a time when private enterprise required very high-level blessing indeed.

The key to financial success in Russia in those early years
after the fall of Communism lay in access to the government.
Russia was a vast treasure house of raw materials and commodities priced at a fraction of the world market price—like
Loutchansky's early fertilizer gold mine—and available for export *if* a sufficiently powerful official would authorize an export
license.

Sometimes the means to get that license were tortuous and
ingenious. In 1992, the city of New York received an unex-
pected offer from Russia. The "Columbus Company," of which
Nordex was a shareholder, proposed to donate a giant statue
of Christopher Columbus that would be larger than the Statue
of Liberty, made entirely of copper. The copper was the key,
because the artist of choice, a politically well-connected Georgian sculptor named Zurab Tsereteli, proposed to work with a
very highly refined form of the metal that is very expensive and
normally reserved for use in the electronics industry. Russia
had a large stockpile of this material and its export was forbidden.

No less a person than Prime Minister Victor Chernomyrdin,
a frequent visitor to the baroque palace on Prinz-Eugen-
Strasse, gave the order to allow the export of the raw material,
waiving all licensing requirements and export taxes. Thirty
thousand tons of copper thereupon left Russia, enough to build
at least thirty of the proposed monuments. However, no such

statue was ever built. The consignment was last seen on the docks in Rotterdam.

Chernomyrdin was not the only high official who enjoyed a warm relationship with Nordex. Yuri Luzhkov, the powerful and much feared mayor of Moscow (a friend and patron of the sculptor Tsereteli) lent his weight to the Columbus deal. Luzhkov controlled Glavsnab, the Moscow city agency in partnership with Nordex, which subsequently transferred $23 million in cash and interest-free loans to Nordex for unexplained reasons. Oleg Soskovets, the czar of the Russian metals industry (noted for the high mortality rate among its executives) and later a First Deputy Prime Minister in the Yeltsin government, was of profound help in Loutchansky's steel and other metals ventures.

"Nordex," observed the intelligence official who drew up the German file on Nordex, "is an example of the enrichment of criminals and politicians at the expense of an economically and politically weakened state." By 1993 Ukraine certainly qualified as such a state. By comparison, Russia itself looked like a healthy economy. The new country's rulers made little attempt at reform and, most seriously, Ukrainians depended on Russia for its entire supply of oil and gas. But Ukraine was not paying the bill for this supply, and by the fall the Russians suspended deliveries. Loutchansky organized a barter deal by which he would arrange for Russian oil deliveries and take payment in the form of commodities such as sugar, steel and fertilizer. Grateful Ukrainians hailed him as the savior of their country and received the Nordex chief in Kiev as a visiting head of state. Assuming his account of the message that President Clinton asked him to convey to the Ukrainian President at this time is true, the former professor of economics and felon was now taking on a diplomatic role.

Less savory aspects of the deal emerged only later. A large percentage of the fuel shipped in was promptly resold by the government officials with whom Nordex was dealing, leaving the Ukrainian people holding the bill. The Prime Minister, Yefim Zviahilsky, felt it necessary to leave the country in a hurry to avoid questions regarding personal profits from various sources of $25 million. Loutchansky showed what a loyal partner he can be by sending his personal aircraft to pick up the traveling statesman. He also brought a Kiev associate, Vladimir Bortnikov, to Vienna. Bortnikov was in urgent need of Austrian medical attention due to the five bullets that business rivals had pumped into his body. Ukrainian law enforcement wanted Bortnikov to stay in Kiev and answer some questions, a move swiftly frustrated by Zviahilsky, who personally spirited the wounded man out of the hospital and onto the Loutchansky jet. A Bortnikov partner was not so lucky, being arrested at the border while carrying Bortnikov's diplomatic passport and an enormous sum of money.

If anyone asked, Loutchansky was quick to portray himself as purely a victim in the affair. He had rescued Ukraine from a freezing winter without fuel and had not been paid for it. This did not explain, however, why he had felt it necessary to assist in the precipitous emigration of Zviahilsky and Bortnikov. "It's not that Zviahilsky was associated with organized crime," remarked a foreign financial adviser brought in later to help try to clean up the mess. "Under him, the government *was* organized crime."

The BND report disseminated to Allied intelligence services spoke of evidence that pointed to involvement by Nordex in "the international weapons trade as well as in narcotics and nuclear smuggling across the Baltic."

Nuclear smuggling in the Baltic was much on the minds of intelligence agencies at the time the report was written, owing to the strange case of the beryllium in the Lithuanian bank vault.

In the spring of 1993 a savage mob war had swept through Klaipeda, the chief port of the newly independent Republic of Lithuania. Like the other Baltic States, Lithuania was a major transit point for commodities smuggled out of Russia. The borders were essentially unguarded and few questions were asked. Police were puzzled as to the reasons for the bloody shoot-outs, but they eventually concluded that it might be connected with the four tons of beryllium ingots packed in twenty-seven crates they discovered, after an anonymous tip-off, in the vaults of a Vilnius bank. A major smuggling operation was underway; local criminals had tried to muscle in on the action and been gunned down for their pains.

Beryllium, a gray metal lighter than aluminum but stronger than steel, is very valuable. It sells on the world market for about $600 a kilo and is used in missile inertial guidance systems and other sophisticated electronics applications. However, it has another property that makes it of even greater value to nuclear weapons builders. When the fissile material, such as plutonium, reaches critical mass, the precursor to a nuclear explosion, a great number of neutrons are released. The greater the number of neutrons, the more efficient the process of fission. Beryllium is an excellent neutron reflector. If the plutonium core of a weapon is surrounded by a shell of beryllium, neutrons created during the fission reaction are reflected back into the sphere, enhancing the chain reaction. A bomb designer can produce a satisfactory explosion with far less plutonium—or uranium 235—than he would otherwise need. Any country seeking to build an efficient weapon will therefore want to go this route. For example, in the late 1980s when the Indians suddenly began buying large amounts of beryllium the CIA concluded that India was trying to build more sophisticated nuclear warheads.

The beryllium hoard in the bank vault had originally come from a Russian nuclear research institute in Obninsk, sixty miles south of Moscow. Like nearly all such facilities in Russia, the Institute of Physics and Power Engineering had large stocks of poorly guarded nuclear materials, including plutonium and enriched uranium and very little cash. When a businessman in Yekaterinburg (known as Sverdlovsk in Soviet times) made an offer to buy nearly four and a half tons of the institute's beryllium stockpile early in 1992, they were only too happy to oblige. The businessman had links to Minatom, the Russian nuclear ministry, and used a Minatom letterhead to place the order.

For financing, the businessman turned to a local trading firm which had, at the very least, close links with powerful Mafiya organizations of the region, including a particularly fearsome enterprise known as the "Central Group."

Such weighty assistance was necessary because the export of the beryllium was illegal without special permission. The Russian government was committed to restricting the sale abroad as a nuclear-weapons-related item. However, with the Central Group lending its powerful support, the licenses were duly issued. In June 1992 the consignment was flown to Lithuania, lodged in the vault of the Innovation Bank in Vilnius and advertised, quietly, for sale. After a long delay, an obscure Austrian company made an offer to buy the entire cache for $2.7 million. But the trail did not end there. The Austrian company had in turn found another buyer in Zurich. The customer agreed to pay $24 million—ten times the market price. The twenty-seven crates in the Vilnius bank were about to be flown to Switzerland when the police swooped down. Despite entreaties from the United States, the Russian government adamantly refused to take the illegally exported beryllium back.

Intelligence officials across Europe and in Washington following the beryllium trail could never prove the identity of the mysterious buyer in Zurich, but many of them, including CIA officers specializing in nuclear smuggling cases, expressed the firm conviction that one company was heavily involved in the deal: Nordex.

The files were getting longer. More pages were added in 1994 when a cargo plane en route from North Korea to Teheran touched down at an airport in Ukraine. Inside were launchers for Scud missiles. The plane belonged to Nordex. Other entries in the dossiers focused on Nordex associates, such as a London-based Bulgarian consultant named Ognian Doinov, who had also worked with Robert Maxwell, the Czech-born British media magnate who mysteriously drowned during a yachting cruise and posthumously was found to have embezzled hundreds of millions of dollars from his own companies. Back home in Bulgaria, Doinov's brother Emil was suspected of being one of the leading black market suppliers of oil and gas to Serbia, a profitable enterprise in view of the United Nations embargo on that country.

The smoke around Loutchansky was getting thicker, but frustrated officials could not find evidence that would enable them to bring criminal charges against what one former high-ranking official called "the most dangerous man in the world." The intelligence that generated such paranoia, such as electronic intercepts or the agent in place, was far too sensitive to be brought in front of any court. Instead, they set out to make his life as difficult as possible.

In the spring of 1994 Loutchansky applied to enter Canada. Up until that point the globe-trotting entrepreneur had been accustomed to jetting wherever his business took him, but now he was about to find that things were changing. An urgent message from Washington prompted the Canadian immigration office to ask some hard questions about the "source of his funds." Whatever answer he gave, they refused to be satisfied. Later that year his jet taxied to a halt at London's Heathrow Airport. Instead of waving him through, stony-faced immigration officials invited him to a small office for a talk. The interview turned out to be a long one, as the officers grilled him about every aspect of his business and past. They made it clear that the questioning could go on for a long time. After six hours Loutchansky had had enough. In the words of the record of the incident entered into the British National Intelligence Computer, he "elected to leave," putting on his coat and striding angrily back onto the plane for Vienna.

That same year, Loutchansky applied for Austrian citizenship. He was confident of success, especially in view of the high-priced and influential legal help he had retained. The United States speedily informed the Austrians that their would-be fellow countryman was suspected of nuclear smuggling. His application was denied. Washington was by now monitoring his every move. He had high hopes of a multibillion-dollar deal with the American USX steel group in Kazakhstan until the U.S government brought pressure to kill the venture. A mining scheme in Kazakhstan with a Canadian group met the same fate, as did plans for a brewery in Moscow, financed from Wall Street, and an oil deal with Mobil Oil.

In July 1995, the Democratic National Committee, apparently oblivious to anything but the possibility of a political donation, invited him back to Washington for another dinner with President Clinton. Outraged protests from the CIA caused the invitation to be hurriedly withdrawn, much to Loutchansky's disgust. The world was closing in on him. The one place where his application for citizenship succeeded was Israel, obligated to accept him as a Jew under the Law of Return. The Israeli police duly noted how skies over the eastern Mediterranean darkened with charter jets in February 1995, carrying such leading lights of the Moscow underworld as Iosif Kobzon (described by the CIA as the "Tsar and kingpin" of the Russian Mafiya) as they flew in for Loutchansky's lavish fiftieth birthday celebrations in the resort town of Eilat.

Israeli intelligence was also taking a keen interest in Nordex. Mossad was very active in Russia and regularly liaised with the CIA on cases that touched on their turf. In Loutchansky's case they received a specific request, which they were happy to oblige. Anyone suspected of shipping nuclear materials or components to the Middle East was a top priority for the Israelis. Ever since the Israeli air force bombed the Osirak nuclear reactor in Baghdad in 1981, they had been waiting for the bomb makers in Baghdad or Teheran to rise again from the ashes.

To all the accusations hurled or leaked against him, Loutchansky defiantly answered that no one had ever brought a criminal charge against him (apart from his spell in the Soviet jail) and that he was a victim of a disinformation campaign mounted by old enemies in the KGB. His spokesman got so used to answering queries about the boss's alleged criminality that he took to opening conversations with references to "mafiosi and criminals," which, he insisted, "Nordex absolutely is not." It was all very unfair. "The KGB has said terrible things. We've had no dealings with nuclear materials, money laundering, prostitution, weapons. Dr. Loutchansky is a nice guy. He's got the feeling he's got no human rights. He feels lost, exploited."

The CIA and its fellow agencies remained unconvinced. Despite all the heartfelt denials, CIA Director John Deutch went on the record in describing Nordex as "an organization associated with Russian criminal activity."

No one could be sure that the campaign against Nordex had stopped a pipeline of nuclear weapons components coming out of Russia. But there was increasingly vivid and horrifying evidence that enough deadly material was lying around in the ruins of the Soviet state to supply any number of would-be bomb makers.

8

Q CLEARANCE

Southeast of Munich, Lake Constance forms the border of three countries, Germany, Switzerland and Austria. It was here in May 1994, in the medieval village of Tengen, that German police stumbled on the purest plutonium to come on the market. This was not a sting. In the course of searching the house of Adolf Jaekle, a fifty-two-year-old suspected counterfeiter, detectives found six grams of rare super-grade plutonium 239. Jaekle had stored this lethal sample of top-quality bomb material in his garage. The local constabulary had no idea what it was. Fortunately, none of them tasted it to see if it might be narcotics.

Jaekle swore he was given the sample by an eclectic trader in nearby Basel. Willy Jetzler dealt in mercury, gold and diamonds. He insisted that his trade did not extend to plutonium and was never charged. Jaekle was tried and convicted. The case was closed. The question of how he came upon top-grade Russian plutonium and what he intended to do with it was

never properly answered. The detectives found two very interesting pieces of evidence in the Jaekle house. There were bank
records of his account at the Golden Star Bank in Vienna.
Golden Star was owned by the government of North Korea.

In a chest of drawers, they also found two business cards
belonging to Russian scientists. They gave their address as the
Kurchatov Institute in Moscow.

Three months after the Tengen seizure, two White House
physicists boarded a plane for Moscow to assess security at
the aging nuclear complex just inside the Moscow city limits.
Lieutenant Colonel Fred Tarantino was a stocky, handsome
physicist-soldier, who had put his advanced degree to work in
the netherworld of "black programs" at the Pentagon. He had
served in the basement corridor that was the nerve center of
the Strategic Defense Initiative, better known as Star Wars, trying to devise a way to shield the United States from incoming
nuclear missiles on hair-trigger alert. This was not his first trip
to Moscow.

In 1991, when he was still a major, Tarantino was given the
mission of completing a deal to buy an advanced Russian nuclear power plant designed to be shot into space. Code-named
Topaz, it could power space-based lasers and military satellites.
A year before, Topaz had been a top secret program. Now in
the crumbling empire, it was up for sale. The Pentagon wanted
it fast. Two weeks after leaving Washington, Tarantino was
shepherding home two huge C-5 transports loaded with Topaz
hardware.

With his few hours to spare on that trip, Tarantino strolled
around Red Square with his interpreter. Below the onion
domes of St. Basil's Cathedral, he found old women begging,
holding out their hands in the hope of a few coins. The major
took four dollar bills, wrapped each in a ruble note, and embar-
rassedly asked the interpreter to pass them to the beggars. They
rushed after Tarantino, struggling to kiss his hands. They were

crying. "This country is ruined," he thought. "We have to get them some money."

He would recommend to headquarters to make an offer for the highly enriched uranium space reactor fuel stored at the research center at Podolsk, not far from Moscow. His idea got short shrift in Washington. Topaz was high priority. Ordinary enriched uranium was not. In October 1992, he learned that an employee at the Podolsk research center had walked out of the main gate with one and a half kilos of that same weapons-usable reactor fuel in a suitcase.

By September 1994, Lieutenant Colonel Tarantino was detailed to the White House. As he stepped off the plane in Russia with his White House credentials, the dark-haired, athletic Tarantino looked less like a physicist than the officer in charge of a Special Forces outfit. His companion looked more the part. Frank von Hippel, a third-generation physicist, with wisps of hair trailing over his domed head, was a distinguished envoy. Von Hippel was the soft-spoken Deputy for International Security at the White House Office of Science and Technology Policy. He was Lieutenant Colonel Tarantino's boss and Jessica Stern's in-house mentor. If his White House credentials impressed the Russians, the physicists among them respected him for other reasons. His Nobel Prize-winning grandfather James Franck, having fled Nazi Germany, helped give birth to America's atomic bomb.

As a child, von Hippel sat at the feet of both his grandfather and Niels Bohr, a giant in the wartime Manhattan Project. It was Bohr who warned his American colleagues that the Nazis were secretly pursuing a weapon of mass destruction that must be matched at all costs. His campaign led to Albert Einstein's letter to President Franklin Roosevelt urging a national war effort to build atomic weapons. Both Franck and Bohr were refugees from Hitler's Europe and could have easily landed amidst the physicists who found refuge in Moscow and Arzamas 16 rather than Los Alamos and the Metallurgical Laboratory in Chicago. The legacy of the bomb makers gave von Hippel a deep sense of responsibility for what they had wrought. He was appalled by what he found in Building 116 at Moscow's Kurchatov Institute, named for the father of the Russian bomb.

The White House physicists found themselves in a room that housed a zero power space reactor with fuel that was 97 percent enriched uranium, enough for several bombs. It was kept in lockers. The physicists stared in disbelief. *High school lockers.* The uranium looked like metal washers, packed in tubes. The institute guides took some of the tubes of uranium washers and casually poured them out onto a platter. Von Hippel could pick them up by the handful. It did not give him a good feeling about their security. There was nothing but a padlock on the door.

One hundred and fifty pounds of weapons-grade uranium was guarded with a padlock. In other nooks and crannies in the building there were two hundred pounds more. The senior Russian scientists who had the keys earned thirty dollars a month. Thirty dollars a month was an exiguous sum in the new Moscow. It bought coffee for two at the Metropole. The temptation to scoop up some weapons-grade uranium washers was very great.

"I could just throw these washers into my pocket," von Hippel thought to himself. He and Tarantino could see the concrete fence around the main building was crumbling. There were holes in the walls big enough to climb through as a shortcut to the cafeteria and no armed security force. Twenty-eight rooms at the institute housed bomb-grade materials.

It turned out that at Kurchatov nobody had ever taken an inventory. All they had were the receipts from when the material was delivered, piled up in a shoe box. Von Hippel and Tarantino had the same reaction: "My God, there's a problem here," the sort of problem that police stumbled on along the Swiss-German border.

The Kurchatov scientists whose cards were found in the counterfeiters' chest of drawers at Tengen claimed they had simply rubbed shoulders with the man at an international trade fair. Their explanation was plausible. After all, for revenue the institute now depended on selling scientific expertise abroad. In the post-cold-war cash crunch, the scientists were roving salesmen anxiously looking for business. There were no charges filed.

The need for the desperate scientists to market themselves combined with the shabby security at Kurchatov grabbed the attention of top Washington officials. Charles Curtis, Deputy Secretary of Energy in the Clinton administration, knew that Kurchatov was wholly dependent on income from abroad. Curtis and others in the plush executive suites in Washington could see that the Kurchatov Institute scientists were strapped for money. "The imperative for interaction with other countries, those who would value and pay for scientific knowledge, is certainly a security risk."

Von Hippel saw the Kurchatov Institute as the tip of the iceberg. Baku and the disintegration of the Soviet Union focused people on the warheads. How bad the nuclear materials situation was dawned on people later. As physicists and safeguards specialists sat down to study the Russian security system, they found the terrible truth. "There is no system," von Hippel said bluntly.

The White House physicist remembered decades before when the nuclear facilities in the United States were in the same state of disarray. Von Hippel's friend Ted Taylor, a Los Alamos physicist, sounded the alarm in John McPhee's *The Curve of Binding Energy*. In the early 1970s Taylor's revelations of abysmal security got an embarrassed official hearing. There was an emergency response, code-named: Operation Cerberus. In a matter of weeks they installed portal monitors to record who was entering and leaving the secure areas. At the Pantex plant in Texas, where America's nuclear weapons were assembled, there were no portal monitors. For von Hippel, the security system at Pantex and other U.S. nuclear sites had not been quite as bad as conditions in Russia but it was "pretty lax." When the physicist was at the Argonne lab, there was a ton of plutonium on site for a zero power breeder reactor, similar to the one at Obninsk, the Russian closed city where material was leaking out to Prague and Landshut. Entering Argonne, Frank regularly held up a playing card behind a muddy windshield and was waved through the gate. A playing card got him inside the perimeter with enough plutonium for two hundred bombs.

Before landing at the White House, von Hippel had earned his Ph.D. from Oxford and had labored for ten years in the esoteric world of theoretical physics. His field was elementary particles. He had found a berth at the University of Chicago, Cornell and Stanford during the convulsive years of the Vietnam War. Like his grandfather, whose condition for helping to create the bomb was a channel to the President to argue how and where it should be used, von Hippel believed physicists should use their knowledge to sway governments. His family's direct experieince of the Nazis' warped use of science was branded on his conscience. At Stanford, when the young assistant professor discovered that the Johnson administration proposed to deploy antiballistic missiles in the suburbs, he protested. When the suburban residents learned that the antiballistic missiles slated for their neighborhoods would have nuclear warheads on them, they got nervous. They became receptive to scientists like Frank. That attracted the politicians, which in turn generated a national debate.

Citizen scientist von Hippel found himself being roused at 4 A.M. to confront busloads of masked police who had come to flush out demonstrators sitting in to protest secret research for the war effort on campus. The physicist deftly pacified both sides to avoid a bloody confrontation. After his Stanford days, he moved to the Argonne National Laboratory and the Academy of Sciences before settling at Princeton. He served on the research faculty and the faculty of the Woodrow Wilson School. After twenty years as a Princeton "policy physicist" he was summoned to Washington.

Once inside the White House, he entered the exclusive world of Q clearance, those cleared to know the nation's nuclear secrets. Membership in this nuclear elite was a rude awakening. Von Hippel's chain of command went through the President's affable science adviser, Jack Gibbons. Frank found himself at war with the National Security Council.

When Jessica Stern arrived at the NSC, the Princeton physicist, the outsider, broke through the enemy defenses. Jessica was a natural ally. They understood each other as scientists. Their friendship bridged the yawning chasm between the benign and ineffective science clique and the more political and far more Machiavellian national security crowd. Soon it was "Jessica and Frank" plotting at Au Bon Pain, along with Frank's assistant, Matt Bunn. Frank confided in Jessica that some very hard-bitten national security bureaucrats had made the physicist's life hell. He was trampling on national security turf that belonged to the National Security Council. Frank could see that even though he had forgotten more about nuclear weapons than most staffers in the White House knew, they were damned if they were going to cede him any power. They were scared to death of losing their jobs. Protect your turf, von Hippel learned. He was politely counseled to work through his superiors, who would battle on his behalf. Frank was skeptical. He saw Gibbons as well-meaning but too mild and ineffective. The President's science adviser was marginalized, the same fate that had befallen science advisers ever since the Nixon adminstration.

Even treading water on the inside was a struggle. Frank found it hard to have ideas in the shark pool. The White House was disorganized and chaotic. Everything was done on short notice, forty-eight hours, twenty-four hours, sometimes twelve hours. Everything was a scramble. Frank felt "walled out" by the NSC. One weapon his opponents used to keep him off balance was secrecy. The eminent physicist was astonished to find that the NSC began to classify meeting notices.

He told Jessica what her superiors were doing. They classified meetings and somehow forgot to invite Frank. When he found out, the NSC men would then start investigating the leak. "They are threatening everybody," he told Jessica as a warning. "They say they will investigate whoever is talking." Frank found this maneuvering bizarre. Talk about misuse of the secrecy system, he thought. They were going to get the FBI to find out who leaked. Even though the physicist was supposed to be an addressee. It was a very funny kind of game they were playing.

The physicists' smug enemies "inside" the White House failed to calculate von Hippel's ability to make his own potent allies. One of them was in the raised cube at 1000 Independence Avenue that is the headquarters of the Department of Energy. On the fourth floor, there was a set of sliding bullet-proof glass doors. The sign read: "Card Reader Controlled Door. Only Q, T, L, S Badges Through the Door." Q stood for Q clearance, T for top secret and S for secret. Beyond the barrier, the commodious office in the corner with hundreds of bulging files stacked on the tables was the lair of Ken Luongo.

With jet-black hair and the bulky figure of the lifelong Washington staffer, Luongo was in charge of nuclear nonproliferation. On Capitol Hill, where he worked for Senators Proxmire and Levin and the House Armed Services Committee, he had ample experience of hand-to-hand combat with obstinate bureaucrats. He also believed something had to be done about plutonium and uranium bleeding out of Russia. He wanted to stop the flow because he was convinced that "there is a not too distant event which inevitably is going to happen, which is going to be devastating. Either in this country or in some other country if somebody gets their hands on this material." Luongo was deadly serious. He and Frank spoke the same language.

"I mean, we spend billions and billions and billions of dol-

lars defending against God only knows what potential danger,"
Luongo liked to say. "Here you have something so real and so
close that we can't even see it." When he first moved into his
DOE office as a political appointee, a year after the debacle of
the shredded top secret "Russian Fission" documents, he
thought the threat was so "in your face" that people could not
see its magnitude, except for a very few people, literally a handful. Among them was Frank von Hippel.

Luongo and von Hippel had first met when Luongo left the
Hill for the Union of Concerned Scientists. When he landed the
Department of Energy job, one of his first calls was to Frank at
the White House.

"Frank, I'm inside the government now."

When Ken and Frank sat down in Room 490 at the White
House Office of Science and Technology Policy, they thought,
"What are we going to do?" They saw themselves as outsiders
in a sea of Republicanism, appointees from the Reagan and
Bush presidencies, leftovers hanging on in key positions.
"These people don't give a shit," said Ken with disgust. "What
do they care?"

"I am suspect right off the bat to these guys on the National
Security Council," thought Ken, "because I come from liberal
Hill members and from outside the government." "Oh, what
the fuck do you know?" he could hear them saying. "You've
never worked inside the government. You're some kind of political appointee moron." Luongo and von Hippel developed a
strategy. At DOE, Luongo had money, ideas, willpower. Frank
had inside access. So that was the nexus. They saw themselves
as the only ones who could carry out this work. Meanwhile
Frank and Matt Bunn, having forged an alliance with Jessica
Stern, could hammer away at the White House day and night.

If the Princeton physicist was a threat to White House bureaucrats jealously guarding their territory, he was a welcome
official visitor in Russia's secret cities. The Russian scientists
knew von Hippel. He had first visited the plutonium-producing

reactors at Mayak inside Chelyabinsk 65 in 1989, in the first thaw of relations with Gorbachev's Soviet Union. Frank thought the unmarked fenced city of 100,000 was a beautiful place. The handsome wooden dachas of the first physicists in residence were still standing. The birch forests of the Ural Mountains framed the town. He bought a map of the area. It was eerie that the map showed the peninsula where the city was built as an uninhabited forest. Officially, Chelyabinsk 65 and the Mayak reactor complex that had produced the plutonium for the first Russian bomb did not exist.

There were two lakes. The one downstream, Lake Karashai, was so contaminated with radiation that a half-hour stroll on its shores was courting death. On von Hippel's first visit, he was escorted to the second lake upstream. When he was taken out to an island, Frank thought he was in a fairy tale. There was a table, with white linen under the birch trees, laden with food. They served fish from out of the lake. There was an ample store of good wine. Before dinner, the seventy-year-old director of the lab tore off his clothes and jumped in the lake. The physicist watched to see whether the director survived and then followed his host into the water.

After the island banquet, von Hippel was taken to two of the Mayak reactors. He was astonished to see that the containment building for the reactors, meant to be the protective shield for the outside world in the event of a catastrophic meltdown, had a wall of windows. He discovered that if the electricity went out, they did not want to grope around in the dark. So it really was not a containment building at all. There was no protective shield.

It was the first time the townspeople had seen Westerners. Because of their classified bomb work, they were forbidden from traveling abroad. Entry into their secret world was denied, even to Russians who were forced to apply for a visa to Chelyabinsk 65 thirty days in advance. More often than not they were turned away.

Five years later, when von Hippel returned with his official White House credentials, the subtle changes he found were for the worse. Now the closed cities wanted to stay closed, to keep out the raging crime outside the gates. The day before he arrived, the deputy director was murdered. This time when the White House physicist entered the enclave, he passed a neighborhood where they were building huge houses. He was told they were selling for $200,000. How could that be? This was a place where salary plus benefits was $1,000 a year.

"How do these people get that kind of money?" Frank asked his guides.

"Those are *the night people*," he was told.

It seemed awkward to push much further. They were black marketeers inside the fence. Only 10 percent of the population was employed by Mayak as nuclear physicists or technicians. The rest contributed to infrastructure, food, services, maintenance. Some of that had been turned over to the free market, with the night people, whom residents discussed in hushed tones, as the profiteers. The secret city, with its treasure trove of nuclear materials, its facilities for making bombs, had been invaded. The walls of the fortress, the vacancy on the map, a whole division of MVD troops from the Interior Ministry, ten thousand men, could not stop the night people.

When von Hippel walked into the Mayak nuclear storage facility, he saw the urgency of the problem. Spread out before him were 12,000 stainless-steel containers packed with plutonium. The containers looked like foot-high coffeepots. Each pot had a stopper. Here was all of their civilian plutonium and an estimated 150 tons of weapons plutonium. It was piling up. The room with the 12,000 coffeepots was not even designed to store nuclear materials. It was a chemical storage building, built of cinder blocks, rather than the required reinforced concrete. It had windows and it had a big ventilation duct. A concern of Frank's party was that the duct was big enough to crawl through.

There were two-foot trenches dug into the floor to reduce the radiation levels. The plutonium-stuffed coffeepots were stacked in two layers, covered with a light decking to walk on. In that one room, thirty tons of plutonium sat virtually unprotected.

"Nagasaki had six kilograms of plutonium," mused the physicist as he surveyed the staggering quantity of plutonium at his feet. "So I'd say, with two of those coffeepots, you could make yourself a bomb." There were the makings of 6,000 bombs in one cinder-block room with windows.

There was so much nuclear material in the room it did not require heating. The coffeepots radiated heat. Their cinder-block home with its indefensible windows was secured with a single padlock. A caretaker with a key would appear when summoned. There was no intrusion detection, no portal monitor. The one protection they did have was that everyone passed through a changing room. In principle, if they watched you changing, they could see if you had anything. But they didn't watch von Hippel changing.

There was no system of ID cards, no electronic sensors. Von Hippel and his team sped back to Washington and ordered a portal monitor, motion-activated TV cameras, walkie-talkies, a retinal scan, hand geometry. They discussed laying fiber optics over the trenches. All of this equipment was supposed to be dispatched posthaste and installed. But it was not until nine months later, in June 1995, that its virtues were first demonstrated to the Russians. The Defense Nuclear Agency, the Pentagon office responsible for moving the equipment, "screwed up," thought Frank. A year and a half after the trip, von Hippel was not even sure that the measures so desperately needed had been put in place. There was an agreement that it was supposed to be installed. He did not know if it was. After he visited Mayak, Frank was sure, heads rolled for allowing the Americans in. Minatom got cold feet and decided they had seen too much. Mayak was once again off limits.

The sticking point between Moscow and Washington was money. A government-to-government program, administered by the Pentagon's Defense Nuclear Agency, was failing miserably in the race to secure Russian facilities. The Defense Nuclear Agency was determined that not a cent would be paid to a Russian. We'll give them equipment, but we won't give them money. "That," thought von Hippel, "was an impediment to progress." The Pentagon was busy installing fancy monitoring equipment in three facilities, in Russia, Ukraine and Kazakhstan. On paper, it looked impressive. Money was disbursed to American Pentagon contractors. The only problem was, the facilities in question had no weapons-grade uranium. They had no weapons-usable uranium. The material was useless to a bomb maker. The effort was utterly futile, except as an exercise in Pentagon pork.

"We don't want any more of this low-enriched uranium stuff," von Hippel told his White House colleagues. He was trying to break the logjam and started by inviting the Russians to the White House for lunch. He pressed his guests to talk about specific facilities. He urgently needed a better understanding of where they were drawing the line. It turned out the Russians wanted to exclude weapons materials. But they were happy to have von Hippel work on "weapons-usable" materials, uranium from civilian facilities that could be used to make a bomb. It turned out there was a whole set of facilities the White House could very productively spend money on. The counterpart of the Argonne National Laboratory was Obninsk. The 363 grams of plutonium intercepted at the Munich airport came from Obninsk. Von Hippel worked out a list and went back to the interagency group and said, "I think we've got twenty million dollars' worth of work we can do here."

There were handshakes and agreements, but American inspectors were turned away at the gates of Victor Mikhailov's nuclear empire. Minatom would not budge. Frustration in Washington was mounting. The crisis called for unorthodox measures. Someone had to figure out how to hire Russian contractors and pay the Russians directly. The Defense Nuclear Agency rules were: don't give the Russians any money. That way, joked Frank, DNA could verify that the Russians weren't stealing any money. By not giving them any. The Defense Nuclear Agency was insisting, for example, that Arzamas 16, the jewel of the Russian nuclear establishment, open up its books. Arzamas scientists recoiled.

"My God," they told Frank. "This really is a spy program."

Ken Luongo decided to resort to guerrilla tactics. He raided Department of Energy accounts for money. For Luongo, the goal was very simple. "We have never secured one kilogram's worth of weapons-usable material in collaboration with the Russian Federation or any other former Soviet state," he argued. "If we don't break the psychological bubble and get moving, there's no way this thing is ever going to take flight."

Luongo and his boss, Charles Curtis, chose to lay out two million dollars to fix the dire security at the Kurchatov Institute's Building 116. The contractor would be a former high-ranking Russian Army general who ran a Minatom offshoot called the Eleron Institute. Eleron had all sorts of gadgets, intrusion detection devices. They had a man trap. It weighed you to see if there was one person in the trap. The general proudly displayed his wares to the White House physicist.

"You know," he told Frank, "we've had some big jobs. Like the Hermitage. We've also had a fifteen-thousand-kilometer job."

"What was that?" von Hippel asked.

"The Iron Curtain," said the general.

The job that Luongo and von Hippel calculated would take the Russians a year took two months from start to finish. Workmen were laboring overtime in the snowdrifts. When sufficient cash was involved, the importance of the work captured the Russians' attention. There was a fence, there was a sensor, there were cameras. Luongo was stunned by the progress. General Michen was waiting for him, a short bear of a man with lots of gold teeth and white hair. Snow was heaped on the ground. The paths were slick. The general grabbed him and did not let go for about an hour and a half. They walked around the building, inside the building, into the reactor areas, man traps, portal monitors. There had been a remarkable transformation.

The wedge in the door that von Hippel and Luongo had achieved by throwing the Russians some business was not enough for them to declare victory. "I'm not relaxed about any of this," Luongo told Frank, scanning the vast piles of classified documents, the rising sediment of the U.S. government response to the problem. "This is a huge problem. It is an enormous problem and there is not enough money to solve it. There is not enough money that this Congress will give you to solve the problem. There is not enough money that the United States can generate for this problem."

Luongo and von Hippel both knew there were some seventy facilities with nuclear materials suitable for making bombs. Kurchatov was only one of them. If Kurchatov had tons of material, other storage sites had tens of tons. There was a crushing weight of responsibility on their shoulders to keep up the momentum, to improve the glacial pace of the protection that was so badly needed.

Von Hippel and his assistant, Matt Bunn, began having powwow sessions with Jessica Stern. Occasionally the venue would shift from Au Bon Pain to an Italian restaurant, Note Bene. Frank helped Jessica to get educated. The physicist was amazed that you were able to get much more responsibility at the National Security Council if you came in not knowing anything than he was apparently able to get at the Office of Science and Technology with his extensive background in the subject. The representatives from the trenches of the two warring White House factions agreed they would attack the problem from all sides.

Stern took the smuggling side, border control, law enforcement. She carved out new territory by setting up new groups, like the Materials Protection Control and Accounting Group, to prevent the hemorrhaging of fissile material in Russia. Another spin-off was the Nuclear Smuggling Response Group, a mechanism for rapid communication, to make sure that State, CIA and the FBI did not give conflicting instructions. Frank concentrated on any conceivable means to forge cooperation between the Russians and the Americans to protect the plutonium and uranium at the source. He even invited a delegation of Russians to see an American plutonium storage site in Hanford, Washington.

The Russians were shocked. Where, they wanted to know, were the troops? Where was the fence around the city? "Guards, guns and gates" was the shorthand for the Russian vision of security, adequate within the confines of a smoothly running police state. With the breakdown of the Soviet state, it was a Potemkin system, vulnerable from the inside. Arzamas 16 was a city of 90,000 people with double chain-link fences and access point controls. Each sensitive facility with weapons-usable nuclear materials was gated and guarded by Interior Ministry troops with fixed bayonets. The Russian secret city was tight as a drum with respect to the security problem they had designed the system to address: keeping intruders out and keeping people in. It did not guard at all, von Hippel and Luongo knew, against the insider threat of people simply walking out with material.

Von Hippel, Stern and Bunn at the White House and Luongo at the Department of Energy knew that to get out of the morass of bureaucratic infighting, principally battling the Pentagon, they had to attract the attention of someone further up the chain of command. This White House underground was, in von Hippel's grim assessment, "a few guys trying to move this thing forward with several layers of disinterest above them."

When Ken Luongo tried to get the Pentagon to fork over

fifteen million dollars from their nonproliferation account to make the same kinds of quick fixes that had transformed the Kurchatov Institute, his poaching was regarded by the Pentagon's Office of Cooperative Threat Reduction as a declaration of war. Luongo had to go up against the Department of Defense, which was in the throes of killing this effort because they did not like Minatom. They did not believe you could work with Minatom, or the defiant Minatom chief, Victor Mikhailov, who tormented Washington bureaucrats by smoking heavily in their air-freshened offices.

On top of that, the Pentagon was hearing from the Congressional Appropriations Committee subcommittee chairman that this was not real defense work. The Pentagon did not like giving money away where Congress did not want it to go. Compared with the hundreds of billions of dollars thrown in the defense trough, this was a pittance. Fifteen million dollars. And it was a brutal struggle. Ken called it a long, stupid, difficult battle.

The Department of Energy was ready with their blue-bound "Action Plan" drawn up in a secure basement chamber on Independence Avenue by twenty-five nuclear safeguards experts from the labs, Livermore, Los Alamos, Sandia and Oak Ridge, and Ken Luongo. Across the vast nuclear landscape of the former Soviet Union, they knew what equipment they wanted to put where.

But while they brawled for the money to install cameras and monitors, Frank von Hippel understood that the comforting hardware was not enough. There was a much bigger problem that got lost in the shuffle of equipment lists and contracts. Regardless of how many clamps and locks and cameras were installed, a task that he expected would take a decade, the people inside, indeed the senior people inside, were outside Washington's control. The inmates of the secret cities, the fine physicists at the institutes, remained, after all the blood and sweat expended in Washington, the wild card.

Von Hippel thought the fact that, as far as he knew, there hadn't been a hemorrhage of a lot of material was thanks only to the dedication of these people. It was going to take years before the system was in place. And even with mountains of equipment there, the physicist knew it still didn't stop a defector. He thought of his own experience at the Kurchatov Institute. He had watched the miracle of securing enough uranium to build several bombs. He had visited several times and therefore, like the staff of the institute, was known to the new guards diligently manning their posts. With all of the gadgetry in place, the physicist's arrival was marked by warm recognition and bonhomie.

"Oh, it's von Hippel," the guards said as they waved him through the man trap.

The purpose of the device was to weigh a guest on entering and weigh him on the way out. If there was a noticeable discrepancy, it was logical to conclude the visitor might be carrying contraband. But when the guards saw von Hippel had his suitcase, they said, "Oh, sure, take your bag." They were equally negligent as he walked out into the Moscow street. A handful of 97-percent-enriched uranium washers in his pocket and by Russian standards he was a rich man.

Von Hippel knew that installing high-tech equipment and sensors was only half the battle. Actually, stabilizing the labs economically was the other half. The paychecks were failing to appear. The housing began to buckle and leak. The clinics were short of medicine. Without an injection of funds, the night people, already doing a brisk trade inside the gates of the atomic cities, would hold all the cards. The physicist noticed that an expensive Mercedes was often parked on the institute grounds.

Already, another huge supply of bomb-grade uranium was sitting unprotected in one of the former Soviet republics. Kazakhstan, where the Soviets had exploded countless bombs at their desert test site and where the sensitive materials used in atomic bombs were produced and stockpiled, was being used as offshore headquarters for legions of Russian black marke-teers. The newly independent country also had excellent rela-tions with the Islamic Republic of Iran.

9

SAPPHIRE

When Elwood Gift visits the Department of Energy headquarters on Independence Avenue he dons a necklace of plastic security cards. Office workers who spot the dapper middle-aged scientist striding through the lobby mark him out as someone with access to the offices with coded locks. In February 1994 he walked into one such office on the fourth floor and picked up a secure phone to call his boss.

Gift was tired. He had just landed after flying direct from a central Asian city so remote and secret that very few Americans had ever heard of it, let alone been there. But what he had discovered in a dimly lit vault could not wait until he flew home to Tennessee. "We're going to have to get that stuff out of there," he said, once his boss came on the line. The "stuff" was over half a ton of highly enriched uranium, enough to make ten atomic bombs. "There" was a vault, guarded by a middle-aged lady, in a half-ruined plant in the city of Ust-Kameno-gorsk, Kazakhstan.

Gift's journey had begun a month before, when a highly classified message oozed out of a scrambled fax in an office of the Y-12 plant at Oak Ridge National Laboratory in the mountains of eastern Tennessee. Walking into the National Security Program Office at Y-12 requires just as high-grade a security clearance as the fourth floor at DOE, because it functions as Oak Ridge's equivalent to Z Division at Livermore. The fax came from one of Ken Luongo's "action officers" and it was addressed to Alex Riedy, the director of the office and Gift's boss. It stated that the American embassy in Almaty, capital of the three-year-old Republic of Kazakhstan, was reporting rumors that an enormous cache of bomb-grade uranium, left behind from a secret program of the Soviet Navy, was sitting virtually unprotected at the Ulba Metallurgical Plant in Ust-Kamenogorsk. Riedy was asked to send an expert to Kazakhstan as fast as possible to check if the story was true. Gift, an unflappable Marylander with a neatly trimmed mustache and an easy laugh, had got the job despite his sixty-three years.

It took him a month even to reach Kazakhstan. That part of central Asia is never easy to get to in January. The temperature drops to 20 below and stays there. Blizzards sweep across the steppes. Roads and airport runways are blanketed with sheets of ice and towering snowdrifts. At such times even the Russian Air Force refuses to fly into the country.

Finally the weather cleared enough for the Oak Ridge scientist to set off on the long journey, changing planes in Frankfurt and Almaty. Two years before he had been to Moscow, fast shedding its soviet grimness for Western-style hotels and restaurants. This place was very different.

The best word to describe Ust-Kamenogorsk is "hell." It lies on the Irtysh River at the edge of the windswept eastern desert of Kazakhstan, a hundred and fifty miles (and downwind) from the old Soviet nuclear weapons test site at Semipalatinsk. In Soviet times it had been a closed city, off limits to foreigners and officially known as "Mailbox Ten." The snow that covers the streets and drab apartment blocks in winter is gray and dirty. All year round a massive plume of black smoke spews from the chimneys of Ust-Kamenogorsk Zinc, a vast lead zinc smelter sprawling on the edge of the city. The Ulba plant, next door to the zinc smelter and Gift's destination, is even more enormous. From the upper windows of the central office building it stretches as far as the eye can see in every direction. Only to the east does the dim outline of the foothills of the Altai mountain range break the monotony. Row after row of huge warehouses, each the size of multiple football fields, sit silent under thick webs of power cables. Some contain the debris of a failed effort to produce goods for the Soviet consumer market—tens of thousands of electric toasters that no one will ever buy. One side of the plant is littered for hundreds of yards with pieces of machinery, left to the elements since the mid-1980s, when an expansion project was abandoned. Clusters of rusting cranes and other construction equipment litter the open spaces, as if the workers had broken for lunch and never gone back. Everywhere there is the sound of fluttering wings as thousands of pigeons fly in and out of the huge buildings through scores of broken windows. On the edge of the complex a shattered building stands as a monument to a 1990 explosion that scattered a deadly toxic dust over the city and its people.

This was the cheerful scene that greeted Gift when he drove past the sliding steel main gate and guards dressed in an assortment of scruffy uniforms, the day after he arrived. The guards flashed their gold teeth but did not search the car, because he was with Vitali Mette, the plant director and the most powerful man in the city. Mette was one of the very few people who knew who Gift was and why he was there. Like most people in Ust-Kamenogorsk, Mette was not a Kazakh, but a Russian. Once he had been a submarine commander in the Soviet Navy and there were rumors in the city that he had also been close to the "competent organs"—the KGB—but these were stories he preferred not to mention to the American scientist sitting beside him. As far as the rest of the 16,000 men and women in the workforce were concerned, Gift was just another visiting bigwig, probably from Moscow.

They drove through the plant, skirting the clusters of rusting machinery, until they came to a low building with three locked doors in a row. A solitary middle-aged woman in uniform with a pistol at her belt stood outside in the snow. A plant official unlocked the first door and Gift stepped inside.

He found himself in a vault about twenty feet wide and thirty-five feet long. From the twenty-five-foot ceiling the dim bulbs shone on hundreds of steel cans of differing sizes, most of them about the size of quart cans of tomato juice, stacked everywhere. Some were on wire shelves, some sat on the floor. Others were on plywood platforms. There were no windows, which Gift thought was just as well, considering the lethal quality of what he thought he was looking at, but there was another door at the opposite end—unguarded.

The next door opened to a similar sight, and the next. Gift had no idea how many hundreds of cans he was looking at. No one had been here for a long time and the dust lay thick on the shelves. Gift asked to see the detailed records of what was stored here. Back at Y-12, such information would be instantly accessible on a computer database. Here it consisted of sheets of paper in the hands of Vasili, the man who originally compiled them. "I am younger than you," he said to Gift later, "but you are better preserved." He flourished the "declarations," covered with cryptic notations comprehensible only to him.

Walking through the vaults and scanning Vasili's handwritten lists, Gift began selecting cans at random and handing them to the small group of plant executives hurrying after him. He wanted samples from each of these cans, he told them. In fact, he would like an analysis on some of them done right away. This news was going to hit Washington like a bombshell.

In the plant laboratory Gift watched as the workers opened a can and took out a dark solid pellet. He handed over a file that he had brought with him from Oak Ridge and one of them sawed off a small piece. As the file rasped away, a dense shower of sparks flew out and arced down to the ground. "Oxygenation," thought Gift, recognizing it as a sure sign of uranium, which oxygenates very easily. Then the lab workers dropped four samples he had selected into nitric acid. They were carrying out a routine test known as a "nondestructive assay." The tests confirmed the records: the material was uranium enriched to 90 percent—perfect for making bombs.

"If the United States doesn't take it," said Mette, "there are probably other countries who would."

No one had been thinking of bombs when these pellets originally emerged from the plant's production line. In the early 1970s the Soviet Navy secretly began work on a new type of nuclear submarine, code-named Alfa. It would travel so fast and deep underwater that the American attack subs would never be able to catch it, thanks to a new type of reactor that used very highly enriched uranium. The Ulba plant got the order to produce the very special fuel pellets.

As it turned out, the project was a technical disaster. Navy crews nicknamed it "Goldfish" because it would have been cheaper to build out of gold. Eventually even the commanding admirals admitted that the concept was unworkable and the entire project was abandoned. Down at Ulba a large amount of fuel had already come off the production line, and when the cancellation order came from Moscow, the managers simply moved the uranium into the vaults and closed the doors. They stayed closed as the cold war flared and waned in the 1980s, as Gorbachev struggled desperately to reform the decaying Communist system, as the Soviet Union fell to pieces. The next time they were opened, Ulba belonged to the new country of Kazakhstan and the ties to Moscow were gone. The uranium in the vault was just as potent as ever.

But by 1992 a senior Kazakh official had learned the secret and the bankrupt government in Almaty realized that it had something very dangerous but also very valuable on its hands. Later some officials claimed that they had tried to send it to Russia but the Russians had refused to take it. That left either those countries that might be anxious to get hold of a hoard of material more or less ready to be turned into a bomb, or the United States.

While his colleague was tramping through the sooty snow-drifts, the thirty-six-year-old Riedy was already working on the next step in his Oak Ridge office. He was going to have to put together a team to go to Ust-Kamenogorsk, package up all the nuclear material that Gift was inspecting and somehow get it to the United States. He had to be careful whom he talked to about it, because Washington had made it very clear that this was a covert operation. Riedy was used to secrets. Oak Ridge, five miles from his house, was where the Manhattan Project had built the world's first plant for enriching uranium. The thousands of workers who labored around the clock to construct the huge facility had not known they were helping to make an atomic bomb. The name of the plant, Y-12, meant no more than its grid reference on the map. By the time Riedy came to work there in the early 1980s the veil of secrecy had lifted a little, but he and most of his colleagues carried plastic badges that identified them as "Q-cleared," possessed of nuclear weapons information. Their specialty was arcane: they were the experts in the technology and production of enriched uranium. Whenever U.S. intelligence, or anyone else in the government, came across a sign that someone in the world was betraying an unhealthy interest in bomb-grade uranium, the call went out to Y-12.

By the end of the cold war the calls were specifically coming to the National Security Program Office, a small group of fifty people whose members tend to downplay their intelligence role in favor of vague references to "arms control." Most of the time, says Riedy, "we work with paper. This [the expedition to Kazakhstan] was going to be something real."

Riedy had already seen something of the real world outside Tennessee. In the aftermath of the Gulf War he had been recruited for the UN inspection teams that ventured into Iraq to penetrate the secrets of the nuclear weapons program that Saddam Hussein had brought to the verge of completion before the American bombs began to fall. That experience was certainly far removed from paper analyses, playing cat and mouse with an unfriendly government determined to protect its lethal secrets as much as it could. Alex Riedy does not like to talk about his feelings. The most he will admit about the experience of ferreting out Saddam's nuclear secrets under the noses of the dictator's murderous gunmen is that it had been "stressful."

For Riedy, however, this was going to be a different challenge. Though he had been in the field in a dangerous place, he had simply been part of a team. Now he would be leading people who had never been in the field to do a job that had never been done—and it had to be done quickly.

This was the most exposed hoard of nuclear material the United States had ever come across, and there were people who wanted to get it. The CIA had been warning for years now that the Iranians were "actively shopping" for material to make a bomb. Every week, more reports of these Iranian expeditions were piling up on the desk of the Agency's Deputy Director for Intelligence. A lot of them seemed to be concentrating on Kazakhstan.

If the other side was not to get there first, the American plan had to be kept behind closed doors, but at a Washington meeting, Riedy was appalled to see government officials filing into the room carrying folders boldly labeled "Kazakh HEU"— highly enriched uranium. The operation, he concluded, needed a code name. Talking it over with Gift, he threw out a word. "Sapphire." Gift thought it had a nice ring, so did the bureaucracy up the line. The operation was now officially Project Sapphire.

Washington wanted a fast operation. The quicker the team could be out of Kazakhstan, the less chance there was of a leak. Gift's estimate of the number of canisters in the vault was around 360. If they were lucky, everything could be packed into a single shipping container and carried on one of the air force's big C-5 transports. Fourteen people working flat out could do the job in two weeks.

Back in Washington the bureaucrats were bickering. Everyone agreed that the material would have to come out of Kazakhstan and that the Kazakhs should be paid, but that left plenty of room for argument. Pentagon officials did not want the cost to come out of their budget. The Department of Energy was worried that the environmental lobby would object to bringing bomb-grade material into the United States, so they wanted it to go to Russia instead. It all added up to delay.

Meanwhile, Riedy was starting to get disturbing reports from Kazakhstan. There might be a lot more in those vaults than anyone had known. He decided he had to see for himself.

In early August he strode into the vaults in Ust-Kamenogorsk and started counting. Long before the end he realized with a sinking heart that he was going to have to go back to the drawing board. Gift's estimate and all the other calculations had been wildly wrong. There were not 360 canisters ranged along the wire shelves and on the wooden platforms, there were three times as many. In fact, there were 1,050. That finished any hope of slipping into Kazakhstan with fourteen people and packing everything up in a shipping container inside two weeks. The only way to do it was to open all the old canisters, measure very carefully what was inside and then repack everything in American containers that they would have to bring with them. He was going to need more people, a lot more time.

That same month Lieutenant Colonel Mike Foster, operations officer of the 9th Airlift Squadron at Dover Air Force Base in Delaware, found himself summoned to a classified briefing.

He was told he would be flying the team in and the material out of Kazakhstan. He was also told that this operation had a higher national security priority than an invasion of South Korea.

Riedy was looking hard to fill his expanded team. His own outfit, the National Security Program Office, consisted mostly of analysts. They knew a vast amount about enriched uranium production and how to look for the telltale signs that someone was trying to get hold of the equipment to manufacture it. But that was mostly a paper exercise carried out in air-conditioned offices behind high-security coded locks. This operation was going to need professionals who worked with nuclear materials, hands on, every day. There were plenty of workers with the skills he needed around the Y-12 plant, people who understood the invisible dangers lurking inside the half ton of dark gray metal waiting for them on the other side of the world.

Uranium 235 is a fissionable material, meaning that its atoms emit stray neutrons. When nuclear scientists talk about a "critical mass" they mean that there is enough fissionable material together in one lump (or mass) so that the neutrons being emitted by the material will reliably intercept the nucleus of another atom and split it, knocking off more neutrons, which will in turn knock off other neutrons. Each time that happens, energy is released. If the process continues at sufficient speed the result is a chain reaction and a nuclear explosion ensues. Too much U-235 dumped in a can and they might be lighting up Kazakhstan. Riedy penciled in a slot for criticality experts.

He also had to look for "health physics" specialists, because uranium 235 gives off alpha radiation, which attacks the living cells in a human body. The workers were going to have to be well shielded, but even then they would still be in danger from the air they breathed. Riedy's samples had revealed that the canisters contained more than enriched uranium. A lot of the material was blended in with beryllium and that was very bad news. Anyone working with beryllium has to be very careful indeed not to breathe in any dust, because the likely result will be berylliosis, in which the victims' lungs seize up and they slowly but inevitably choke to death. Doctors in Ust-Kameno-gorsk knew all about berylliosis, for the Ulba complex had been the major producer for the entire Soviet Union. It had been one of the beryllium plants that exploded in September 1990, sending a fine dust drifting across the city and its 400,000 inhabitants.

When Riedy started asking for volunteers he didn't mention the beryllium explosion. In fact, he didn't even mention Kazakhstan. The people he was talking to had Q clearances, but he still kept the pitch vague. "Would you be willing to work on a project in a foreign country that would involve being gone for about four weeks?" Just enough to get them interested. If they volunteered he told them a little more, but not much. By the end of the recruiting drive he had twenty-five people, specialists in packaging and shipping enriched uranium, laboratory experts, specialists in measuring the properties of nuclear materials, an expert in "nuclear accounting," an engine mechanic, an electrician, a doctor. Everyone had a vital skill, although slipping into a foreign country on a covert operation was not part of their job description. Many were "good old boys" who had barely been out of Tennessee. The chief packaging expert had a beard. Riedy told him the beard would have to go. They were going to be working in a place where a close-fitting respirator mask could make the difference between life and death.

Now Riedy had to worry about making sure he had everything he needed to operate a laboratory eight thousand miles away in a place that was well out of the reach of Federal Express.

That was why, in late August, Riedy began to re-create a small corner of Kazakhstan in eastern Tennessee. Every day behind the locked and guarded doors of Building 9729, an anonymous warehouse at the Y-12 plant, the team put on yellow plastic contamination suits, fitted the breathing masks as tightly as possible onto their faces and set to work inside a carefully marked-off narrow space, sixty feet by twenty with a twenty-five-foot ceiling—the exact dimensions of the room in the Ulba plant where they would have to operate. Riedy had inspected it during his flying visit at the beginning of the month. At the time it had been piled high with money. Because Ulba was a metalworking plant the government of Kazakhstan had ordered it to mint millions of coins for the newly indepen-dent country. By the time the job was finished the soaring rate of inflation had rendered the entire stock worthless, so the coins, like the uranium next door, had been locked away. The plant managers were quite happy to clear them out to make room for Americans who were offering dollars—real money.

What Riedy had to figure out was how to get a "hood" from Oak Ridge to that far-off room. When technicians at Y-12 are working with nuclear materials they do it in sealed containers with long gloves fitted to holes in the sides. The men and women who spend their days this way talk of working "in the hood," just a few millimeters of heavy plastic between them and metallic lumps and powders that must never be touched.

The hoods at Y-12 were rigid, heavy pieces of equipment, permanent fixtures in antiseptic rooms. He was going to have to build his own portable version. Scrounging around, he found a supply of plastic thick enough to shield whoever was on the other side from alpha rays. To hold it rigid he turned to scaffolding, with the plastic contraptions sitting on tables. The tables would have to come with them too—maybe Ulba would have the right size and strength, maybe it wouldn't. The inside of a hood has to be under negative air pressure. "You pump with a light vacuum," explains Riedy, "so that air from outside flows in. You don't want it the other way around where pres-sure [inside] is higher than the outside air so the air would leak out." To make sure that absolutely nothing got out of the boxes Riedy scrounged around for what he refers to casually as "Hepa filters"—high-efficiency particulate air filter system, so fine that not even a radioactive particle, still less a speck of beryllium, could escape. That might not be enough. Everyone working in or near the hoods would have to wear their yellow contamination suit, complete with breathing apparatus. They would have to be constantly monitored to make sure nothing was migrating into their bodies.

Riedy had to think about more than high technology. The lighting in the room at Ulba was barely bright enough to read by, so he had to find fluorescent lights. Heaters—they could be working in subzero temperatures. They would need electrical generators. Fuel for the generators? No, that was something at least that the locals could supply. Would there be forklifts at the site? Better to bring their own. What was to happen if someone with a key specialization got sick? Riedy started cross-training his people, so that everyone could do someone else's job. Most of the group still did not know where they were going. Riedy's wife didn't know either, even though she too worked at Y-12.

In little more than six weeks of eighteen-hour days Riedy had put together a mobile nuclear laboratory, recruited his team and trained them in every step of the operation. By the end of September he was ready. He was also getting anxious. The air force was confident they could get them in and out of the battered airfield at Ust-Kamenogorsk, but winter would start to close in sometime after the middle of November. Only one thing was holding them up now. The President of the United States himself was going to have to sign off on the operation and so far there had been no word from the Oval Office. The bureaucrats were still wrangling. To make sure he wouldn't lose any time when the word did come Riedy trucked everything he was going to bring to McGee Tyson Air Force Base in Knoxville, a few miles from Oak Ridge.

In those last few days another group of specialists began to slip into Oak Ridge. Bill Nickels arrived from Las Vegas, along with two tons of classified satellite communications equipment. He had the job because he is the resident communications expert for the nuclear bomb squad, the last line of defense if nuclear materials ever leak out of a forgotten vault in Kazakhstan and come to the United States in the form of a bomb. The mission of the Nuclear Emergency Search Team will be to find and defuse the weapon before it's too late. This was not the first time Nickels had been recruited for a covert overseas mission to retrieve nuclear material, but they had been quick operations. This would be the longest.

Commander Paul Shaffer of the U.S. Navy, on the other hand, was used to spending a lot of time in outposts of the old Soviet empire even more remote than Ust-Kamenogorsk. Shaffer had once spent his working days underwater in a U.S. Navy nuclear submarine playing cat and mouse with the attack subs of the Soviet enemy. Now he was assigned to the On Site Inspection Agency, a product of various arms control treaties with the dying Soviet Union and its successors. Shaffer's job was to go to once secret bases and check that there are no more missiles, or tanks, or bombers there than the other side claimed. That made him an instant expert on how to deal with officials, especially those who might be a little late in getting the news that the cold war was over. Shaffer himself speaks "just enough Russian to get into trouble," but he brought a three-man team of skilled navy linguists with him. Now they were combing specialized dictionaries for the Russian terms for phrases like "neutron flux."

Late in the afternoon of Friday, October 7, President Clinton finally signed a Presidential Decision Directive authorizing the operation. The instant he got the word, Riedy started moving everyone to the airfield. The day before, the team had finally learned that they were going to Kazakhstan. In fact, Riedy decided to bend the ironclad security rules and let the twenty-three men and two women tell their families a few bare details about where they were going and what they would be doing.

They could say they would be in Kazakhstan "to assist the U.S. embassy." Nothing more.

The man who was going to take them to Ust-Kamenogorsk and, hopefully, bring them back was less diffident when he briefed his own team. Now that there are few wars to fight, it is often the air force transport crews—"trash haulers," as the fighter pilots sometimes derisively call them—who get the interesting jobs. Mike Foster had the roving commission to take the C-5s that live at Dover Air Force Base in the flat fields of central Delaware whenever the air force has a new and different transport request. His job was to take his planes into places like Somalia, where the reception committee might be shooting at him, or Bosnia, where the airfields had been wrecked by years of civil war and there were none of the maintenance comforts of home. This time it would be Kazakhstan.

Calling his own carefully selected crews together for a final briefing, Foster made it simple: "This stuff is coming to America one way or another. Either it's going to come here in two C-5s or it's coming in the back of a pickup truck or in a cigarette boat with a terrorist riding shotgun, maybe to a mall where your wives are shopping."

Early in the morning of October 8 the first of the huge black transports, 247 feet from nose to tail, lumbered down the runway and lifted its massive bulk into the air. Followed by two others, it droned steadily eastward, landing in Spain only to refuel. The cavernous cargo holds of the C-5s, big enough to carry tanks, were crammed with 130 tons of equipment. The team traveled upstairs in the troop-carrying sections, forty seats facing backward.

As they started to descend over the Kazakh desert some of the team tried to get a look through the two tiny portholes, all that a C-5 offers in the way of sightseeing facilities, but the glass was gouged by years of scratches. The unknown country below was invisible.

For Foster, touching down on the 8,000-foot-Ust-Kamenogorsk runway was like riding a bucking bronco. Once on the ground, the air force did not linger. The weather was still warm, but winter was coming to central Asia. Mike Foster was wondering what would happen if the snow and ice had arrived by the time he came back. Looking through the nighttime darkness at the desolate stretches of the Ust-Kamenogorsk airfield, he did not see much sign of deicing equipment, without which his fleet would be effectively marooned in bad weather. "What do you do to clear the runway?" he asked. Someone pointed to what looked like a pile of junked machinery sitting in the middle of the field, including an antique truck with a jet engine on the back. "They can't be serious," he thought, and took off, hoping that the team would be finished before he had to worry about snow, ice and jet-powered trucks. On the ground the plant director announced, "Either you get out by November or you're here until April." Riedy hoped he was joking.

On the eighteen-mile night drive across the steppe to the city Bill Nickels noticed that the road had been cleared just for them. Police cars with flashing lights blocked every intersection. "Wasn't this meant to be a low-profile operation?" he thought.

Riedy and the team had trained endlessly at setting up his portable hoods back in the warehouse at Oak Ridge. Now they had to do it for real and they had just three weeks to meet the weather deadline. Outside, beyond the grim walls and broken windows of the plant, Kazakhstan was sinking into hunger and desperation. Millions of acres of farmland were eroding into desert. The wheat harvest had been a disaster. Food prices were going up 30 percent a month. That month hungry crowds started to gather outside City Hall shouting, "How are we going to live?"

Riedy had no time to think about that. He had to worry about the fifty nuclear weapons' worth of material in those vaults—worth enough to somebody to buy bread and more for half of Kazakhstan. Set up the lighting system, set up the heating system, assemble the hoods. Most of the room was marked off as the "Hot Zone." Anyone inside that area had to be wearing their yellow "C suit" at all times. In case anyone forgot, multiple signs proclaimed: "Radiation—Keep Out." The alarms were rigged, ready to go off if the radiation level started rising and everyone had to get out fast.

Finally they were ready. There were three hoods—glove boxes—lined up in the vault. Working from the original paper list of what was supposed to be there, he had figured out the order in which he wanted to pack the uranium. A Kazakh plant worker, one of the few who were in on the secret of what these foreigners were here to do, brought the canister. At the door, one of the health physics experts on the team stopped him and measured it for radiation. Everyone inside the room was wearing their yellow zip-up suit, shoe scuffs to cover their shoes and safety glasses. Most of them were wearing their respirator and some had on two pairs of gloves. Someone else checked the serial number against the list. After it was weighed the person at the end of the line tore open the heavy Velcro seal on the air lock and put the canister gently inside.

The next job was to get the canister open. They were bolted shut, requiring a wrench and screwdriver to prize off the long sealed lids. That was easy enough in the open air, but now it had to be done while peering through the semi-opaque plastic wall of the hood and protective eyeglasses and working the tools while wearing two pairs of gloves underneath the rubber gloves that led in from the hole in the side of the box. Empty the canister into a tray, making very sure that no more than thirty pounds went in—everyone knew what would happen if a package went critical. Weigh the tray on the high-accuracy digital scale. Pass the tray through an air lock inside the hood to the next person in line, who empties the tray into a quart-size American stainless-steel container. Crimp the lid tightly shut with the electric crimper set up inside the hood. Decontaminate the outside of the canister. Pass it through the last air lock, and weigh it again.

That was their life for six weeks, twelve hours a day, six days a week. Every morning they left the hotel in a guarded bus when it was still dark. When they drove back in the evening it was dark again. The physical labor was constant and repetitive, but at the same time the smallest slip could have lethal consequences. As the weeks wore on, the tension and stress grew higher and higher. Worst of all were the days when they had to wear their respirators for the entire shift. No one had ever done anything like this for so long. Sometimes the inside of the plastic hood got coated with toxic dust, fixed there by static electricity, and they would have to stop and try to clean it off. Always they had to worry that the filters were working and that nothing at all was leaking out.

Some found the culture shock too much to bear. On only the second day one of the youngest members of the team announced that he had "made the wrong decision" in agreeing to come and he wanted to go home. No chance. The young man became a recluse. Other team members tried to console him by spending long hours talking about his family and distant Tennessee, or playing chess with the set he had bought in a local market.

That was only one of Riedy's problems. He had been promised total cooperation from the plant, but he soon discovered managers who had not changed their old Soviet attitudes. They were the ones who delivered a traditional *"nyet"* when he asked for something. That was when he turned to Shaffer. The tough navy commander was used to getting senior Russian generals at strategic nuclear missile sites to live up to written agreements, when to threaten and when to charm. No one could afford to wait around for things to sort themselves out, because, as Riedy likes to say, "time was not a friend." The first snow had fallen on the second day, before they had even started work.

The team was handling material that was practically ready to go into a bomb. "The uranium metal was in little slugs. There was about a hundred sixty kilograms of that, and that's pretty good stuff," reminisces Elwood Gift. "You can't get it better than that." There was also about thirty kilograms of uranium oxide powder, known as UO_2. "That's pretty fine stuff too. All that was very, very good weapons material just by itself. Nothing needed to be done to it." Speaking as a professional, he thinks that converting the powder to metal might have been a "little bit of a problem," but "within the capability of any country," not to mention "a lot of subnationals"—terrorist groups. Even the material that was mixed with the beryllium would hardly have been much of a problem to a determined bomb maker. "Dissolve it in nitric acid, not a complicated procedure."

The cover story for local consumption was that this was simply a group of experts from the International Atomic Energy Authority who were taking an awfully long time on the job. They were staying at the Irtysh Hotel, Ust-Kamenogorsk's finest and normally a favored hang-out of very mean-looking characters who have found a way to prosper, even in Ust-Kamenogorsk. (Sometimes the chandeliers in the grander rooms on the upper floors start to tremble and the front desk reports, "Either it's an earthquake or the plant blew up again.") The choice at the bar lies between bad cognac, vodka that tastes like kerosene and the flat local beer. Single travelers are normally advised not to venture in there, but while the Sapphire team was in residence the other guests never seemed to check out. The more alert Americans eventually concluded that they were sharing the hotel with a special security squad shipped in for their protection.

Sometimes the interpreters would relay news of what was happening in the city. A leader of a pro-Russian faction had been kidnapped and thousands of his followers were demonstrating against the Kazakh government. There were rumors that Russian intelligence operatives were involved in a plot to destabilize independent Kazakhstan. Nobody knew for sure. Ordinary people were complaining about the price of bread, the breakdown in the medical system, the radioactive wasteland bequeathed by the Russians over much of the country.

Two weeks into the mission Riedy and Gift had to worry about a different kind of pollution. They discovered that some of the material was suffused with hydrogen. That was serious, because in the language of nuclear fission hydrogen is a "moderator," slowing down the neutrons and making it easier to get to criticality. The only solution was to persuade the plant to take it away and bake it. But it came back not in powder form, as they had expected, but caked into hard lumps. Now the workers on the hood line had to spend hours breaking it into small pieces before they could pack it up. Then the plant director announced that there was quite an amount of highly enriched material left in the actual production line. Would Riedy like that as well? He could only say yes. Ulba had already turned out to have far more bomb-grade uranium than its paperwork indicated. So much for Soviet nuclear accounting.

The first snowfall had come while they were still unpacking. Those early winter storms came and went, but they were a foretaste of what was to come. Far away in the operations room at Dover, Delaware, Mike Foster was anxiously awaiting the word to go back and get everyone out. In the secure NSC offices at the White House and across Washington, the few people in the know were just as anxious. Sapphire was running two weeks behind schedule.

The pace picked up. By now the team was ready to throw anything into the drums—old fuel rods and other bric-a-brac. Better to be safe than sorry. At last, one week before Thanksgiving, Riedy checked the final canister out of the hood. The loaders packed it into the last of the fifty-five-gallon drums marked "Fissile Radioactive Material" and they were ready to go. Not everything they were going to take actually was fissile material, for Riedy had decided it was better to err on the side of caution. The team packed just about everything they had touched that might be worth bringing—scrap metal, empty fuel rods. No one wanted to have to come back to Ust-Kamenogorsk.

Foster set out to get them with four C-5s. One of them was loaded with deicing equipment. From what he had seen on his last trip, the Kazakhs would not be able to help much if the weather turned really bad. When he landed in Spain to refuel, word came that there was a weather front moving through central Asia. He had no way of knowing for sure if Ust-Kamenogorsk would be closed down by the time he got there. Everything was put on hold for a day.

On the ground Shaffer and the dour ex-KGB officer who ran security at the Ulba plant were reconnoitering a safe route to the airport for the cargo. This would be the perfect time for a hijack, with all the material carefully packed up and easy to handle. They checked the roads, likely ambush spots, radio coverage along the way. Certain parts of the city, advised the security boss, were best avoided. The ditches were lined with trucks that had skidded off on the ice—highway salting and sanding had yet to come to Kazakhstan.

The C-5s set out on the last leg. Almost immediately, bad news came over the radio. One of the planes was having equipment problems and was turning back. That was the aircraft with their entire stock of deicing equipment on board. Foster began to pray even harder that the weather would be kind. He was getting two different sets of weather forecasts, each contradicting the other. Nickels had set up his high-tech communications gear at the airfield and was sending back weather reports to the Pentagon, from where they were being relayed back across the world to the planes, but there was no meteorologist on the team who could tell the anxious Foster what was going to be happening at Ust-Kamenogorsk by the time he landed.

Late in the day the "extraction team" finally began to touch down. Foster was relieved, it looked like the weather would be fine enough to get going in the morning. He and his crew went to get some rest. A few hours later he woke up and peered out into the darkness. His heart sank. There had been a ferocious ice storm and now it was raining hard. Ice on the runway was getting steadily thicker and the deicing equipment was thousands of miles away. He had no expectation that the jet-powered truck he had laughed at six weeks before was going to help. All he could do was hope for the best. Still hoping for the best, he gave the go-ahead for the loading.

A heavily guarded twelve-truck convoy crammed with the radioactive barrels pulled out of the Ulba plant. Foster had only one plane on the ground so far—the others were still on their way—so this was only half the load. The dangerous trip would have to be repeated. The entire highway had been closed to traffic and lined with police and elite Kazakh Army units. Every available light had been turned on.

At the airfield the air force contingent watched with amazement as the truck with the jet engine on the back trundled onto the ice-sheeted taxiway. After a couple of misfires it roared into life. The joke was on the Americans, because within seconds the roaring jet exhaust began to blast away the thick layer of ice. Massive chunks flew through the air. The airmen laughed at this "brute force deicing," but it was working. There was ice on the plane itself, which could be cleared with chemicals, but there was no ladder at the airfield long enough to reach sixty-five feet to the top of a C-5's tail. Suddenly, the Ust-Kamenogorsk fire brigade clattered through the gates, hurriedly requisitioned from downtown. Nothing like this had ever been seen on a USAF base, but nothing mattered as long as it worked. The second plane landed and another convoy set out from the plant with the rest of the material. Any potential hijackers stayed out of sight.

By the end of the day it was done. The first C-5 maneuvered cautiously to the end of the runway and started its takeoff roll.

If the pilot had to abort the takeoff and the ice had not all been cleared, it would have been impossible to stop. Foster watched through the lashing sleet and rain as it bounced down the uneven concrete and then lumbered into the air. He followed on the last plane out. After forty-five days Sapphire was coming home.

No one had wanted to ask countries along the way if they could drop by with a consignment of bomb-grade uranium, so the journey was nonstop direct to Delaware. Every few hours the huge planes would buck and jump as they maneuvered up to a KC-10 tanker to take on another load of fuel.

Nearly a full day after lifting off from Kazakhstan, the first C-5 touched down at Dover. Suddenly the operation was covert no longer. The Secretaries of State, Defense and Energy made a joint appearance to announce the triumph. Alex Riedy went home to his wife and two small children in Oak Ridge.

But it was not over yet.

•

A few months after the Sapphire team had gone back to their quiet lives in Oak Ridge, a group of executives from the huge chemical engineering firm of Babcock and Wilcox in Lynchburg, Virginia, journeyed to Kazakhstan and made a discovery that sent shock waves through the CIA and the White House.

The executives had been scouring the far reaches of the fallen Soviet empire for raw material for the nuclear power industry. Now they had come to Semipalatinsk, where for miles around the desert was seared and cratered from hundreds of nuclear blasts and the scattered civilian settlements spawned more mutant births than anywhere else in the former Soviet Union. The Americans chanced on an unlocked, unguarded building. Inside were two tons of a nuclear material no one in the United States had ever seen before. It was the remains of a very secret Soviet space program, more ambitious and dangerous than anything ever seriously attempted by

NASA. The Russians had been building a nuclear rocket. This was the fuel, two hundred kilos of it—bomb-grade uranium 235.

The Americans took pictures, returned home and got in contact with the CIA. "We've been taking [satellite] pictures of this place for twenty years," said the spooks. "Is that what's inside?" The reaction at the National Security Council was: "Jesus Christ!" How much more of this stuff was going to turn up? Could the U-235 be extracted from the rest of the fuel? Did the Russians want it back? No locks on the doors? How much would it cost this time? There were going to be a lot more Sapphires. Whatever the trouble and expense, no one wanted the other team to get there first. Riedy's group had already come across their footprints.

During the weary weeks at the Ulba plant, one of the team had taken a walk around some of the nearby buildings. In one warehouse there stood a pile of containers that appeared ready for shipment. Each one had an address neatly stenciled on the outside. The writing was Cyrillic, but it was easy to spell out the destination: Teheran. Iran.

The news went straight onto the scrambled fax in the communications trailer parked fifty yards from the vault. Bouncing off the satellite, it flashed to the Pentagon, igniting a firestorm of excited questions from the other end. The plant managers hurriedly explained that the containers held only beryllium and that they had already decided not to send the shipment. The report was instantly and highly classified and none of the high Washington officials brought it up at their triumphant press conference. The Sapphire team were warned never to discuss what they had found. It was much too real.

Jessica was about to find out how close the danger was.

10

MIKHAILOV'S SECRET DEAL

At 8:30 A.M. on March 7, 1995, Jessica Stern sat down at her desk in her basement vault office, switched on her computer, tapped in her password and settled down to scan the overnight cable traffic. Thousands of encrypted messages flowed into the White House Situation Room every day around the clock. By the time she arrived in the morning the overnight shift would have sorted out the ones she should see and routed them to her classified mailbox. Most, whatever the impressively coded classifications at the top, could be swiftly dumped. But she had learned to pay close attention to regular and detailed messages from a science attaché in the Moscow embassy named Ken Fairfax.

There was one of these waiting for her this morning. Jessica brought it up on the screen and started to read. Then she froze. "My God," she thought.

Twenty-four hours before, a call had come into the science office on the eighth floor of the yellow U.S. embassy building in the heart of Moscow. "I have something interesting for you to see," said the voice at the other end of the line. It was the news Ken Fairfax had been waiting for. He grabbed his coat and hurried out of the building. Driving through the main gate onto the Garden Ring Road, he saw the militiaman in the guard post pick up the phone. The cop was alerting the watchers that a designated target was leaving the building. They had started doing that a few months after he arrived in Moscow—a mark of respect. Russian counterintelligence had realized that he was a man worth following.

Fairfax, approaching the end of his second year in Moscow, knew that it was pointless to try to shake off the followers. They were too good for that. He was banking on the fact that they would not connect the man he was going to see with the source of the document that would be changing hands.

For months, Victor Mikhailov, Minister of Atomic Energy of the Russian Federation, had been slipping out of Moscow on his executive jet and heading two thousand miles south to Teheran. The Minatom boss was grimly pursuing a billion-dollar prize—a huge order for nuclear power reactors. But the man he was dealing with wanted more. Reza Amrollahi, Vice President of the Islamic Republic of Iran and chairman of the country's Atomic Energy Organization, was building a nuclear weapons industry. The reactors offered by Mikhailov might be some help toward that goal, but for the Iranian they were not the objective of the deal. He wanted to be able to produce his own enriched uranium and weapons-grade plutonium. If ever that technology was safely within the Iranian border, then the way would be clear to build bombs—lots of them. Fairfax had been hearing rumors that Mikhailov, desperate to get a profitable deal for the reactors, might actually agree to give the Iranians what they wanted.

The CIA office in the embassy could not believe that Mikhailov was capable of such an outrage. They had lots of good arguments on their side. Passing weapons technology to the

Ayatollahs would certainly bring down the wrath of the U.S. government on Mikhailov's head. It would threaten the whole U.S.-Russian relationship. Iran was close to Russia's southern border; it would be madness to help them get nuclear weapons.

"Mikhailov would never dare do such a thing," one intelligence official protested to Fairfax. "That would be just too egregious."

"Well," replied the slight young diplomat from Kentucky, "he's an egregious kind of guy."

They still did not believe him. He needed hard evidence to prove that he was right. A few days before the phone call that brought him hurrying out of the embassy, a trusted source had suggested that it might be possible to get hold of a document that would put the matter beyond doubt. His friend did not himself work for Minatom but was in touch with people high up in the nuclear organization who hated Mikhailov and were terrified at the prospect of a nuclear Iran. Now, heading urgently to a carefully chosen meeting place, Fairfax felt he was on the point of proving his case.

At first glance the two sheets of paper his source handed over hardly seemed explosive. Two months before, on January 8, 1995, Mikhailov and Amrollahi had signed a contract "to complete the construction of Block No. 1 at the Bushehr nuclear power plant" a few hundred miles south of Teheran on the shore of the Persian Gulf. What Fairfax now had in his hand was a "protocol" to that agreement, signed on the same day, outlining related aspects of the contract. To the uninitiated it might pass as simply a straightforward business document. But to Fairfax, the implications were momentous.

Buried in the middle of Section Six, Subparagraph Four was a reference to the "signing of a contract for the construction of a centrifuge plant for enrichment of uranium."

That on its own was deadly serious. A centrifuge plant was one of the most efficient systems for enriching uranium right up to the purity required for a bomb. There were strict international controls on the export of these plants even if they were intended purely to produce fuel for civilian power stations. Mikhailov and Amrollahi had agreed that the plant would be sold "according to conditions" comparable to "contracts concluded by Russian organizations with firms in other countries." On the face of it this sounded as if such deals were normal and internationally accepted. But Russia had sold only one enrichment plant to one other country—China. Under international treaty, sales of nuclear technology to countries that already have nuclear weapons are governed by a different and looser set of rules than those covering sales to states that do not possess nuclear weapons. China had nuclear weapons. If the Iranians were getting a uranium enrichment plant under the same conditions as the Chinese, then the international controls were irrelevant.

Running his eye further down the list, Fairfax picked out something even more sinister. In Section Seven, Paragraph Two, there was another innocuous-looking phrase referring to "the construction of a desalination plant in Iran," similar to plants Russia had sold to other countries. Selling a desalination plant to a semi-desert country to extract drinking water from the sea might seem perfectly benign, but the young American immediately recalled one crucial background fact. The only country with a Russian desalination plant was Kazakhstan, at Aktau on the Caspian Sea. The plant at Aktau yielded a lot more than fresh water. It was a *breeder reactor,* producing plutonium on a massive scale. Not only that, it was an experimental system and the plutonium in the "blankets" that periodically came off its core were far purer than the product of ordinary military production plants. "Ivory grade," physicists called it.

The rest of the protocol outlined other pledges granted by Mikhailov that were hardly less threatening. He was going to help them mine their own uranium. Iranian nuclear technicians would be trained in Russia. Amrollahi would get the research reactors he had been looking for. It was little wonder that Mikhailov had kept the whole agreement secret, not just from the world but even from his own government. In fact, the American was getting his hands on the document at about the same time that Boris Yeltsin's senior national security advisers heard the news. It was an extraordinary coup.

Fairfax hurried back to the embassy. There was an urgent cable to write. He hoped someone in Washington would be paying attention when they read it in the morning.

It was the word "centrifuge" that made Jessica freeze. "This is really important," she thought. This was the Iranian bomb. "Why isn't everybody screaming?"

She was hardly the first person in the government to get to work. A lot of people were on the same cable distribution list, yet no one was calling. There was no urgent meeting going on in her boss's office, no excitement over at the State Department or the CIA or any of the other departments that were meant to be on a sharp lookout for news like this. The phones were quiet.

"Maybe I've got it wrong," she thought suddenly. "Maybe this isn't what I think it is." Before talking to anyone else, she needed to get an expert opinion. Waiting until it was time for the West Coast to be at work, she picked up the secure phone and put in a call to Bert Weinstein, head of Z Division. She knew that the Department of Energy intelligence people did not like her doing this. Z Division was their own private resource and they liked to keep all communication with the nuclear intelligence experts out at Livermore closely confined. Jessica didn't care.

Weinstein was a sharp scientist and a respected weapons designer, but his present job brought with it a certain bureaucratic caution. He wanted to see the copy of the protocol sent by Fairfax before he committed himself. That brought Jessica up against the bureaucracy of the classification system. It was forbidden to send such material out of the building without going through a cumbersome set of channels and that took time. Jessica fumed as the government machinery slowly ground its gears. This was a chance to understand the truth about Minatom and its frightening master.

It had been three years since General Bill Burns faced down Victor Mikhailov in his office in the massive building on Ordynka Avenue and forced the boss of the Russian nuclear complex to accept his terms. Since then the U.S. government had kept a wary eye on the fiery minister and done what it could to help him keep the nuclear genies he controlled in their bottles. Minatom had become a very important factor in U.S. national security calculations.

The problem was that no one knew very much about the vast but secretive nuclear organization. Almost up until the end of the cold war, U.S. military intelligence officers on the tenth floor of the embassy listed Minatom's massive headquarters as a "Central Statistical Office." The system of secrecy built up decades before by Stalin's fearsome secret police chief Lavrenti Beria as protection against U.S. spies was still holding up. Since 1991 Mikhailov himself had become a familiar figure, dreaded in Washington offices for his habit of puffing Marlboros by the packful into the faces of clean-living Clinton administration officials. But, even when drunk, he gave very little away. His subordinates were almost totally unknown quantities. Despite all the vast resources of the 80,000-strong U.S. intelligence establishment, Minatom had remained very much a closed book. Ken Fairfax was making it his job to open it up. Jessica thought he was one of the most remarkable people she had ever met.

Only a few years before, Fairfax had been on a path very far removed from the dark intrigues of the Russian nuclear complex. Fresh out of college and weighed down with student loans, he was seriously in need of money. He made his way to the software industry of the San Francisco Bay Area, joined an information systems firm, rose rapidly to become a vice president, quit, started his own business working off his kitchen table and was soon turning over a million dollars a year. In a few years he would be running a major corporation. He hated the idea. Living the '80s dream, he cherished an unfashionable goal. He believed in public service. So in 1987 he sold out to his partner, abandoned cyberspace and joined the State Department. In the summer of 1993 he was ordered to Moscow.

Shifted to a new and unknown world, he was officially designated as a science attaché charged with monitoring developments in the field of Russian nuclear power, particularly reactor safety. These were routine and unexciting tasks, but Fairfax is a man of rare intellectual energy, ever ready and able to penetrate to the heart of a subject that interests him, whether it be gourmet cooking (the three-star professional chefs of Washington rate him as a peer) or, once installed in dreary diplomatic housing an hour's hard commute from the office, the unknown country of Minatom.

There was no particular reason for Victor Mikhailov to take notice of the arrival of an unknown and apparently unimportant diplomat in a minor posting. Nor, for that matter, had anyone in the embassy science office paid much attention to the Russian nuclear chief and his organization. Despite the fact that Minatom employed a million people, the office had no Rolodex for the nuclear ministry. Fairfax found that the only relevant phone numbers on hand were those for the minister's assistant and the head of the ministry's International Department. No one knew how, for example, to get hold of the director of Tomsk 7, all-powerful in his own far-off secret Siberian city and the custodian of 23,000 plutonium nuclear weapon pits. Certainly no one had ever been there and met the man or his counterparts in such equally inaccessible enclaves as Krasnoyarsk 26 and Sverdlovsk 45. A few intrepid explorers had managed to get glimpses of this unknown country. Frank von Hippel had managed to get to Mayak—Chelyabinsk 65—back in 1989. The brilliant Los Alamos weapons designer Steve Younger had bonded with the Russian bomb makers at Arzamas 16. One or two stray scientists had made hurried descents on Chelyabinsk 70, the mysterious rival to Arzamas deep in the Urals. What lay beyond and what indeed was going on in these strange cities was largely unexplored and unknown. Fairfax set out to unwrap the enigma.

He had arrived at the right time. Minatom was running out of money. That summer, Younger had a hair-raising conversation with the director of Arzamas 16. "We are desperate," pleaded the official. "We have got to have money. You are driving us into the arms of the Chinese." Arzamas was not the only place where people were getting desperate, which was why plant managers and institute directors were inclined to be a little more receptive to a sympathetic young American diplomat.

Unfortunately, finding out what was going on in the largest storehouse of nuclear weapons and material in the world was not a high priority in the embassy science office. In the beginning, Fairfax found that his official duties consisted of the mindless chore of fixing appointments and preparing paperwork for the congressional delegations that poured into Moscow in an endless stream. Nevertheless, he set to work to penetrate Minatom from the bottom up.

He began by submitting an armful of requests to visit the far-flung secret cities and other Minatom outposts. There was no response from the ministry. As he anticipated, his letters were gathering dust in some official's pending tray. But the requests gave him the excuse to call the ministry at every opportunity, gleaning every scrap of information he could about people far down in the organization, their first names and patronymics, their direct lines. He haunted formal receptions, ever ready to exchange business cards and set up a more discreet meeting over lunch at a later date. Slowly, he got to the point where a friendly Minatom bureaucrat on the other end of the line would mention when a delegation from some desolate plant in Siberia or the Urals was coming to town.

Finally, his networking efforts paid off with an invitation from the director of Tomsk 7 to come out for a visit. Such a trip had to be cleared with the Ministry of Foreign Affairs, which monitored the activities of all diplomats like himself. The ministry bureaucrats were outraged at the notion of the American's invitation. Fairfax soon discovered the reason why—no Foreign Ministry official had ever been given permission to visit the secret outpost at Tomsk. He ultimately prevailed on the bureaucrats to let him go. Other invitations soon materialized. On one occasion, when he made a trip to the weapons center at Arzamas 16, a Foreign Ministry official came along to "mind" him. It turned out that this was the first time the Russian had ever been allowed inside the fence.

The key to his success was the realization that he had something valuable to exchange. Time and again he would come across a lonely group of Minatom physicists engaged in groundbreaking research who were desperate for cash. Quickly, he would refer them to a laboratory or business in the United States who were interested in the research and had plenty of money to spend. There were scientists at Arzamas who, thanks to the role of high explosives in nuclear weapons design, were the world's experts in "directed" explosives—an area of great interest to the U.S. oil industry. Fairfax arranged the connection. A starving physicist in the Urals knew more than anyone else about the intricacies of deep borehole disposal of nuclear waste. Fairfax found American funding for her research.

The engaging diplomat was becoming a familiar and trusted figure in the world of the "Atomshi," men and women who only a few years before had been the pampered elite of the Soviet system but were now staring into a bleak and empty future. Now he was getting to know Minatom as well as the people who worked there. He could chart the factions and rivalries within the huge complex ruled by Mikhailov. He knew who hated and distrusted the minister, and why.

It was not only Jessica, reading his cables with rapt attention far away in the White House, who appreciated his skills in penetration. One day, he noticed the militia guard at the gate reaching for the phone when he left the embassy. The same thing happened the next time he went out. The counterespionage specialists in the FSB (the Federal Security Bureau, once the much feared Second Directorate of the KGB that had harassed Jessica in her Moscow days) had taken notice of this unassuming diplomat who did not show up on any of the normal lists of intelligence targets.

The surveillance teams got plenty of exercise. Fairfax, moving from meeting to meeting, was rarely in his office. Without attempting professional countersurveillance techniques, he found it entirely possible to keep encounters discreet when necessary. His Russian contacts, habituated to discretion by life under Communism and the KGB, would instinctively speak in coded generalities when the need arose, or scribble a sensitive piece of information on a scrap of paper to confound the eavesdroppers. Increasingly, such messages concerned things that the minister hoped would stay secret, not only from the Americans but also from his own government. Mikhailov was operating as an independent power, with his own foreign policy.

That policy was directed at making money, for Minatom and, so some in Washington suspected, for Mikhailov himself. (A few years before, officials in both countries had been locked in discussions about transferring a million dollars to finance a design study for a plutonium storage site. The United States was anxious to get the work going as quickly as possible. "No problem," barked Mikhailov down the phone. "Simply send the money to the following bank account in Liechtenstein." The Americans pondered what the minister was doing with a private account in the tiny European enclave noted for the discretion of its banking system.)

Whatever his personal incentives, Mikhailov had to find foreign sales. He saw himself and his empire besieged by American competitors. "We are at war with the United States," he growled at visitors. "A *hot* war." They might be stealing his markets for nuclear fuel and equipment in Eastern Europe and North Korea, but there was one country where the Americans had cut themselves out—Iran. The Iranians wanted something that he alone could sell them.

It had all begun in the days when the Shah ruled Iran and the Western world was rushing to fill his shipping bag. His Imperial Majesty not only lavished billions on the most advanced fighter planes, ships and tanks; he also harbored ambitions of becoming a nuclear power. By the time he lost his throne he had drafted plans for no fewer than twenty-three nuclear power stations. More covertly, he gave orders to start work on a nuclear weapons program. Thousands of young Iranian physicists were sent to study in the United States and Europe. None of the eager Western vendors appeared to find anything amiss in this. The French Atomic Energy Commission even accepted a $1 billion loan to build a uranium enrichment plant in return for a promise to allow the Iranians full access to the related enrichment technology.

At first, the Islamic revolutionaries who toppled the Shah and took over the country had neither the time nor the money to follow up on his nuclear ambitions and they canceled all the contracts. The two reactors that the Siemens Corporation had actually started building at the time of his downfall rusted in the sea air and sand of the Persian Gulf. One of them was heavily bombed by the Iraqis during the eight-year war between the two countries.

In 1987, however, as long-range Iraqi missiles rained down on Teheran in the final stage of the war, the Iranian nuclear program was stirring back to life. For years a research reactor that the United States had supplied back in the 1960s had barely operated because the fuel was long spent. Now the Iranians sought out fresh supplies of fuel from Argentina. In 1988

President Rafsanjani actually spoke publicly about the need for his country to develop weapons of mass destruction. Over the next few years the CIA began to get stray reports of Iranian emissaries moving around the world, cautiously exploring the supply lines for components and technologies necessary for a bomb. They were in Beijing negotiating to buy a research reactor from the Chinese; they were buying a calutron (another uranium enrichment method which the Iraqis had put to good use); they were seeking to buy another research reactor from the Indians; there were reports that the Pakistani military had agreed to help with weapons technology.

It was becoming apparent that an Iranian bomb program was not just the dream of fanatical Ayatollahs, but an idea that appealed to the most moderate pragmatists in the government. Ataollah Mohajerani, a Vice President of Iran, was one such moderate. By training, he was a literary critic, who cared for nothing better than discussing the finer points of Joyce's *Ulysses* or the novels of William Faulkner in his spacious book-lined office. Yet in October 1991 he proclaimed, "If Israel should be allowed to have nuclear weapons, then Muslim states should be allowed to have the same." By that time the effort had been put in the hands of his fellow Vice President, Reza Amrollahi. The Iranian ambition was clear.

Despite Iran's dire economic straits, brought on by years of bloody and exhausting war with Iraq, mismanagement and corruption and, not least, the U.S. embargo on trade relations, Amrollahi appeared to have a huge budget and a direct line to the center of power in Iran. The CIA, tracking the activities of his burgeoning organization, discerned that the Iranian nuclear chief was following an astute policy of not trying to do too much too soon. Eventually he would have to start building the massive plants and other infrastructure necessary for full-scale nuclear weapons production, but at that point—even if the buildings were carefully camouflaged—the Americans would be sure to find out. An even tighter embargo, perhaps even a blockade or a bombing attack, would surely follow. If Amrollahi had not acquired all the components and materials he would need by then, it would be too late. Instead, the Iranian set out on a stealthy buying expedition. His aim was to gather in everything that would be needed, whenever it became available, in preparation for the day when the final work would begin. However, he was not the only Iranian official engaged in a nuclear weapons project.

Amrollahi's goal was not just to build a bomb but to build a self-sufficient nuclear weapons industry. However, the Etallat, the Iranian intelligence service, controlled by the ruthless Ali Fallahiyan, had its own role to play in acquiring the means for a bomb. While the Atomic Energy Organization was painstakingly assembling the means to produce the essential fissile materials, Fallahiyan looked to the chaos of the former Soviet Union and pondered whether it might not be a good idea to try a shortcut.

Early in 1992 the CIA began picking up reports of Iranians visiting nuclear installations in the former Soviet Union. They were, the intelligence directorate concluded, agents of Fallahiyan. Although they were apparently reconnoitering likely sources of fissile material, or even nuclear warheads, in all parts of the old U.S.S.R., their attentions were concentrated on Kazakhstan. They were sniffing out where the supplies were and who might be prepared to do a deal. In 1992 they paid a call on the Ulba plant at Ust-Kamenogorsk. The Agency picked up their tracks at Semipalatinsk, the old nuclear test site, and, most ominously, at the breeder reactor at Aktau. So consistent and clear was the pattern of the Iranians' interest that CIA Director Bob Gates actually went public in 1992. "The Iranians," he said, were "actively shopping" for a nuclear weapon or materials. But Fallahiyan and his men were undeterred. Soon rumors were circulating in Almaty, the Kazakh capital, that the government was actually negotiating with Iran to supply a quantity of fissile material. The price on offer was $300 million.

Nothing came of it—the Kazakhs calculated that with Western oil companies pouring investment dollars into the country the cost of getting caught in an irregular deal was not worth it. Nursaltan Nazarbayev, the President and unchallenged boss of Kazakhstan, authorized an arrangement with the United States—the deal that led to Operation Sapphire—for less money but with a lot of goodwill thrown in. Confusingly, however, Amrollahi's officials were also crisscrossing the same territory. They were not charged with buying enriched material, but with gathering anything that might be needed for the eventual Iranian nuclear weapons production line. The containers filled with beryllium—irreplaceable as a neutron reflector in a sophisticated nuclear weapon—that the Sapphire team came across in 1994 addressed to Teheran were one legacy of an Iranian Atomic Energy Organization buying trip. So was the beryllium that turned up in the Lithuanian bank vault in 1993, part of a mafia smuggling operation which CIA officials believed was linked to the infamous Nordex Corporation.

The Americans might stop him in Kazakhstan and elsewhere, but Amrollahi had his sights set on bigger game. He was stalking Victor Mikhailov, who, he knew, was desperate for cash. As bait, the Iranian dangled the billion-dollar order to complete the reactor complex at Bushehr. They had judged their man correctly.

The contract was bait because the light-water 1,000-megawatt power plants that Mikhailov was trying to sell were far down the Iranians' list of priorities. They would be a cumbersome source of materials for a bomb, and besides, Iran, as the Americans never tired of pointing out, is flush with oil and gas. It defied credibility that the Teheran government would want to invest scarce resources in building up a source of energy, nuclear power, for which they had no need and which they could not afford. The project made sense only if Mikhailov, lured by the prospect of the reactor sale, could be inveigled into supplying what the Iranians really wanted: essential technology for their bomb program.

Fairfax agreed with the CIA that Mikhailov did not actually want the Iranians to build a bomb. But his sense of the Hawk's megalomaniacal personality told him that the nuclear czar had absolutely convinced himself that he could stay in control of this dangerous game.

The cable that Jessica stared at with incredulous eyes that day in March proved that he had been right. But she was having a hard time getting the rest of the government to pay attention. She had finally managed to get the text of the protocol to Z Division, but Dr. Weinstein insisted on going by the book and transmitting his analyses up the chain of command to the Department of Energy. From there it eventually made its way back to Jessica's office. Her reaction had been correct; the weapons experts at Z Division agreed that the centrifuge agreement alone was a deadly serious leakage of weapons technology. More confident now, she sat down and banged out a classified E-mail to her immediate boss, making it as forceful as she knew how. It worked. Finally the official wheels began to turn and very high-ranking officials huddled in meetings. Fairfax's cable was suddenly a very hot potato.

The administration was faced with a tricky political problem. The law required that if a country was found to be exporting nuclear weapons technology to a state not in possession of nuclear weapons, all U.S. aid had to stop forthwith. As the destruction of the records of the "Russian Fission" conference (along with the career of its organizer) had shown, the Clinton team was prepared to go to almost any lengths to give Boris Yeltsin's government a clean bill of health. Just to make matters more urgent, Bill Clinton himself was set to give his Russian counterpart a very visible seal of approval by going to Moscow in May to join in the celebrations of the fiftieth anniversary of the end of World War II. On the other hand, the real possibility of an Iranian bomb in the near future was too terrible to ignore, especially if the press found out.

So far as most people knew, Minatom had merely agreed to sell the Iranians two light-water reactors, with a possible sale of two more, for a basic price of $800 million. That sounded ominous enough, but it could be seen as simply an ill-advised sale, rather than a straightforward nuclear weapons assistance program.

Jessica got a taste of the administration line when she went to a meeting at the State Department the day after Fairfax's cable had arrived. She was still reeling from the implications of the news and expected it to be the main topic of discussion. In preparation she had prepared multiple copies of the protocol to hand around. That was not at all what her peers at the meeting wanted discussed. She was told very sharply to put her copies away—unless she wanted to be up on charges of leaking highly classified information. As the meeting droned on, Jessica felt she was in Oz. Official after official took up the issue of the wretched reactors. Whenever she tried to mention the centrifuge she was hushed for digressing. The chief concern appeared to be that the news might leak. Administration rhetoric in public skirted the enormity of what Mikhailov had actually done.

In the following weeks, as the deadline for Clinton's May trip to Moscow grew closer, a succession of high-ranking U.S. officials made the trip to Moscow to try to talk the Russians into canceling the whole deal. At the beginning of April the Secretary of Defense, William Perry, handed over a classified intelligence report on the Iranian nuclear program, complete with copious details on the buying trips to Kazakhstan. Secretary of State Warren Christopher gave his Russian opposite number, Andrei Kozyrev, the same briefing at a meeting in Geneva. Al Gore went to the Russian capital and added his own persuasions. None of it appeared to make any difference. The reactor issue was becoming a matter of national pride for all

Russians. They saw it as simply a matter of politics; the unscrupulous Americans were trying to kill a perfectly legitimate
commercial Russian victory in a market that the United States
had lost. Those who knew better kept quiet. Mikhailov's friend
Evgeni Primakov, who headed the SVRR, successor to the
KGB's formidable foreign operations directorate, obligingly
produced a report downplaying the possibility of a serious Iranian bomb program. (Two years before, the SVRR had stated
the opposite.)

Mikhailov himself was full of righteous indignation. When
we asked him at that time why Iran, drenched in oil and in the
midst of a world glut, should have such a pressing need for
"peaceful" nuclear power, his indignation knew no bounds.
"What about the United States?" he erupted. "Don't you have
enough oil? You built a hundred and ten reactors. What about
Russia? We are one of the leading countries in the world in
oil and gas but we developed a nuclear industry." Lighting up
another Marlboro, he bellowed that "the galaxy itself is powered by nuclear energy," one of his favorite lines.

Still no one had mentioned the enrichment plant or the plutonium reactor. There had been no leaks in Washington. When
the news finally broke, it came from a voice of conscience in
Russia.

Amid the ambitious, unscrupulous and sometimes sinister
personalities of Boris Yeltsin's court, Alexei Yablokov, former
chairman of the Soviet branch of Greenpeace and president
of the Moscow Society for the Protection of Animals, was an
unlikely figure. While so many of the others schemed and intrigued in a ceaseless struggle to gain power or make money,
this white-haired professor, one of the world's leading zoolo-
gists, was driven by different concerns. His cause was the mor-
tally wounded environment of Russia, a landscape ravaged by
decades of heedless exploitation, thousands of square miles so
poisoned that it was dangerous to set foot there. His despair
was fortified by personal tragedy; both his parents and his first

wife had died of cancer. He had remarried, but his second wife was dying of the disease.

Among the leading culprits, as the professor never tired of pointing out, was the nuclear industry, where the best, most technically accomplished people were "morally broken" because of their unqualified dedication to the cause of nuclear energy.

Mikhailov regarded Yablokov with a visceral hatred, losing no opportunity to denounce him as a lunatic. The Hawk was a dangerous enemy to have in Moscow, but Yablokov survived because he had not only the moral authority of a selfless environmental campaigner but also a powerful friend in Boris Yeltsin. The connection had been forged in the days when Yeltsin, dismissed in disgrace from the Soviet Politburo in 1987, was building a new power base as a Russian regional politician. As he challenged the Kremlin, Yeltsin was drawn to Yablokov and the force of his denunciations of Communist ecological mismanagement, appointing him his Special Counselor on the Environment and Public Health (a novel concept in Soviet times). When the world turned upside down in 1991 and Yeltsin himself moved into the Kremlin he did not do much for the environment but on the other hand he did not abandon Yablokov. This was why Mikhailov had to contend with the fact that his vehement critic was lodged in the offices of the National Security Council, a stone's throw from Red Square. From here the professor fought his battles with the help of a range of contacts in the Russian establishment and high-level supporters overseas, including Vice President Al Gore. Bitter as the nuclear boss might be at the scientist's well-informed assaults, he could not touch him.

When the news broke of Mikhailov's reactor sale to the Iranians, Yablokov was outraged. The clinching news of the deals outlined in the secret protocol was still known only to a few, even in Moscow, but the scientist found even the reactor transaction highly dangerous. Mikhailov was claiming that there was no way that these light-water nuclear power plants could help the Iranians build a bomb. Yablokov knew that this was not true, that plutonium extracted from the spent fuel of such a plant could be used to make a weapon, even if it was less satisfactory and harder to deal with. He dug deeper into the details of Mikhailov's Iranian negotiations, drawing on a network of sources that extended even into the heart of Minatom itself. Finally, someone who shared his concerns—Mikhailov was later convinced that it was Al Gore himself—leaked him the text of the secret protocol. The full enormity of what Mikhailov was doing dawned on Yablokov. Urgently, he put in a call to the Kremlin. He felt sure that Mikhailov was lying to the President, repeating his usual line that there was no danger in the deal and that the American protests were motivated purely by commercial jealousy.

Yablokov was convinced that if he could only speak personally to Yeltsin he could get at least the worst parts of the deal stopped. But his calls to the President's office went unanswered, blocked by Mikhailov's allies. The only way, he eventually decided, of getting the attention of the one man who could stop Mikhailov was by going public. He called the editor of the widely read and influential paper *Izvestia* and offered an exclusive.

His article appeared in mid-April, six weeks after Jessica had sat stunned by Fairfax's discovery. His mention of the centrifuge was the first inkling for the outside world of Mikhailov's covert agreement. Washington now started raising the issue in public. Predictably, the news led to calls for the cancellation of Clinton's Moscow summit with Yeltsin.

Clinton went anyway. With him on Air Force One was a thick briefing book on the Iranian sale over which Jessica had labored long and hard. After reviewing thousands of Russian Army troops marching past the world's leaders in celebration of the World War II victory, Clinton sat down with his Russian counterpart to do some serious talking.

While the United States protested the reactor sale in the strongest terms, he said, the related deals, including the centrifuge, were absolutely unacceptable. There was no way that friendly relations between the United States and Russia, not to mention the large amounts of aid flowing to Moscow, could survive if they went ahead. To emphasize the point, he brandished an actual copy of the protocol. Yeltsin could only give in, assuring his visitor that the centrifuge and the nuclear desalination plant were dead.

Since so much attention had been focused on the question of the reactors, it was not generally recognized how crucial Yeltsin's concession had been. Mikhailov added to the confusion by putting his own spin on the affair, claiming that the secret protocol had never been a real agreement but in fact a clever invention designed to excite the Americans and draw their fire before being dropped as a "concession." One Moscow paper, *Nezavisimaya Gazeta,* reported that the CIA had learned of the deal by intercepting Mikhailov's communications with Teheran. Ken Fairfax was happy to leave it at that.

Jessica knew better than that too, but she had more important things on her mind. For the first time, she and her friends in the White House had gotten Bill Clinton worried about loose nuclear material in Russia.

THE OVAL OFFICE

T he President was stunned. Twelve days before, a truck
bomb packed with two tons of homemade explosives had
blown apart the Murrah Federal Building in Oklahoma City
and killed 168 people. Now he was being told that all across
Russia, stocks of plutonium and bomb-grade uranium were sitting in barely guarded stockpiles. Unless something was done,
and soon, there was a chance that the next truck bomb might
be nuclear.

The intense, bearded scientist who was effortlessly commanding the attention of everyone in the crowded Oval Office
had just said that the Russians had no way of knowing whether
any of this deadly material had been stolen because they had
no idea how much they had stashed away in the first place.
"Jesus," muttered Bill Clinton to himself. Even worse, it
seemed that efforts to try to deal with the security situation at
the Russian labs were being stymied by officials in his own
government. At the end of twenty-five minutes, the President

found himself staring at a vivid graphic depiction of what a homemade one-kiloton bomb parked on Pennsylvania Avenue would do to the White House.

Jessica watched him intently. All around her were ranged powerful officials who enjoyed access to the President on a daily basis—the Vice President, the White House Chief of Staff, the National Security Adviser, the Deputy National Security Adviser and a host of others. She had been working in the White House for all of eight months and this was the first time she had been inside the Oval Office. Yet this meeting was taking place only because a small group of committed people like her, most of them young, had decided that the only way to alert the government to a terrifying situation was to go to the top.

Getting there had not been easy. For months, she and her allies in offices around the White House had been getting together at places like the nearby Au Bon Pain or Nota Bene around the corner on 15th Street to discuss their frustration. The news from Russia kept getting worse, but hardly anyone in the upper ranks of the government seemed willing to stick their neck out to do something about it. Jessica herself had recently fought to get her superiors to pay proper attention to Ken Fairfax's news about the impending sale of Russian nuclear weapons technology to Iran. Frank von Hippel and his friend, the straight-arrow soldier Fred Tarantino, had sent urgent cables from Moscow about bomb-grade materials there for the looting, only to see them vanish into the bureaucratic morass. Matthew Bunn had stories of high-ranking officials with multibillion-dollar budgets refusing to release comparatively tiny sums that could make all the difference to a crumbling Russian lab.

When Jessica had first arrived in Washington and realized what was happening, she had blithely reached for what seemed an obvious solution. The President had the power to issue a Presidential Decision Directive that required the government to take action on an issue. The problem was clear and the solution seemed obvious, so she began asking the representatives of the various federal agencies who came to her Nuclear Smuggling Working Group meetings to start coming up with proposals for a Decision Directive. She was quickly disabused. Senior officials, sensing an upstart threat to their prerogatives, slapped her down hard. Gradually, she began learning how to get things done.

Today, in the Oval Office, she occupied a prized place on the sofa a few feet from the President. Sitting next to her was a genial, unassuming man with years of experience in government, one of those who had taken swift action when news of her initiative on the Decision Directive had leaked out. Dan Poneman was a survivor, joining the NSC staff back in the days of the Bush administration and somehow staying in place when the Clinton people moved in. He owed his place in the Oval Office that morning to his title of Senior Director for Nonproliferation. There were a lot of reasons why he might not be enjoying the meeting. Some of her friends believed he had fought hard to prevent it.

No one really disliked Dan, an affable lawyer who had originally found his way to the White House via the Department of Energy. He had a kind word for everyone and worked long hours, often late into the night. The only problem, so his detractors complained, was that nothing much seemed to get done.

Poneman, for example, was responsible for overseeing the deal to buy 500 tons of highly enriched uranium from Russian nuclear warheads that Bill Burns had extracted from Victor Mikhailov back in 1992. This was still the most important effort to deal with nuclear bomb material in Russia since the end of the cold war, but the years were dragging by and little of the deadly uranium had been shipped. A lot of people blamed Poneman for not making things move faster. "You know," he announced cheerfully to one complainer, "I wrote that damn agreement and I can't remember a darn thing about it."

One problem with the deal was that the agent at the U.S. end was a government-owned corporation called the United States Enrichment Corporation, or USEC, which was due to be privatized and become a fully commercial entity. Critics in and out of the government believed that the corporation's responsibility to speed the flow of bomb material out of Russia was losing out to USEC executives' ardent pursuit of a healthy balance sheet. (Basically, thanks to government subsidies, it was cheaper for USEC to enrich uranium for sale to the power industry itself rather than buy the material from the Russian warheads.) One critic wrote that among the reasons for the consequent lack of movement "appear[ed] to be the low level of attention that the HEU deal received from the Clinton administration's senior national security officials . . ."

Poneman was, however, energetic in one area. He jealously defended his authority as the man in charge of all questions relating to proliferation. That included the leakage of nuclear weapons or materials from Russia, the issue that the impatient members of the underground thought should override petty considerations of turf and interagency responsibilities. As a seasoned survivor, Poneman knew that he should not antagonize powerful people in other agencies. If, for example, the Pentagon or the State Department dragged their feet, he would not risk making enemies to get things moving. At the same time, he zealously defended his own turf against attempts to encroach on it from below. It appeared that in those late nights in his office he was carefully editing and redrafting urgent memos sent to him for forwarding to those above him in the chain of command, including the President himself. All too often they never got any further.

To people who thought that even the possibility of someone taking advantage of Russia's ruined state to get hold of a nuclear weapon, or the materials to make one, was the most vital security issue facing the United States, this was more than frustrating. One man who had seen messages on the crisis in the

Russian nuclear institutes vanish into the quicksand of the Senior Director for Nonproliferation's office summed up the feeling this way: "Can you imagine what would happen in this country if someone got hold of a bomb and set it off here. It wouldn't just be the destruction. It would be the end of democracy. We would have a police state so fast you wouldn't believe it. This has to be stopped at the source."

One person who not only understood what was at stake but also seemed capable of finding a way to get things done was Matthew Bunn. Years before, as a very young graduate student at MIT, he had been fascinated by the question of ICBM accuracy and what that meant for the superpower nuclear standoff. By the time the Clinton team moved into office Bunn was working at the National Academy of Sciences and already delving into the parlous state of the Russian nuclear materials stockpile. Frank von Hippel recruited him to work with the Office of Science and Technology Policy at the White House, recognizing, as did most people who came across him, that this young man in his early thirties was extraordinarily effective not only in mastering arcane technical details but also in getting things done. He had the gift of being able to get along with practically anybody, from Russian nuclear officials to hard-bitten traders from the nuclear fuel corporations. He and Fred Tarantino, though, as someone said, "designed to hate each other" as an arms controller and a career military officer, immediately became fast friends. Jessica quickly assessed him as an invaluable asset. Quietly, she began inviting him along to her smuggling group meetings at the NSC to sit alongside the emissaries from the CIA, the FBI and other potent agencies.

Powerful though the NSC might be, it was not very useful for getting things done if officials up the chain were not interested. As the friends mulled the problem, the answer seemed clear. They had to find a way to get to the President. He was the only person who could cut through the undergrowth of regulations and interoffice disputes and make things move. But

Jessica had already found that there was no way to get to the Oval Office through the NSC—the fate of her effort to write a Decision Directive had proved that.

It was Lieutenant Colonel Tarantino who came up with the answer. One day he pointed out to Bunn that their own relatively powerless agency, the science office, might actually have a role to play. "Jack Gibbons," the President's science adviser, he pointed out, "has the same rank as Tony Lake." He had as much right as the National Security Adviser to go straight to the boss.

They mulled it over. It was a promising idea, but Gibbons, their boss, was not exactly the forceful personality they needed to fight this one through. Finally, however, a solution appeared. In addition to the science office itself there was an institution known as the President's Council of Advisers on Science and Technology. At the time, despite its imposing title, this was a moribund entity, not having done anything since Clinton came into office. As such, it was an ideal vehicle for the underground's plans. Powerful figures in the NSC, the Pentagon or elsewhere would not feel threatened by an initiative from such an obscure group. On the other hand, if they could attract some influential names to write a report under the council's auspices, it would be that much easier to get to the Oval Office.

To lead the inquiry, Bunn reached out to a friend with unassailable qualifications. John Holdren, a professor at Berkeley, had been fighting nuclear battles for years. Back in the early 1980s he had been a leading figure in the campaign against the U.S. breeder reactor on the Clinch River in Tennessee (stoutly defended at the time by a young congressman named Al Gore). An acknowledged world expert on the disposal of nuclear waste, he also had a deep knowledge of the Russian nuclear scientific establishment thanks to decades-old friendships with eminent physicists like Evgeni Velikov, head of the Kurchatov Institute. To flesh out the team the two of them went looking for people who were too high-powered for their work to be ig-

nored but at the same time were active enough to actually con-
tribute something. They avoided anyone already known for
being publicly vocal on the issue—"loose nukies," as one high-
ranking Pentagon official liked to call them.

Among those they recruited was General Bill Burns, the first
official to negotiate with the Russians on safeguarding weapons material and the only American—though neither of them
knew this—to have defended an American nuclear base against
terrorist attack. Norman Augustine, a titan of the U.S. military-
industrial complex as CEO of the defense giant Lockheed-Mar-
tin, was someone whom no one on the NSC would dare keep
away from the President. Also in the group were Sally Ride,
America's first female astronaut, and Ruth Kempf, an expert
on nuclear materials security from the Brookhaven National
Laboratory.

As anticipated, no powerful figure initially objected to this
obscure committee getting together to investigate the safety of
nuclear materials in Russia. By the time it dawned on relevant
officials in the NSC and elsewhere what was happening, it was
too late. The machinery was up and running and, in addition,
they were reviewing an intelligence report that laid out in stark
terms just how dangerous the situation had become.

Officially, the highly classified report had been the work of
a group known as the Joint Atomic Energy Intelligence Committee, the JAEIC, made up of analysts from all the various
intelligence bodies in Washington. In fact, it was almost entirely the work of one man: Jerry Dzakowic.

When Jessica had set off for Washington in the fall of 1994,
Jerry had stayed behind at Z Division, "working in the weeds,"
as he liked to put it. Not long after his partner settled in at
the NSC, a tasking order arrived at the windowless Livermore
building from the JAEIC. They wanted a systematic assessment
of the state of nuclear materials security in Russia. Habitually
modest, he told anyone who asked that he got the job because
he was "standing in the wrong place at the wrong time." In

reality, he was selected because he was the best. Accordingly, he sat down to assess all the disparate pieces of intelligence and anecdotes about the state of the Russians' stockpiles of nuclear materials in hard, quantifiable terms.

Being what he calls a "mathematician scientist type," Jerry was not satisfied with the way intelligence agencies, including his own, had been looking at the problem. "People were saying, gee, we don't think Russia has good control of the situation. This just tried to quantify that a little more."

He started by sketching out a "matrix," with all the known Russian nuclear facilities down one side of the paper. Then, working across the paper, he put down known "attributes" of each facility, such as whether the materials on hand were properly locked up, who had the key and so on. This involved a lot more than counting and labeling. Suppose there were two different accounts of an accident at a nuclear installation. One gave a more frightening picture than the other. Which one was to be believed? Jerry had a true analyst's "feel" for ferreting out the truth. With all the intelligence collection resources in the U.S. government at his disposal, he soon found himself looking at a frightening picture. He did not strive to make the report that eventually went up the line to Washington scary. He just tried to make it truthful. As he recalls, with a characteristic little laugh, things were "probably a little worse than I expected." The starkest truth that emerged was the Russian government's total ignorance of how much bomb-making material they had produced and where it was. Time and again he found instances of barrels of material turning up unexpectedly. "Somebody maybe stored them as waste, then retired and forgot about it, and there was no inventory requirement." This was the uncomfortable truth that was to stun Bill Clinton.

Jerry's quantified assessment of the problem was confirmed and buttressed by the witnesses summoned by Holdren and Bunn before the committee when it began meeting in January 1995. They were the scientists and lab technicians who had been over to Russia and seen firsthand the wasteland of the nuclear sites. At one all-day meeting, one of these travelers flashed up a slide showing containers of U-235 secured only with a wax seal.

"Wait a minute," said Augustine. "Anyone with a stamp could open the container and then replace the seal."

"That's exactly the point!" cried the physicist.

One expert with extensive experience with the Minatom labs recalled a conversation he had with the director of the research institute at Obninsk, where the amount of fissile material on hand was small compared with the big military installations at places like Tomsk 7 or Krasnoyarsk 45. How long, he asked, would it take to do a complete inventory?

"If I had all the money and help I needed?"

"Yes."

"About seven to ten years."

By the end of March, three months after they had set up, the report was ready. Each member of the committee had written a portion, all of which was then reworked by Bunn. The highly classified document gave a picture that was a lot more frightening than anything the public had been told. It starkly concluded that "the global problem of nuclear theft and smuggling is among the most serious and urgent security threats that the United States faces in coming decades."

All that remained now was to fulfill the purpose of the whole exercise by using the report to reach the President. That turned out to be easier said than done.

As word seeped out into select offices of what the apparently inoffensive committee was reporting and recommending, there were the first salvos of a counterattack. Suddenly, it seemed that the one thing in the world that the President of the United States should not have to hear about was the threat of nuclear materials leaking out of Russia, nor should he be asked to authorize measures to try to stop it. Subtle but effective bureaucratic maneuvers, second nature to experienced officials, were being deployed to keep the issue away from the Oval Office. The science office, the titular overseer of Bunn's effort, was assailed with suggestions that a simple briefing of Lake, or even Poneman, would suffice. The President was a busy man, with a host of problems more important than the possibility of nuclear terrorism to worry about.

The most threatening assault came in the form of a letter to Tony Lake from the formidable John Deutch, Deputy Secretary of Defense. Deutch had somehow been inspired to warn against the very idea of bringing the report to the President's attention. He thought it a wholly bad idea that the President should hear arguments in favor of cooperation with Minatom to increase security at the Russian nuclear labs (Victor Mikhailov had made himself an especially hated figure in the Pentagon).

To some of those who had worked so hard to give birth to the report, the root cause of their troubles seemed clear: the report's unsparing summary of the problem made it plain that people had not been doing their jobs, one of them being the NSC's Director for Nonproliferation, Dan Poneman.

In the end, despite all this high-level pressure, Tony Lake and Chief of Staff Leon Panetta decided to give the go-ahead for Bunn, Holdren and the others to have their day, or at least an hour of the President's time.

The night before the meeting, Holdren and Bunn worked late. They would be presenting a subject of deadly importance, but to produce the necessary effect they had to put on a theatrical performance.

They distilled the report down to a crisp lecture that would take about twenty-five minutes to deliver. Holdren would be doing the talking with the aid of a series of charts studded with "bullet points." Bunn would be flipping the charts.

A chart showing the effects of an Oklahoma-type bomb (two tons of explosive) and a one-kiloton nuclear weapon set off next to the railings in front of the White House was their most dramatic visual display. They had originally planned to bring it up in the middle of the address, but they found that discussing the details of the explosions took up a lot of time. "Let's just bring it up at the end and let it hang there without saying anything about it," said Bunn.

They prepared other props. At Obninsk, home of the Russian Institute of Physics and Power Engineering, there were thousands upon thousands of small disks containing plutonium or highly enriched uranium, each about the size of a dollar coin. With minimal safeguards then in place it would be easy for someone to slip a handful into their pocket and walk away. Now Holdren put one of the disks (not containing dangerous material) in his jacket pocket.

Nuclear leakage from Russia had been getting a lot of press. Bunn had carefully collected as many of these articles as he could find and now he clipped them together. They made an impressive pile, two inches thick. He made sure that an especially ominous *Time* magazine cover blazoning the menacing message "Nuclear Terror on the Loose" was on top.

The next morning at eleven o'clock the crowd assembled in the President's office. As soon as everyone was in place (except for Gore, who turned up five minutes late) Holdren started in. His delivery was powerful, "like a laser-guided bomb," thought one of those present, "directed straight into the President's brain."

He began by laying out the threat. How the difficulty of obtaining plutonium or highly enriched uranium was the major obstacle that prevented most countries or even terrorist groups from building a bomb; how small an amount they would actually need to make one, small enough to be carried by one man out of a poorly guarded facility; the places in Russia where there were no proper safeguards against theft; the vulnerability of trains carrying not just materials but even weapons across the vast country; the places where the guards were not being paid; the amounts that were available even to a casual thief.

Here, barely pausing for effect, he reached into his pocket and casually flicked the nuclear fuel disk onto the table in front of Clinton.

As Bunn went on silently turning the charts, Holdren laid out the thefts that were known to have already taken place and the Russians' ignorance of exactly how much they were supposed to be guarding—the point that elicited the President's startled exclamation. Having laid out the dimensions of the threat, Holdren threw in the clincher. Picking up the wad of press clippings, topped by *Time*'s alarmist nuclear terror cover, he tossed them onto the table. "Mr. President," he said, "the public is concerned." Clinton gave a thoughtful look at the evidence that this was becoming a popular issue with the voters.

Then he moved on to what was being done to try to stave off disaster. Thanks to cooperation between U.S. and Russian laboratories there were two hopeful initiatives in place— security upgrade programs at the Kurchatov Institute in Moscow (the fruit of Ken Luongo's efforts the previous year) and at Obninsk.

Now it was time to move on to the key point. What was being done was not nearly enough. A lot more could and should be done, but it was not happening. The work had been delayed and, in a phrase that may have sent a chill through the heart of the man sitting next to Jessica, "is still being delayed" by disputes between different government agencies.

Finally, he laid out what was needed. Controlling this nuclear material had to be made a matter of critical and urgent national security priority for the United States. Someone had to be given the job of seeing that all the programs to improve matters were properly run, without obstruction. The President had to make sure that the money to get the job done would be on hand and safe from budget cuts. Lastly, the issue had to be made a central factor in relations with Russia. If the effort was not made now, Holdren reminded the audience, and terrorists or a state like Iran or Iraq were able to get the essential materials for a nuclear weapon, any possible defenses would be very expensive and unlikely to work.

Bunn turned over the last chart, the one that showed what a small, crude device would do to the White House and the rest of central Washington. It did not need any comment. The President simply stared at it.

Three weeks later, Pennsylvania Avenue in front of the White House was permanently closed to traffic, forever blocking the main crosstown artery in the nation's capital.

Holdren asked for questions. Clinton went back to the point that had evoked his exclamation. "Jeez," he said, "I understand that the security is bad, but this is the first time I've understood that they don't even know if something's been stolen."

Gore spoke up, suggesting that since the President would be meeting with Yeltsin in Moscow in a few days, they should be prepared to talk about getting the Russians to cooperate on improving their nuclear security. Lake started to object on the grounds that it was too late to introduce the subject. Gore abruptly cut him off. It was clear that the chilling talk had had a powerful effect on the two men in the room who counted.

Clinton and Gore both latched on to the fact that wrangling in Washington was holding up efforts to increase security at the Russian nuclear sites. As he was leaving the room, Clinton turned to Lake. "I want this resolved by tomorrow," he snapped.

Word of the order flashed around the small group that had worked so hard to get this far. It seemed that they had made their point.

Bunn got a further indication of the impact of the meeting that afternoon when he got an urgent message summoning him to help rewrite the statement that would be issued after Clinton's meeting with Yeltsin. The summit was still a week away, but for the relevant bureaucracy this counted as doing things at the very last minute. Passing one National Security Council office, Bunn overheard a staffer on the phone to a colleague, complaining about the changes. "This is what happens," he groused, "if the President speaks for himself."

Although the President had spoken, nothing he had said about agreeing to the ideas put forward at the meeting could be implemented until it took the form of a Decision Directive. For a few weeks after the Oval Office get-together there was no sign that any such directive was going to be written. At this point Jessica seized the initiative. She announced to Poneman that there was going to be a directive and she was going to write it. Over a long weekend she did just that, hammering out a draft. She had come a long way since the previous fall.

However, an order, or set of orders, like this had to be ironclad. President Clinton might have made his intentions clear, but officials and agencies were adept at finding loopholes in even the most clear-cut instructions that would allow them to avoid doing whatever it was they disliked. Accordingly, Jessica and Bunn agreed to make it a cooperative effort. Each of them drafted and redrafted versions, swapping them back and forth after long nights of effort. By the end, they had each rewritten the document thirty times.

Finally, on September 20, Bill Clinton put his signature to Presidential Decision Directive 41. The key provision in the directive she and Bunn had crafted called for the NSC to put in place a single official with responsibility for making sure that all the various programs to increase security for nuclear materials in Russia were being properly run. Jessica knew just who should get the job.

After his coup in getting hold of Victor Mikhailov's secret agreement to sell nuclear weapons technology to the Iranians, Ken Fairfax had remained in the science attaché's office in the Moscow embassy. But he was suddenly plagued by ill health. None of the doctors he talked to could quite understand his symptoms. He thought it was possible that after spending so much time in Minatom's nuclear facilities, he had been "cooked" and was now paying the price. It was time to come home.

With the help of energetic lobbying by Jessica, Fairfax was given the newly created job on the NSC Nonproliferation Directorate of trying to plug the leaks in Minatom's nuclear storehouse. She felt it was the most important thing she had accomplished in all her time in the White House.

Everyone agreed with her about Fairfax, even Poneman, who found that at the end of the exercise he had resisted so energetically he ended up with his bureaucratic domain actually enlarged. He was pleasantly surprised, remarking later that he had "not appreciated until afterward the galvanizing effect an outside panel could have." Not everyone who had been involved in the battle, however, thought that they had really made much of a difference. "We have absolutely no idea how much plutonium, how many warheads may have already left Russia," said one. "Even if the Russians knew, they wouldn't tell us. There are plenty of people out there who want a bomb."

Anyone who doubted that had only to look to a country that clearly wanted a bomb very much indeed.

12

THE PHOENIX

Not long before midnight on February 27, just two months before President Clinton was briefed on the disastrous state of Russian nuclear security, an Iraqi nuclear physicist stole out of his Athens apartment to make a promised call to a London newspaper. Khidir Abdul Abas Hamza was half dressed. He wore slippers for the hundred-yard dash to the phone booth. "I'll be back in five minutes," were the Iraqi defector's last words to his wife.

She was not reassured. Hamza had told her that he had spirited some fifty pages of top secret Iraqi documents out of Baghdad, damning evidence that would prove beyond a shadow of a doubt, when spread across the pages of the London Sunday *Times*, that Saddam Hussein was building a nuclear weapon.

"If the world does not stop him now," the scientist said to his long-suffering wife, her nerves frayed from traveling under an assumed name and moving from one safe house to another in the netherworld of the Iraqi exile community, "it will be too late."

Hamza claimed his documents detailed a nuclear bomb program that had survived wave after wave of 2,000-pound bombs and Tomahawk cruise missiles in the 1991 Gulf War. With skilled subterfuge, the 20,000 scientists, engineers and staff employed in Saddam's quest for the bomb had played an elaborate shell game to defeat the efforts of the UN nuclear inspection teams ordered to comb Iraq after the bombing.

Before his excursion to the phone booth, Hamza had already faxed the London paper a few pages from his documents cache with Arabic markings that matched the top secret classification stamps on documents carted away from Iraqi installations by United Nations inspectors. A former counselor in the presidential center for nuclear energy under General Hussein Kamel Hassan (Saddam's son-in-law), Hamza said the official secrets had been in his possession for seven months, since he and his wife slipped out of their well-appointed home near Celebration Square in the Harithiyah district of Baghdad and fled into exile.

The couple made their way north across the inhospitable desert, where the 130-degree heat of August was broken only by eerie whirlwinds. They managed to evade Republican Guard checkpoints and cross the parched no-man's-land into the mountains of Iraqi Kurdistan, then a protected zone with American A-10 aircraft screaming overhead to inspect the landscape for Saddam's tanks. Their route took the Hamzas through Salahaddin, where the scientist met General Wafiq-el-Samaraai, another Iraqi defector, who had attempted a military coup against Saddam. Then on October 3 the scientist and his wife crossed the Turkish border, driving through the medieval villages of eastern Turkey and up to Istanbul. There they secured false papers and headed for Greece. In Athens, the scientist moved often, relying on expatriate friends to shelter them. Once closeted in the one-room apartment in the Glyfada district, the Hamzas rarely appeared in public except on short outings to buy food.

The scientist's wife was convinced that they had not escaped the long arm of Baghdad. Two men were staking out the apartment, one of them unusually tall with the thick mustache favored by Saddam's cadres. Surely, she thought, they were agents of the Mukhabarat, the dreaded Iraqi secret police.

"Look back at these people," she told the nuclear scientist. "They are following us." He ignored her. She panicked too easily.

The night of February 27 she panicked again. Fifteen minutes after her husband left the apartment where they had been sequestered for weeks to make his long-distance call, she disobeyed his orders and ventured into the night. The phone booth was empty. The street was deserted.

"I saw his slipper in the street. I understood at once that they had got him."

The scientist's wife called London.

"They have killed him," said the distraught woman. "And they are going to kill me."

In trying to piece together what had happened, Greek authorities noted that just before Hamza disappeared, an Iraqi secret policeman called Farouz Hajazi had been spotted in Athens. A unit under his command was suspected of having carried out the abduction. Immediately after the night at the phone booth, the Iraqi ambassador and military attaché Issam Saud Khalil was recalled to Baghdad.

The scientist's wife told investigators she set fire to her late husband's incriminating documents to save her own life. With the file incinerated, it was impossible to say what had been lost. The police had to take into account the possibility that the explosive documents never existed. Iraqi exiles desperate for cash were capable of staging a hoax. But the few official-looking pages faxed to London seemed like plausible evidence that the Iraqi bomb project was far from dead. If they were faked, the Hamzas would be actors in a drama staged by some faction of Saddam's opposition or a Western intelligence agency.

"He was the genuine article. He was involved with the program," said Ambassador Rolf Ekeus, the soft-spoken Swedish diplomat who until July 1997 chaired the UN Special Commission set up to dismantle the Iraqis' nuclear and chemical weapons program. "But the Iraq program is highly compartmented." When Hamza emerged from Iraq, he had only part of the picture. At the phone booth he may have gone underground, like scores of other Iraqi defectors now going by false names, resettled by foreign intelligence agencies. "It's very complicated and shadowy. Who you talk to. Who you don't talk to. Who is handling you. Who is moving you," says Ekeus. "I think he's alive and well." The abandoned wife returned to Baghdad.

The importance of the mysterious telephone booth defector was the evidence he left behind, slim but convincing, that Iraq was determined, in spite of the very high stakes of concealing a nuclear program, to have a bomb. UN sanctions had strangled the country and still Saddam refused to give up. No one wanted to believe it. The received wisdom was that the Iraqi program for weapons of mass destruction had been dismantled. At least Saddam's bomb-making factories had been shut down. The International Atomic Energy Agency in Vienna wanted to give the Iraqis the benefit of the doubt. But the three pages of documents faxed to London gave details of a flourishing weapons design group and a materials research department in Baghdad. They outlined internal Iraqi government orders to hide nuclear materials from the American inspection team leader David Kay, one of Ekeus's top men in the field.

Hamza was not the only scientist with ties to Saddam's nuclear program to be silenced on a foreign street. Two years before, in December 1992, a nuclear physicist employed by the Iraqi Ministry of Military Industries was vacationing in Amman, Jordan. Muayad Hassan Naji al-Janabi had made up his mind to defect. With his wife and two children, the physicist was on his way to pick up visas for Libya. A gunman dressed in black raised a pistol with silencer to al-Janabi's head and fired. The authorities in Jordan believed he was gunned down by Iraqi intelligence to prevent him from spilling nuclear secrets.

Nuclear physics was a hazardous profession. Both the murder in Jordan and the disappearance in Athens set off alarms in Washington. The nuclear weapons team assembled by Saddam Hussein, with its core of 7,500 physicists and engineers, was still in place and defection was rewarded by death. Something in Baghdad was still worth hiding. The Iraqi leader's obsession with a nuclear weapon combined with the disintegrating controls in Russia, Iraq's long-standing supplier of military hardware and training, was very worrying to Jessica's White House Nuclear Smuggling Working Group, to officials in the Clinton administration's terrorism office and to the men whose job it was to dismantle the Iraqi bomb project. What was worse, the White House had top secret information that a tasking order had gone out to Iraqi intelligence to buy a nuclear warhead or bomb-grade materials.

The only stricture in the tasking order was that the Iraqi intelligence men should not get caught. In the brutal Iraqi security apparatus, run by Saddam Hussein's second son, Qusay, the foot soldiers knew that getting caught would mean execution.

For David Kay, the UN's chief field inspector for Iraq after the Gulf War, Russia was the worst nightmare. A good connection for Russian plutonium or uranium—a connection that in the spring of 1995 some Washington intelligence and terrorism specialists privy to National Security Agency intercepts believed already existed—could undermine all of Kay's years of painstaking work. The depth of his concern could not be understood without an appreciation of how massive and sophisticated the program was that he and his colleagues uncovered and how feverishly the Iraqis worked to block his every move.

Even after Kay and the UN teams had labored for five years under the terms of the Gulf War cease-fire to shut the Iraqi nuclear threat down, they could not shut down Russia. In 1995, they stumbled on a Russian military smuggling ring doing a brisk business shipping guidance packages for extended-range missiles from Russia to Baghdad. The highly sophisticated guidance "cans," including gyroscopes, came from dismantled Russian submarine-launched ballistic missiles. This was equipment for very long-range missiles that could carry a nuclear warhead. For Kay, the fact that some were stopped in Jordan and others were produced for inspectors after being dumped in the Tigris River in Iraq meant that "we really don't know how many got through. How many shipments were there?" The Iraqis had purchased the goods at bargain basement prices. The missile guidance packages still had serial numbers on them. The Russians said the Iraq-Russia deal was the work of a black market smuggling operation rather than a sanctioned government sale. But someone had official access to nuclear missile stores. Someone decided to sell it. This was not someone who cut through a fence and grabbed it, stole it and smuggled it out. How far would the Russians go to service their old customer?

The Russia connection was very disturbing to Kay's boss, Rolf Ekeus. In fact, the Iraqi forays into Russia were the most sensitive intelligence on the plate of the UN Special Commission. "These gyroscopes were from dismantled nuclear weapons. They were dismantled and stored. Of course, the most disturbing thing is, if one could pick up that component of a nuclear weapon, one is concerned how they control other aspects. That is for me the most nagging question."

The UN diplomat was very uncomfortable with the implications. "In the Russian complex, Iraq managed to buy components from a nuclear weapon." They had the route, the contacts, the transport, the bags of cash. They might, for all Ekeus knew, now have a nuclear warhead. The Swedish diplomat regarded this matter as so sensitive that he was in direct touch with the Russian Foreign Minister, Evgeni Primakov. "They say they are investigating." Ekeus seemed less than convinced.

"Primakov says, 'No state organ of Russia is involved. No state organ.' " Ekeus smiled faintly. "We've reached a wall." The Russian ties to Iraq were so extensive and so deep. "The Iraqis adopted the Soviet system. Their ability to hide and deny. They import the technology but also the lies."

•

The Iraqi nuclear weapons program was so sophisticated that details of their warhead designs developed on the eve of the Gulf War were highly classified. In the past, the Iraqi nuclear program had no trouble attracting patrons. In 1980, the cafeteria of the French nuclear training center at Saclay outside Paris was crowded with eager Iraqi physicists in white lab coats learning how to operate a French nuclear reactor called Osiris, named for the Egyptian god of the underworld and judge of the dead. It was a small, elegant 40-megawatt research reactor. France was building an exact replica in Iraq called Osirak, which long before completion came under intense scrutiny from the intelligence agencies in Washington. Osirak as a source of bomb-grade materials marked the beginning of a nuclear arms race with Israel. In June 1981, Israeli F-16s thundered over Baghdad and demolished the Osirak reactor with 2,000 bombs.

The Israelis made it clear they would do everything in their power to halt the Iraqi bomb program. By 1989, Jerusalem was once again leaking intelligence that Baghdad was within two years of producing a bomb. The accelerated program was costing billions of dollars. Few people knew that the Iraqis had found an oil-rich partner to help foot the bill. A former high-ranking American diplomat in the region was privy to an explosive secret that was tightly held in Baghdad and Washington. The silent partner was Saudi Arabia.

The alliance was made public when a top Saudi defector, Muhammad Khilewi, abandoned his UN post in 1994, producing documents showing payments of up to five billion dollars from the Saudi treasury for Saddam Hussein to build a nuclear weapon. Between 1985 and 1990, up to the time Saddam invaded Kuwait, installments of the generous gift to Saddam from the princes' coffers were paid on condition that some of the bombs, should the project succeed, be transferred to the Saudi arsenal.

The Fahd-Saddam nuclear project, according to the former senior diplomat, was also known to the CIA. "I knew about it," the diplomat says matter-of-factly, "and so did they." A senior White House official, asked about the Saudi government's involvement with the Iraqi bomb project and American complicity, told us, "They did spend billions on the Iraqis. It was a different world. We were ready to overlook a lot of things the Saudis were doing for the Iraqis. It's consistent with all the other terrible things we did at the time" to shore up Saddam.

The "terrible things" included an unchecked flow of high technology for his bomb project. A senior U.S. official at the Department of Energy in Washington who ran the office of export controls found out in 1989 that nuclear detonators of the most advanced kind were being shipped from the United States to Baghdad. When he complained about the violation of export laws and the alarming sophistication of the bomb program judging by this equipment, he was fired from his job and exiled to the classification department, the Siberia of the Department of Energy. Saddam was moving full speed ahead on a program supplied at least in part by U.S. companies. The White House was mute. President Bush responded to the alarming Israeli reports by saying he did not want to give credibility to the reports that Iraq had a crash program to build nuclear warheads.

Washington's insistence on ignoring the problem led to a

very awkward moment after Saddam invaded Kuwait in the summer of 1990. The Department of Energy's chief of Foreign Intelligence, Jay Stewart, was asked for an emergency assessment of the Iraqi program. Stewart did not know whether Saddam had succeeded yet or not. Did he have a bomb? Stewart knew that Saddam had an arsenal of Russian delivery systems. There were Scud B missiles, Frog-7 rockets, TU-22 bombers along with TU-16s and MiG-23s. Did he have a warhead that would turn them into deadly tactical nuclear weapons? It was a critical piece of intelligence for an army preparing to go to war with Iraq.

Stewart and his staff scrambled to gauge the scale of Iraq's Manhattan Project. What they found was startling. At the same time, it was obvious. The Iraqis had launched their crash program to build a nuclear weapon with vintage American blueprints declassified in 1949. Thousands of freely available pages detailed a long since abandoned method for building an atomic bomb. Declassified American design plans that predated Hiroshima had become the Iraqi bomb.

No one could believe it. The first evidence traveled out of Baghdad hidden in the suits, socks and sports coats of American hostages. It was invisible to the naked eye.

In the tense weeks leading up to the bombing of Baghdad in January 1991, the Iraqi leadership decided the best way to ensure that their military and industrial factories and depots would not be destroyed was to plant small groups of hostages—oilmen, engineers, salesmen who had been doing business in Iraq—at strategic facilities. One group of hostages was billeted at the Tuwaitha Nuclear Research Center southeast of the capital. The daily rounds of the Tuwaitha hostages included a workout in the gymnasium, visits to the Research Center doctor to prove they were in good health, and transport on Tuwaitha nuclear workers' buses. They were unwittingly gathering critical evidence.

When Saddam changed his strategy and released the hos-

tages, their first stop was Jordan. There, an American government official met the Tuwaitha veterans with a peculiar
request. "I'm from the U.S. government. Trust me," he told
them. "Give me your clothes."

Everything they had worn at the nuclear research center
was analyzed. Tiny flecks of highly enriched uranium showed
up in the cuffs, collars, the pockets. The strange thing was,
these uranium samples had isotopic characteristics that had
not been seen since 1945. This uranium could only have been
produced by a means of enrichment called electromagnetic isotope separation. Yet during World War II, that method had
consumed most of the U.S. government's silver supply, empty-
ing Fort Knox, before it was rejected as a practical way to make
a bomb. The silver had been melted down to build giant magnets. Gaseous uranium in the form of uranium tetrachloride
was injected into a magnetic field and spun around in a vacuum until uranium isotopes of different weights were flung out
into collectors. Massive amounts of electricity were used. The
expense was astronomical. The method was exhausting. Uranium 235 was scraped off the walls by legions of young women,
each armed with a toothbrush.

It was not possible, thought the nuclear experts evaluating
the evidence from the hostages' clothes. The Iraqis could not
be using calutrons. Z Division colleagues of Jerry Dzakowic assigned to watch Iraq dismissed the idea as absurd.

A few nights into the air war, Tuwaitha was heavily
bombed. Eight F-117A stealth fighters evaded Iraqi air defenses
and flattened the research center's laboratories and three of the
four reactors. By accident, air force targeteers discovered two
other key nuclear facilities for uranium enrichment, Tarmiya
and Ash Sharqat. They were damaged but not destroyed. U.S.
Air Force claims that "100 percent of the nuclear facilities in
Iraq that we knew about" were destroyed was wildly optimistic.
Al Atheer, Iraq's Los Alamos, was left intact.

The mystery of the uranium in the hostages' suits began to

make sense in May, two months after the bombing campaign ceased, when there was a gruesome car crash on the road from Baghdad to Mosul in the north. A burned body was left in the wreckage. It was the corpse of an Iraqi nuclear physicist, or so it was made to appear. The physicist had staged his own death. He meanwhile fled with his wife and brother to Iraqi Kurdistan, and told marines at the Dohuk checkpoint, "I am Saddam Hussein's top nuclear scientist. I want to defect now."

The party was dispatched to a Munich safe house. In his debriefing, the defector revealed that Iraq was indeed using the calutron method. They had ingeniously adapted the antiquated U.S. plans, obtained under the Freedom of Information Act, solving the insurmountable technical difficulties of 1945 with 1980s technology. Moreover, the enrichment facility was still up and running.

The $3 billion two-square-mile complex at Tarmiya north of Baghdad had been fortified and camouflaged well enough to survive. Building 33 was stuffed with calutrons, the giant magnets. The defector's statement was put before two top American scientists, one of whom was Richard Garwin, chief scientist at IBM. They rejected the story as fantasy. How could Iraq succeed where the United States had failed?

A few days later, a satellite photo interpreter noticed a detail that proved the defector was telling the truth. Saddam's nuclear secrets were unraveling quickly. The spy satellite recorded a series of images that looked like a massive cleanup of bomb rubble just outside the Tuwaitha research center fence. Junked equipment was buried in the desert. Coincidentally, David Kay's team of UN inspectors was just about to arrive at Tuwaitha. "As the team left the site," Kay remembers, "the photo interpreters on the next satellite pass noticed that the Iraqis were digging up the material they had buried before" to hide from the inspectors. "Then they made a connection. A photo interpreter said, 'Those shapes. I saw those objects during the bombing campaign.' They're very large round circular objects some nine meters across. So they pulled the pictures."

The same "shapes" had been pulled out of Building 33 at Tarmiya. Photos of the Tarmiya complex were spread out on a table in front of one of the oldest members of the American nuclear establishment, John Googin, a veteran of the Manhattan Project. Googin was eighty-one years old. His specialty was electromagnetic isotope separation. The only intelligence he was given about the building in the photographs was that it might be somehow related to nuclear weapons and it was somewhere in Iraq. The octogenarian walked slowly around the table. He studied the mysterious Building 33 as he walked around again.

"I worked in this building my entire life."

Tarmiya was an exact replica of John Googin's building at Oak Ridge, Tennessee, home of the calutron weapons program. The nine-meter circular objects were magnets. Now Kay and his UN team knew precisely what they were after. This time, no one made the mistake of underestimating the Iraqis.

Kay was impressed. "The Iraqis took the unclassified information on the U.S. calutron program and then they innovated. One of the problems with the U.S. program was isotopes whirling around in a vacuum. In order to collect the product, you had to take it apart. Break the vacuum. Well, anytime you take apart a home appliance, putting it back together again it almost never fits exactly right. It was a horrendous problem in the U.S. program. The Iraqis said, 'This is not so smart.' "

In Baghdad, scientists devised a movable sleeve, an elegant solution. The sleeve was like a large rubber bag inside the chamber. "Open it up, slap in a new bag and a new set of collectors, and the thing goes right back into production." The other critical difference from the Oak Ridge calutron project of 1945 was the existence of modern computers. Iraqi physicists could model and simulate and use them in the process of enrichment. "It was not," says David Kay, "a dumb program."

It was also not in ruins. The spy satellites were picking up movement of the calutrons that had been buried in the sand outside the Tuwaitha fence. They were now lashed to tank transporters snaking across the desert to the military encampment west of Baghdad called Abu Gharib. Kay, who carried a handheld Global Positioning System that gave him precise coordinates of where he was (the reading was fixed by using three satellites), needed constant updates. In order for satellite interpreters in the United States to get in touch with Kay and his men to alert them to movements and new coordinates, they needed a code. Satellite telephones were easy for Iraqi intelligence to monitor. The Baghdad hotel rooms were bugged and routinely searched. The code they used was cumbersome and murderously time-consuming but very hard to crack. It was a book code. The photo interpreters and the inspectors, thousands of miles apart, had the same volume. "We were always joking that we were going to buy sex manuals." This time, it was the autobiography of George Bush.

"There's a way of offsetting the code, so all you talk is numbers. If you're listening in to the data screen it is 6, 7, 8, 5, 4, 3, 2, 1. You then have to offset the pages and the number sequence to add and subtract to come back to words. It's exceedingly slow. If you make one mistake, it turns to gibberish."

The book code worked well enough for Kay and his team to keep up with the German-built transporters with their secret cargo—in theory. But protocol as set by the International Atomic Energy Agency in Vienna demanded that the Iraqi authorities be given twelve hours' notice before the inspections. Twelve hours was ample time for the military to dispatch the calutron convoy to another base. The Iraqi countryside outside Baghdad was a thicket of jealously guarded military zones, whether you were traveling southeast to Basra, south to Karbala and An Najaf or north to Kirkuk. This cat-and-mouse game was impossible for Kay to play successfully unless he could spring a zero-notice inspection. This was against the gentlemen's rules. He would break the rules.

"We would not tell the Iraqis where we were going. I did not refer this decision to Vienna or New York. Partly because I was afraid they would say no. But also, our communications were so insecure. We literally dealt with commercial telephone lines and handy talkies from Radio Shack. They were not secure military communications."

The UN inspection team, tasked with dismantling Iraq's weapons of mass destruction, was very poorly equipped. "The U.S. military at that point wanted nothing to do with Iraq. They didn't want to get sucked back in. Our transport was Land-Rovers that the British Army gave us." The steering wheel was on the wrong side for Iraqi roads. The diesel fuel they needed was only obtainable on the very outskirts of Baghdad, some-times an hour's journey from midtown. Rush-hour traffic was a mess with the main boulevard that spanned the Tigris River trisected by bombs.

On top of that, the June heat at midday was climbing to 135 degrees Fahrenheit. The violent sun, the glare off the desert floor made the inspectors' job hellish enough without the game of deception.

On June 28, Kay would attempt a zero-notice inspection. The night before, when his hosts asked what his proposed itin-erary was for the following day, he was deliberately imprecise. The English language was full of land mines, he thought. Prep-ositions were easily misunderstood. Kay said he wished to travel "toward" the military base at Abu Gharib. The Iraqis thought he meant "to." Everyone was happy. The team turned in at 2 A.M. At four, they received final instructions on the calu-tron positions that had to be decoded immediately. The inspec-tion caravan was due to pull out at five-thirty. Just before Kay walked out of his hotel room, another message came through. He grabbed the Bush memoir.

"We'll try to decipher it on the way to the site," Kay told the others. "Let's go. If we abort, they're going to tumble to what we're doing."

Had the giant magnets for enriching uranium been moved again? Finally the message was clear.

"Good luck. Godspeed." Kay wanted to kill whoever sent that.

The UN convoy rattling down the road at dawn consisted of a bus and two Land-Rovers, one driven by an Iraqi whom Kay did not trust and the other, his own car, driven by the team's communication officer. His last job had been installing electronics on yachts. When business dried up, he answered an ad for a UN job. Kay regarded him as fearless and slightly crazy and indispensable. Six people were piled into his car. Iraqi military escorts, jeeps bristling with security men and their AK-47s, led the inspection party. More soldiers brought up the rear. While they were stopped at an army checkpoint, Kay told his driver to brazenly pull ahead. The Iraqis were confused. Five miles down the road was their supposed destination. The team showed no signs of bolting in the opposite direction. So the convoy proceeded with Kay in the lead. When they reached the base, Kay failed to stop. Following his decoded instructions, he intended to continue for another two miles. Now their minders were agitated. Kay cursed the photo interpreters. They were always reading pictures upside down. A turning with a gate due to come up on the right was in fact on the left. They sped past.

"Pull a wheelie," Kay barked. "Turn across the highway." They hurled around into the gate of another military base. Their chief Iraqi escort, the base commander at Abu Gharib, was livid.

"What are you doing here?" he shouted.

"We demand access," Kay fired back. "We demand that nothing move from this base." When the gatekeeper stalled with talk of permission from Baghdad, Kay became abusive. He was performing, playing the ugly American, threatening to call the UN Security Council in New York on his satellite phone. Finally the inspectors were allowed to climb a water tower just inside the fence.

"You can put three people up on the water tower," said the exasperated commander, "and they can observe the base."

Nine seconds later, their luck improved dramatically. There was movement at the back of the base, what Kay thought resembled dinosaurs in heat. The inspectors on the water tower radioed to Kay.

"These guys are going out the back."

The first Land-Rover that roared off around the base perimeter had a broken fuel gauge. Two miles around the fence line, it sputtered to a halt, out of gas. The second land-rover moved out, collected the stranded inspectors and chased the dust cloud kicked up by the convoy of transporters. They had rammed the fence down on either side of the small back exit and were bouncing over a gully at the gate. One inspector, Rich Lally, made two passes down the convoy and began to photograph the scene. The Iraqi troops on the convoy opened fire over his head. He dove under the seat and reemerged photographing as fast as he could. By the time officials cut off the Land-Rover and demanded the camera and film, the film roll was stashed on Lally's body. He refused to give up the camera.

"The last thing my wife said before I left," Lally told Kay back at the base gate, "was 'Don't lose the bloody camera.' "

"We managed to get the photographs of these calutrons on over eighty trucks," says Kay. "It was a huge convoy. we flushed out the birds." Three days later, the roll of film was smuggled out of Iraq. One set of prints went to London, where six-foot enlargements were strung together in a mural and unfurled for the British cabinet.

"Gentlemen," the London briefer said gravely, "this was the Iraqi nuclear program."

In fact, it was just a piece of it. Since laying the foundations of their nuclear program, the Iraqis had acquired more sophisticated tastes. They wanted a faster, better way to enrich uranium to bomb-grade U-235. The calutrons would enrich the uranium to 20 percent. Gas centrifuges would spin it to 90 percent enriched. They would build the centrifuges, thousands of them in cascades, and produce twenty nuclear warheads a year. By 1987, German companies like the Siemens subsidiary Interatom were busy helping to equip the centrifuge enrichment plant at Al Furat. The centrifuge design was downloaded over open phone lines from German scientists.

Two more German companies, Leybold and Degussa, shipped hot and cold isostatic presses to manufacture shaped charges that would explode the enriched uranium. Presses, vacuum furnaces, a carbon dioxide laser cutter and three electron beam welders made their way to Al Atheer, the vast nuclear weapons development facility south of Baghdad. At least one beam welder may have been exported from the Leybold subsidiary in Enfield, Connecticut, approved for export to Iraq by the U.S. Department of Commerce.

Al Atheer, untouched by Allied bombers, was the jewel in the crown of the Iraqi nuclear program that UN inspectors were piecing together slowly as they seized mountains of documents. Finally they could see the outlines of a multibillion-dollar complex of enrichment facilities and weapons production lines, all under the innocuous code name "Petrochemical 3." What if the Gulf War had not disrupted the frenzied production schedule?

The program as it was conceived had been paralyzed, gutted. But for David Kay this did not mean Iraq had stopped pursuing the bomb. By 1996, after inspectors had carried out hundreds of zero-notice raids in and around Baghdad, he believed that Saddam's physicists were going another route. If their facilities for enriching uranium were smashed, it was of no consequence now that bomb-grade uranium and plutonium were within Iraq's reach. A well-worn smugglers' route ran from Baghdad up through Kurdistan to the Zagros Mountains, hooked into Turkey, and flowed north into Yerevan in Armenia,

Baku in Azerbaijan, the wild mountainous Dagestan, the blasted and lawless Chechnya and then to Moscow. It was a region in chaos. Former CIA Director Jim Woolsey told us his agency had no means of policing territory as perilous and plagued with bandits as it had been in the Great Game.

Smuggling in Iraq, particularly with the burden of UN sanctions, had been refined to an art. By late 1996, there were alarming signs that Iraqi intelligence had moved in on the most profitable contraband traveling these routes, cigarettes. Fabulously rich merchants in Jordan had been elbowed aside by an operation that smelled strongly of Mukhabarat. Controlling transport and black market distribution of cigarettes meant having a network in place that could move anything. Plutonium stuffed in a carton of cigarettes could replace all of the massive calutrons and cascades of centrifuges rusting in the burial pits of Lake Tharthar.

"Look," Kay says with resignation. "The big buildings have been destroyed. This is not to say that there is not some small movable equipment. There is. We never found everything that we knew they had imported. Their explanation was always, 'It was destroyed in the bombing.'

" 'Well, let's see it.'

" 'We cleared the site. We don't know where we buried it in the chaos of the bombing.'

"What we have not dealt with is the most important thing in a weapons program. Not the hardware. It's the scientific talent. If you back to when this program really began, right after the Osirak raid, they had solved a series of difficult problems. The toughest thing is solving it the first time. The second time you know it's solvable. The team has been kept together."

●

The defection of Saddam Hussein's cousin and son-in-law, Hussein Kamel, in August 1995 uncovered fresh evidence of Saddam's perseverance. Kamel packed his bags when Saddam's trigger-happy oldest son, Uday, shot his uncle Watban in the leg. Given the track record in this hot-blooded Tikriti family, General Kamel thought he might be next. The stigma of being branded a traitor was better than a bullet from Uday Saddam Hussein. When Kamel's convoy roared across the western desert and entered Jordan, the former overseer of the Iraqi nuclear program was given a villa by King Hussein. He announced that he had defected and offered to spill the secrets of Saddam's regime. The UN inspectors could not believe their luck.

David Kay's boss, the determined Swedish diplomat Rolf Ekeus from the UN Special Commission in New York, speedily assembled a team of trusted experts and flew to Amman as quickly as possible. Kamel agreed to meet with them right away.

His safe house was the lavish villa of King Hussein's first wife, who died in a helicopter accident. Now the villa was a hive of activity. The phones never stopped. Everyone wanted to debrief the highest-ranking defector ever to flee Saddam's Iraq. When Ekeus arrived, he strolled with the Iraqi general onto the balcony with a distant view of Jerusalem.

"We have been enemies before," the Iraqi defector told the UN diplomat. "Now we meet as friends." Before getting down to nuclear business, Kamel wanted to complain about his brother-in-law, Saddam's eldest son. Uday spent his life in bars, picking fights, drinking, chasing women. Kamel complained that he, on the other hand, worked long hours. He was a teetotaler and a family man. Uday was an aggressive bully. The whole Saddam family, having been squeezed by sanctions, violated by inspections, were full of hatred. They were boiling with hatred.

The defector was hardly a nuclear physicist. But he had been a brilliant manager for the Iraqi nuclear program. In the same way that he had spectacular successes as a Republican Guard commander in the Iran-Iraq war with innovations like mounting machine guns on rubber dinghies in the delta, he knew how to get things done. It helped that his budget was virtually unlimited. He was now ready to talk about Iraq's crash program in 1990 to build a nuclear weapon.

The first intelligence-gathering session got off to a rocky start. The twelve-man team Ekeus had assembled filed into a conference room in the royal palace provided by Jordan's King Hussein for his distinguished guest and sat down along one side of a long polished table. Kamel entered alone and sat down on the other side. Silently, he gazed intently at each of the team members in turn. Finally, he jabbed his finger at the man sitting next to Ekeus. He was an interpreter.

"Are you a Syrian?" Kamel barked in Arabic.

The man looked distinctly nervous. "Yes, I am," he stammered.

"Is your name Tannous?"

"Yes."

"Get the fuck out of here. You have been working for me. I put you on this team. I refuse to be debriefed by one of my own agents."

When it was explained to Ekeus what had happened, the meeting was adjourned. Two hours later, Hussein Kamel received a call from Secretary-General Boutros Boutros-Ghali asking if there were any other Iraqi agents in UN employ that he should know about.

"I'm not surprised," said David Kay. "The UN system is not set up to maintain security. I couldn't even get a secure file cabinet when I took on the job. There certainly were signs that suggested the operation had been penetrated. We go off and do a surprise inspection, expecting to find something, and instead the place would be totally clean, almost as if they were expecting us."

Before Kamel defected, Ekeus was reporting that the Iraqis were in substantial compliance with the UN resolution requiring them to reveal the full extent of their prewar nuclear buildup. Kamel's arrival changed all that, and also, perhaps, explained why Ekeus's men had missed so much before.

After a bad start, Kamel was cagey with the UN interrogators. But Baghdad had no way of knowing, with Kamel rooting out his own spies, that he would be so discreet. Saddam's men chose to turn over a new haul of records, called "the chicken farm documents," to cover what they wagered the top defector would spill. Ekeus was summoned to Baghdad and presented with one million pages of documents. They had been hidden in the extensive farmyard sheds of Hussein Kamel's country estate. The pages detailed a race between two nuclear warhead design teams after the invasion of Kuwait. One was led by General Raad Ismael, the other by Colonel Engineer Modher Sadiq Saba, a brilliant Czech-trained missile engineer. His task was to reverse-engineer a Scud.

"The design work was very advanced, so advanced that we don't dare talk about it too much," says Ekeus. "They had some fifteen, twenty kilos of highly enriched uranium. Enough for one really good blast. The problem was the delivery system." The warhead had to fit into a missile frame just under one meter in width. The Al Hussein Scud, a stretch version of the Russian nuclear weapon (sold with only conventional explosives), had the range to hit Tel Aviv but could not be fitted with the nuclear warhead they had designed. The crash program was to build a new missile before Iraq was attacked. There was not enough time.

But the chicken farm documents made it clear that after the war the Iraqis were both designing nuclear weapons on their advanced computers and carrying out low-grade physical experiments that they could disguise as part of their routine military testing.

Abas Hamza, the scientist who vanished at the Athens phone booth, was right.

The ongoing design work was critical. "At some point," says Kay, "sanctions will come off and they will reestablish the program or they will acquire nuclear materials from Russia. They're putting in place the capability to quickly fabricate a single weapon, if, by hook or by crook, they can gain access to nuclear material. They're trying to work the Moscow connection to get whatever they can get. I'm personally convinced they are trying to acquire nuclear materials."

Notably absent from the cache of one million documents that translators began decoding in 1995 was the Iraqis' "cookbook," the guide to making the warhead. The other conspicuously missing documents were the lists of foreign suppliers. There were also no memos from headquarters, nothing from the MIC (the Military Industrial Commission) or the Ministry of Defense. There was nothing from the office of the President.

The foreign suppliers still constituted the most sensitive issue of all. There were middlemen eager to broker a lucrative sale of Russian nuclear components to Iraq. One month after President Clinton was given the unvarnished assessment of the porous state of Russia's nuclear establishment by Jessica and her colleagues, U.S. Customs raided a warehouse in Queens. Inside was eight tons of Russian zirconium, a metal that can be used in fabricating nuclear weapons. High-grade zirconium is made into finger-sized tubes in a nuclear reactor core. It is used as a safety coating for nuclear fuel rods. Powdered zirconium is also used in explosives. Three Greek Americans, including the former president of the Marathon National Bank in Astoria and the owner of an import-export business with offices in Moscow, were charged with attempting to illegally export zirconium to Iraq. A Customs undercover agent said the importer claimed his contacts included a Russian general and connections in Chechnya. Customs, who posed as Iraqi buyers, said the cache was smuggled from a military stockpile in the Ukrainian city of Dneprodzerzhinsk, sold on the black market, and transshipped through Germany to New York. The Customs men said their secret taping left little doubt that the defendants, who lived on a five-acre estate in Muttontown, New

York, named The Walls of Jericho, knew all along that their high-grade zirconium was to be used in the processing of an Iraqi bomb. The defendants maintained that they were victims of an overzealous Customs sting.

The Customs men were assigned to the legendary Strategic Group at New York's World Trade Center Customs House. They were seasoned undercover men, who had posed over the years as armed merchants to the IRA and the ayatollahs. In 1992, the Strategic Group had penetrated a group of high-level Russian officials and former Polish government arms merchants and intelligence agents who offered to sell nuclear triggers to Baghdad. One had been chief of staff of the Polish Army. Another managed the Russian Mig-29 factory that built the Russian Air Force fighter planes. The Polish intelligence agents were the same officials who had worked closely with the CIA in the 1980s to ship Polish AK-47s to Norfolk, Virginia, and thence to the Contra army in Central America. In nailing the group for a massive intended arms sale to Iraq that including AK-47s, T-72 tanks, Hind helicopters and MiG fighters as well as nuclear triggers, Customs locked horns with the CIA over exposing its old assets. "Oh, man, they hated my ass," laughed one of the Customs men. "Everybody wanted the case kicked. The station chief in Bonn had a picture of me. He used to throw darts at it."

In stopping the flow of nuclear components from Russia to Iraq, Customs in New York was frozen out by the CIA. There was no intelligence sharing. When stories of nuclear smuggling fell out of the public eye completely in 1995, senior Customs agents believed that intelligence agencies, including the CIA, shut down disclosures. Germany's BND Intelligence Service quietly logged thirty-two cases of interested buyers in 1995, sixteen involving states. BND chief Konrad Porzner told a German parliamentary committee that he had definitive proof that two of those active buyers were Iran and Iraq. Details were classified. When two Russians were picked up for nuclear smuggling in Slovakia in the fall of 1996, there were no leaks. A similar case in Vienna was classified. The difficulty for Customs was that the CIA as well as the European intelligence agencies refused to share intelligence with them, leaving them to their own devices. Customs felt understaffed, underbudgeted and overwhelmed.

The Russians simply ignored them. But by late 1995, Victor Mikhailov's stubborn denial that nuclear materials and components were falling into the wrong hands was sharply contradicted by an act of nuclear terrorism in his own backyard, just a few subway stops from Minatom headquarters.

●

Izmailovsky Park was the former summer residence of the czars. The old hunting preserve with three thousand acres of pine forest and meadows now had the best flea market in Moscow. Families flocked there on weekends to pick up souvenirs. There was an open-air theater and a fairground packed with children. In late November the park was dusted with early winter snow. It seemed far removed from Russia's ugly problems to the south in Chechnya.

For months the rebel leadership had threatened to smuggle nuclear materials into Moscow. On November 8, the field commander of the Chechen forces, Shamil Basayev, said he was not bluffing. He had prepared some "trifles as presents" for his Russian enemies. Two weeks later, the field commander sat down for a television interview. He calmly told Yelena Masyuk of Russian NTV that a container packed with nuclear materials was buried on the grounds of Izmailovsky Park.

He gave the Russian television crew instructions on where to dig. This, he said, was one of four "presents" on Russian soil.

It took the journalists twenty-four hours to get a flight out of Chechnya to Moscow and race with the cameras to the park. They fully expected to find they were on a wild-goose chase. Surely this was more disinformation. With cameras rolling, they began to shovel snow. To their horror, they uncovered a yellow carrier bag. Inside was a package that looked like frozen chicken wrapped in plastic bound with black tape. According to the journalists' radiation monitor, the permissible levels of radiation for Moscow was exceeded by a factor of 310.

They called the FSB, the Federal Security Bureau, the successor to the KGB. The next day Izmailovsky Park was swarming with police, emergency medical aid workers, firefighters, a Moscow rapid reaction team, consultants from the Russian Emergencies Ministry and experts from the Radon Science and Production Association. The bomb squad turned up with dogs to detect explosives. The yellow carrier bag, left by the camera team propped against a tree, was placed in a lead container and rushed to an FSB laboratory. The authorities assured the public there had been absolutely no danger. Everyone in Moscow remembered those assurances in the aftermath of Chernobyl.

The FSB announced the container was full of cesium 137. On November 23, the Russian press reported that four containers of radioactive cesium 137 were missing from the Chelyabinsk Region. "The fact that these containers were missing was noticed when a check was carried out at an enterprise in the town of Bakal. Urgent measures have been taken to find the containers."

What the Strategic Group at the Customs House at the World Trade Center knew was that it was just as easy to move nuclear materials and components from Russia to New York and on to Iraq as it was to bury it in Izmailovsky Park. What was alarming about the zirconium case was the ease with which cargo bound for Iraq could be transshipped out of Russia and Ukraine to Queens and then rerouted to an Italian shell company, where Iraqi agents, in this case U.S. Customs, picked up the cargo and shipped it out. The agents from the Strategic Group in New York knew how to smuggle nuclear components to Iraq with no questions asked.

The key was a small town on the southern coast of Turkey called Mersin. For cigarette smugglers, Mersin was the beginning of the black market overland route across Turkey into Iraqi Kurdistan and down to Baghdad. In Mersin, everyone turned a blind eye. "Do you know how many cigarettes go into that dump?" asked a veteran Customs man who knew the territory well. "Do you know how many forty-foot containers go in there? Every son of a bitch in that town would have to smoke a container a week. They stay in bond. No duty for the Turks. They get driven right out to the Kurdish area. The Kurds get it to Iraq. You could easily drop the ceiling of a forty-footer and put two or three nuclear devices in there. You can put anything in that container. You really have to piss off Turkish Customs to get them to look at an inbound shipment of cigarettes."

Rolf Ekeus from the UN Special Commission confirmed that Iraqi intelligence had gone into the business of smuggling cigarettes. In fact, the defector Hussein Kamel told the Swedish diplomat that he, while in charge of the Iraqi nuclear program, personally parceled out cigarettes concessions in Iraq to his friends. In February 1997, Rolf Ekeus flew to Turkey to meet with the chief of Military Intelligence. He expressed grave concerns to the intelligence chief about photographs from U-2 spy planes that showed lines of trucks miles long going across the Iraq border.

"How can you guarantee," the worried diplomat asked, "that nuclear components or materials are not coming in inside these trucks?"

"I know." The intelligence man shrugged.

Ekeus was not satisfied with the response. "He never really explained. He knows what goes in in large terms. But if we talk nuclear, we are talking about things that are too easy to move," far too easy to conceal.

●

Iraq's success at purchasing the guidance packages of Russian intercontinental ballistic missiles gave Ekeus confidence in their smuggling methods. To investigate Iraq's alarming access to goods in Russian warehouses containing dismantled nuclear missiles, Ekeus hired a man he regarded as "the best in the world" at finding out secrets. Nikita Smidovich was a handsome Russian weapons specialist with a full mustache and a remarkable track record at infiltrating the toughest circles in the Russian military. He had cracked the Red Army's secret production of biological weapons behind Mikhail Gorbachev's back.

"This was a dirty secret. The military denied it. Then they called in Nikita," says Ekeus. The Russian was then in charge of chemical and biological weapons affairs at the Foreign Ministry, a post he left in 1991. "He started to interrogate the Russian generals. He uncovered a large part of the biological program. He is of course one of the most hated people in the Russian military." His brief now was to answer the questions plaguing Ekeus. Who was responsible for keeping the inventories? Who was checking? What's the guard system? Why had the Russians not detected the missing guidance packages until Ekeus brought it to their attention?

Nikita Smidovich was stonewalled by his former colleagues in Moscow. This was a criminal investigation, he was told sharply. He was welcome to come to Moscow when they were finished, not before. Between December 1995, when the shipment of missile guidance systems was stumbled on by chance in a 500-kilo air freight shipment from Moscow to Amman, and May 1997, absolutely nothing was forthcoming from Moscow. On the Baghdad end, the Russian had better luck. The Iraqis reluctantly handed over the name of the middleman who had made several trips to Moscow on their behalf. His name was Wiam Gharbiyya. He was in his early thirties, a businessman who spoke fluent English and lived in a Baghdad hotel. Smidovich made an appointment.

When the Russian arrived in Iraq, his host's explanation for ordering strategic missile gyroscopes was simple and elegant. it was all a "mistake." The middleman was inexperienced in missile matters and simply came back with the wrong goods. The "mistake" cost the Iraqi government millions in cash.

Like the Iraqis, Smidovich was a seasoned poker player. The Russian never revealed how much he knew. He was granted an audience with the middleman and listened attentively to Gharbiyya's version of events, vetted by the Iraqi Mukhabarat. The stamps in Gharbiyya's Jordanian passport confirmed that he had made several trips to Russia between 1993 and December 1995. Gharbiyya had excellent connections in the Arab community in Moscow and was able to use the services of a Russian import-export firm there run by three Arabs with a Russian staff.

The 120 guidance packages that Smidovich was sure Gharbiyya had procured in Russia each contained two gyroscopes and one accelerometer. The function of the pineapple-sized gyroscope was to spin in flight, correcting for error in the missile's trajectory—crucial for accuracy in an intercontinental flight. The guidance package would give Saddam the range to hit Paris or Moscow. The Russian gyroscopes that had reached Baghdad had been, thought Smidovich, roughly torn from the missiles that carried them. The fringe of tiny wires on the gyro head was ragged and would require sophisticated rewiring. Who would want to yank the delicate instrument from its platform? Smidovich thought these had been dismantled by black marketeers.

He carefully questioned Gharbiyya in an Iraqi government guesthouse on where precisely the middleman had picked up the nuclear missile parts.

"It was north of Moscow," Gharbiyya told the Russian. "Less than a hundred kilometers. I don't know the name."

Mytischi, a sprawling development center for missile technology that included at least two design bureaus and missile production facilities, was north of Moscow. The middleman claimed he had ventured only as far as the gate. Black marketeers, the "night people," took care of procurement on the inside. Smidovich found this odd. He thought a buyer would want to test the guidance systems. Only the Russian authorities could tell him if Gharbiyya had set foot on the grounds of Myti-schi. It was also curious that nuclear sub missile parts would be at this facility. Why not Miass in the Urals? But, then, the system was very well integrated. And the complicity inside the system was not well understood.

Smidovich pressed the middleman for details. He had been taken to a "church city." For Muscovites, there was only one "church city" in that neighborhood.

The golden cupolas and blue bell tower of Zagorsk, forty-six miles northeast of Moscow, rise from the countryside dotted with brightly painted dachas. The magnificent Trinity Monas-tery of St. Sergius (Troitsa-Sergyeva Lavra) has been a center for Russian religious pilgrimage for five hundred years. The dark blue, starry domes of the Uspensky Sobor, the Assump-tion Cathedral, was built by Ivan the Terrible. Zagorsk is also the home of Russian Matrioshka dolls, the painted dolls within dolls, that have been used to describe the Russian system of security for nuclear weapons. Was there also a missile disman-tling plant, absent from the map? There was silence from Moscow.

What Smidovich did manage to establish was that a "whole system" was in place inside the Iraqi security services to make Russian black market purchases. He, like his boss Rolf Ekeus, found the Russian-Iraqi black market channel "worrying."

On the Russian front, "who is really watching these things?" Ekeus asks. "If you have money, you buy stuff in the warehouse where you have dismantled nuclear weapons. Iraq has so much money. Iraq has shown they can travel with cash in their atta-ché cases. They pay people, get the stuff out, load it, get it through customs, and here we have relatively big things. Nu-clear fuel is so easy to transport. It's so small. The volume is zero. You handle it without a radiation problem. The system is broken, you see?"

The Swedish diplomat who has been prying open the secrets of the Iraqi nuclear program since the cease-fire in 1991 is very distressed about the Russia connection.

"How solid is Russian society? It boils down to that. It's a desperate situation. You know the senior scientist who killed himself. It's a chilling story. For me," in the spring of 1997, "it means the whole system is shaky. Add that to the gyroscopes. The whole moral fiber. What Iraq needs is not much. They'd be happy with twenty kilos. If they could get a hundred kilos" of bomb-grade uranium, "wonderful—that would be five devices."

With the bomb team in place and a workable nuclear weapons design, which Ekeus and International Atomic Energy Agency analysts believe they have, the cigarette cartons full of plutonium or U-235 would complete the picture.

Inspectors repeatedly reported that Iraq was adept at transshipment through neighboring countries and avoiding a paper trail that identified Iraq as the end user. Teams from the UN and the International Atomic Energy Agency also were routinely denied access to certain regions of Iraq. When they tried to overfly southern Iraq in an L-100 fixed-wing plane, Iraqi authorities blocked the effort by denying them takeoff and landing rights at the Basra airport.

When inspectors imported Chilean UH-1H helicopters for a close look at military bases, their flight plans were severely restricted. The Iraqis suddenly invented "free-fire zones" where the inspectors would be risking their lives. Naturally the flights were impossible. Other areas were cordoned off as "presidential zones." Missile equipment was turning up buried under villas belonging to Saddam's elite Republican Guards.

Jessica and Jerry worried that Iraq, with its long-standing relationship with the Russian military, might go a step further. Trainloads of dismantled nuclear weapons were crisscrossing Russia every week. The Russian Defense Minister, Igor Rodionov, was describing the decay of the Russian armed forces as "horrifying." The rot was settling in Russia's nuclear forces, considered by the Defense Minister to be on the verge of anarchy.

The Russians had no idea whether they were missing a warhead out of the thousands of bombs overflowing their depots. Corruption in the officer corps was endemic, soldiers were without adequate food or direction and the safeguards were, like everything else in the Red Army, crumbling from neglect. The army was no longer jealously guarding an empire. Now it was every general for himself.

13

ONE POINT SAFE

The nuclear corridor stretches for thousands of miles in all directions, through the vast empty spaces of the Russian heartland, the flat taiga, the endless birch forests, the hills and defiles of the Ural Mountains. Perhaps two thousand nuclear weapons move along it every year. Once they were destined to soar through space and tear apart cities and other targets on the far side of the world. Now they are loaded on trains and shipped to the plants to be taken apart. They are supposed to be no longer a threat.

Their journey starts at a remote operational base, where the conscripts are paid in chits redeemable at the store—except that there is nothing in the store to buy. The weapons are winched off the top of the missiles by the specialists of the Twelfth Department of the General Staff, trained weapons technicians. Formerly a well-paid elite, they have lately been denied even their monthly bonus of four pounds of sausages.

Carefully moved to the nearby rail stop, the weapons are

228

loaded into a railcar that the former American enemy has spent millions of dollars to make secure. These cars are distinctive, and anyone who knows what to look for will be able to pick out the train from all others passing along the track. An officer taps in the code for the computerized lock that secures the doors. Even if he were receiving his salary, he could still make more driving a cab in Moscow. The special military train moves off through a landscape that may run close to one of Russia's open southern borders, frequented by smugglers, some of whom are infiltrated and controlled by at least one foreign intelligence agency, an agency whose task is to acquire a nuclear warhead. It is a dangerous journey. Someone has been setting off bombs on the southern Russian rail network. Despite special containers and railcars, the weapons may not be one point safe. The commanders of the Twelfth have nightmares that a train wreck could set off the explosives in the warheads, scattering plutonium far and wide.

At the end of its journey the train passes through a barbed-wire fence into the secret city where the weapons will be taken apart. Here too, the workers have not been paid in months. Their union leader talks of a "growth in social tension." The Americans hope that the weapons are indeed being dismantled, even though they have never been allowed to see it done. The nuclear materials in the weapons, plutonium and uranium 235, are worth a lot of money. An American government corporation is buying the uranium, although the Russian Nuclear Minister is scheming to have a close associate gain control of the corporation. The plutonium is shipped to a special storage site paid for by the Americans, but the Russian government has allocated only a third of the money need to guard it.

A colonel watches as one unit of the nuclear force is taken apart. "I spent my life serving the Soviet Union," he says. "Now I don't know who I serve."

There are still 32,000 weapons to go.

•

It is a gray April morning in 1997. Minister of Defense Igor Nikolayevich Rodionov's gleaming limousine sweeps into the center of Moscow. At the end of Arbat Street, across from a popular Irish bar and the offices of a witch grown prosperous selling "love spells," it swings into the courtyard fronting the massive yellow headquarters of the Russian General Staff and the Defense Ministry. As it glides to a stop in front of the huge double doors the guard gives a crisp salute. Deferential aides hurry behind him as he strides to his office. Save for the red, white, and blue that has supplanted the hammer and sickle flag on the roof, he might almost be following in the same footsteps as military chieftains of the past—Zhukov, Malinowski, Grechko, Ustinov—masters of all they surveyed.

The power of the men who occupied the Minister of Defense's office in the Soviet days was almost limitless. This was the ultimate command center for the growing fleets of the Soviet Navy patrolling the oceans of the world with its modern warships and hundreds of submarines. Contingency war plans to send the tank armies of the Group of Soviet Forces in Germany crashing across the borders of Western Europe were crafted here. In 1968 the General Staff organized an occupation of Czechoslovakia by over 200,000 troops in a single day. The Air Armies of the Soviet Air Force and the Air Defense Forces could throw thousands of planes into the sky at any moment. Every branch of the military had nuclear weapons, 55,000 of them at their peak—nuclear artillery shells, nuclear mines, nuclear torpedoes, nuclear bombs, long-range missiles in Typhoon nuclear submarines, the largest in the world. Moscow itself was guarded by antimissile missiles with nuclear warheads. Above all there were the intercontinental missiles of the Strategic Rocket Forces, the elite service manned by the best and the brightest and striking fear into the Americans and their Western allies.

Soviet weapons had fought the Americans to a standstill in Vietnam and had given the Israelis a bloody nose in the October war of 1973. Half the economy of the Soviet Union was devoted to servicing the machine, every year pouring more tanks, planes, ships, missiles into the already bloated arsenals. Five million men were in uniform, their ranks continually re-filled by the 900,000 eighteen-year-olds who twice a year obedi-ently reported for two or more years of compulsory draft duty. Officers were the pampered elite of Soviet society, assured of good pay, the best available housing, a comfortable pension and universal respect. The most senior commanders lived like Oriental potentates, free to indulge their every whim. In the 1960s one admiral in the Northern Fleet, irritated by the untidy look of varying shades of natural rock, ordered an extensive stretch of coastline painted gray. Such high-ranking officers were paid very little, but they had no need of money. The sys-tem took lavish care of them.

Igor Rodionov will never get to decorate a cliff. If he tried he would probably find that the paint had long since been sold on the black market. Bad as things were at the time of the fall of the Soviet Union, when Bill Burns found there was no money to pay for post-Communist officers' cap badges, the state of the Russian military has grown steadily worse. Now, from the very building in which the minister sits, colonels are selling the office furniture out the back door to replace meager paychecks that never arrive on time.

Rodionov himself can remember the days when such things would have been unthinkable, when he was a rising general on the General Staff and later the commander of the General Staff Academy. He was a soldier then, uninvolved in politics. Now he must struggle to survive in a welter of intrigue. The man who sponsored him for the job, General Alexander Lebed, has since fallen from favor in the Kremlin, where the ruling powers are trying to undermine his political prospects by crushing a mafia group that controls the aluminum industry and funds his presidential campaign. Rodionov himself must compete for influence with Yeltsin against the President's defense adviser, a

mathematician named Yuri Baturin, best known for his trans-
lation of *Alice in Wonderland* into Russian. On this April morning Rodionov is right to feel nervous. In little over a month's
time he will be summarily sacked, leaving his successor with
even less money to face exactly the same problems.

The minister has little more control over the military
chieftains down the hall from his office. He only just managed
to get rid of General Vladimir Semenov, formerly the Commander in Chief of the Ground Forces, despite evidence of
what Rodionov called "shady property deals practiced by him
and his wife." For months Semenov simply refused to leave.
He had powerful backing in the Kremlin. So does the former
chief military finance manager, who has yet to be fired even
though he was suspended on suspicion of corruption eighteen
months ago. Charges were dropped against General Anatoly
Kuntsevich, a senior officer in charge of dismantling Russia's
chemical weapons stocks, even though he had been selling the
technology for advanced binary nerve gas weapons to the Syri-
ans. And the Japanese cult leader who planned the deadly sarin
gas attack in the Tokyo subway was claiming in court that he
had bought the blueprints for the sarin factory for $79,000
from a senior defense adviser to Yeltsin.

"An honest person has two options," sighs the minister to a
Russian visitor. "Either join the thieves or go." But the thieves
and gangsters are everywhere in Russia. Businessmen, despairing of the courts, turn to extortion specialists to collect debts
in exchange for 50 percent of the take. Even arguments over a
fender bender on the highway will routinely lead to appeals
to the Mafiya for adjudication. Senior officials openly attend
birthday parties honoring mafia chieftains. Talk-show hosts on
TV have taken to speaking in mafia slang.

Today, the Minister of Defense is bemoaning a newly uncovered case of thievery by his alleged subordinates on a truly dramatic scale. He has just found out that a group of senior

military commanders have coolly sold a billion dollars' worth of weapons out of army stockpiles behind his back. The arms deal included eighty-four tanks, dozens of armored combat vehicles, long-range artillery pieces, small arms, millions of rounds of ammunition. Also part of the consignment were thirty-two R-17 Scud missiles, capable of carrying nuclear warheads. As part of the deal the military entrepreneurs had been able to provide a month-long missile training course at the Kapustin Yar military firing range. The weapons were brought by Armenia, once a Soviet republic on the far southern rim of the old U.S.S.R., close by Iran, Turkey and Iraq. The Armenians were anxious to renew a bitter struggle with the neighboring oil-rich country of Azerbaijan, a conflict that the Russian government has officially been attempting to settle through peaceful negotiation. Since shipping this arsenal by land without official clearance would have required an arrangement with the Customs, the mercenary commanders orchestrating the deal simply airlifted the entire amount, including the tanks, at colossal expense, an expense born by the Ministry of Defense, which unwittingly supplied the giant transport aircraft and their fuel. "Tanks were airlifted!" frets the minister. "Good grief." The enormous shipment had been a total secret until one disaffected insider leaked the story to a Moscow paper.

In the meantime, the military is starving for lack of money, in some cases literally so. In the first three months of the year the Ministry of Finance has handed over only 40 percent of the money needed to feed the troops. That bare statistic did not quite convey the misery of the rank and file. The previous March, in the far eastern city of Khabarovsk, an eighteen-year-old army conscript named Mikhail Kubarsky had dropped dead on Lermontov Street in the center of town. He died of starvation. His unit out in the countryside had not received any rations for weeks and he had wandered into town in search of food. Many of his fellow conscripts have little physical reserves to fall back on. Army doctors examining the new intake of conscripts are classifying fully one in seven as "underweight"—a euphemism for malnourished. Forty-three percent of the draftees are found to be suffering from some form of mental illness. At a desolate far eastern military base at Komsomolsk-na-Amure, not far from where poor Kubarsky died from hunger, two soldiers recently blew themselves up while trying to extract precious metals from the warhead of an air defense missile they had stolen from the ammunition dump. Others take the easy way out—currently half the noncombat deaths in the military are due to suicide.

Even the troops who have just enough to eat may soon be in rags. Already the official allotment of overcoats is one for every five men and now the minister is bemoaning the fact that for the first three months of the year he has received only one-fiftieth of the money he needs for uniforms. There is even less money for new weapons. Such money as has been spent on hardware is often wasted. During 1996, for example, a new heavy cruiser, the *Peter the Great*, was finally launched. It had been planned in the prosperous days of the cold war to be part of an aircraft carrier formation in the Pacific. But while it was still being built, some high-ranking admirals made a cash sale of the Pacific Fleet's only two carriers to South Korea for scrap. So when it was finally launched the navy sent the new cruiser, which had cost $1 billion, to join the Northern Fleet, where there is at least a carrier, even if it has no planes and is rusting at the quayside.

Even Rodionov finds it hard to pretend that he heads a fighting force, though in the spring of 1997 he bravely maintains that the armed forces are still a year away from total disintegration. Just over three years before, his predecessor had told Yeltsin that the rebellious Chechen capital of Grozny could be subdued by a single paratroop brigade "in hours." Instead, after 100,000 people had died, the Russian military had struggled home in abject defeat. In the course of a two-and-a-half-year war the army was reduced to the condition of an armed mob. Drunken tank crews roamed the countryside, threatening to level villages unless they were paid off with vodka. Other soldiers were reduced to begging for food and selling their weapons to the enemy.

In one especially humiliating episode a Chechen guerrilla unit cruised across the border to the small southern Russian town of Budyannovsk, took two thousand hostages and were eventually allowed to return home in triumph. They had passed through the enemy lines simply by bribing the border guards. The following year another invading band of Chechens were briefly trapped in the small Russian village of Pervomayskoye before escaping in safety. Among their besiegers were the elite Alpha antiterrorist unit, hurriedly dispatched from Moscow without food or warm clothes in the 15-below weather. When it was all over, the Alpha team, hungry, frozen and embittered, had to pay their own train fares back to Moscow.

At the end of 1996 dangerous times returned for the citizens of Budyannovsk. The 205th Airborne Brigade was withdrawn from Chechnya, billeted in the town and promptly forgotten by the high command. The officers and men had nothing to do but drink. No one bothered to send their pay. They turned instead to their only possessions of value: their weapons. Hand grenades became the commonest unit of currency, valued at the equivalent of two dollars. The bar owners and taxi drivers of Budyannovsk have learned not to refuse such payment, since irritated customers would simply pull the pin and let the grenade settle the argument.

The rest of the 1.7 million men in the armed forces are hardly in better condition. Apart from the civilian population, this rabble is no threat to anyone, certainly not to potential enemies such as NATO or the Chinese. The high command knows this full well, and they know that everyone else knows too. Consequently, they have made an ominous decision.

Following close behind the minister as he marches to the elevator is a smartly uniformed colonel of the Ninth Department of the General Staff, known as a *shurik*. He is carrying what appears to be a small black briefcase. It is no ordinary piece of luggage. This is the *cheget*, the equivalent of the "football" that goes everywhere with the U.S. President, the ultimate control over the strategic nuclear arsenal.

When opened with the special key carried by the minister himself, the inside of the briefcase shows a flat panel with three displays. When all three are lit up, it means that there is a nuclear alert, enemy missiles are on their way, the Russian President and Chief of the General Staff are opening identical briefcases and all three are hooked into the Kazbek nuclear command and control network. At the top, display panels give urgent information: time to impact; number of incoming. Underneath the displays is a row of five buttons. From the left, three of these denote various nuclear strike plans. Press any one, and a varying number of missiles will erupt from their silos and streak toward their targets. The fourth is a "cancel" button, in case someone changes their mind. Last is the "transmit" button that sends the authorization to launch almost five thousand thermonuclear missiles that are still, today, on constant alert and ready to fire at the first sign of an attack.

The nuclear briefcase is the lingering symbol of Russia as a superpower. It was introduced in the days when the *shurik* attended the chief of a military empire that threw a long shadow, full of menace. Decisions taken in this building were so important for the world that, every night, U.S. military intelligence officers would come and count the number of lighted windows to gauge whether something unusual was afoot. Today, the Americans stay home in bed, Russia is in chaos, but this is still the headquarters of a system as dedicated as ever to waging thermonuclear combat.

Throughout the cold war, the strategic nuclear arsenal had been the ultimate deterrent, a decisive supplement to the enormous nonnuclear military forces. In the early 1980s the Soviet leadership had pledged that they would never be the first to use nuclear weapons. The "doctrine" dictated that only if someone else launched an attack using nuclear weapons would the U.S.S.R retaliate by hurling its own megatons back across the North Pole in response. In November 1993, one month after bloody fighting had erupted in the center of Moscow as Yeltsin quelled a rebellious parliament, the General Staff announced a new policy. From now on Russia's nuclear weapons would be used to deter "the launching of aggression," whether the enemy went nuclear or not. The cold war was over, the country was sinking ever deeper into an uncontrolled morass of corruption and decay, but Russia was, even so, a nuclear superpower. Consequently, over half the strategic nuclear force is on constant twenty-four hour alert. The minister is still one of the very few people who can blow up the world with a briefcase on twenty minutes' notice.

Brilliant and highly trained planners have put a great deal of thought into those few minutes. Even as the United States and the West pour billions of dollars into the Russian economy, the military commanders in Moscow are haunted by the notion that the Americans might launch a surprise nuclear strike and wipe them out before they could retaliate.

The countdown starts at the instant that an early-warning radar or one of the infrared satellites detects the telltale blips of weapons rising out of the enemy missile fields, streaking into space and headed for Russia. By that time the first missiles will already have been airborne for about a minute. In twenty-nine minutes they will start hitting Moscow.

The information is flashed to the Missile Analysis Center at Venyukovski, just inside the Moscow beltway. The duty officer at the center then immediately transmits a warning to the President, the Minister of Defense and the Chief of the General Staff that a nuclear attack is on the way. A small light on the outside of their *cheget* briefcases begins to flash. The three men insert their special keys and open them up. By the time they are patched into a teleconference over special circuits with each other and the commanders of the nuclear forces there are twenty-four minutes to go before the first missile lands.

The warning center confirms the attack. Now a special circuit is switched on, connecting missile headquarters with the missile launch centers deep in silos on the steppes, the mobile SS-25 Topol missiles roaming the countryside and the ballistic missile submarines out at sea or on alert at the dockside. The President and the Minister of Defense then have a maximum of three minutes to decide what to do. Twenty-one minutes left.

Once the two men have agreed to launch, the General Staff starts sending the launch orders together with the "unblock" codes that allow the missiles to fire. Seventeen minutes.

Far away in the missile fields the crews take three minutes to receive the order and verify that it is official. Launching the alert force takes another three to four minutes. Ten minutes to spare, with luck.

The timeline might be stretched tighter still. If the enemy launches a missile from a submarine nearer to the Russian coastline, from the Norwegian Sea for example, then that extra ten minutes disappears. Every second counts.

That is what is meant by "launch on warning," the war plan of both Russia and the United States six years after the end of the cold war. Take more time for reflection and the nuclear mushroom clouds might already be rising over the command centers. It would be too late. To launch *before* an explosion gives clear proof that the attack is real, the retaliatory missiles have to be on alert all the time. This is a nuclear hair trigger, just like the similar U.S. system, and it means that the whole command and control system absolutely had to operate smoothly and without any mistakes at all. There is no margin for error.

With the cold war ended, the United States and Russia felt free to conclude arms control agreements; these were widely assumed to have eliminated the threat of a nuclear holocaust. The START treaty of 1991 called for significant reductions in the number of nuclear weapons the two sides had trained on each other. But that still left each side with up to 8,000 warheads and bombers targeted on the other—quite enough to kill a hundred million people or more. The START II follow-on treaty cuts the numbers down to 3,500 on either side, still enough to destroy two continents. There are no plans to take the missiles off alert, ready to launch on warning.

In January 1994, Presidents Clinton and Yeltsin jointly announced that they had agreed on a move that would lift the threat of instant annihilation from their two countries. Their missiles would no longer be targeted on each other but on some harmless patch of distant ocean. Now, at last, it seemed that the nuclear hair trigger was relaxed. This was the proudest arms control achievement of Clinton's presidency, and he was glad to proclaim it at every opportunity. During his first debate with Republican candidate Bob Dole in the 1996 election he stated confidently, "There are no nuclear missiles pointed at the children of the United States tonight and have not been in our administration for the first time since the dawn of the nuclear age." The President liked the notion so much that during the campaign he repeated the announcement at least a hundred and thirty times.

It was wonderful news. It was also untrue.

Missiles are aimed by a series of instructions fed into their guidance computers on board or at their launch control center. The Russians did indeed set their ICBMs on what they called a "zero flight plan," but the wartime target settings stayed in the computer memory banks. Reprogramming the missiles to head for their aim points in the United States and elsewhere would take precisely ten seconds. Resetting the American weapons would take the same amount of time. In fact, for the Russian missiles, reprogramming was not even necessary. A Russian missile launched by accident or without proper clearance from the high command would automatically head for whatever spot it had been assigned in the original war plan. Whatever

President Clinton may really think, the children of the United States are as unsafe as they have ever been.

On Wednesday, January 25, 1995, the world came close to nuclear war. All because a Russian bureaucrat had forgotten to forward a letter from Oslo.

Norway has long had a peaceful scientific program in which it launches high-altitude research rockets into the upper atmosphere. Throughout 1994, the scientists in Oslo were hard at work preparing for their most ambitious flight yet. Normally the rockets they sent up were modest, single-stage affairs. This time the scientists wanted to study the aurora borealis, the northern lights, and for that they needed to send the instruments at least 900 miles up. The Black Brant XXII was three times as big as anything they had ever launched before. Built in America, it had four booster stages and somewhat resembled a U.S. Trident submarine-launched nuclear missile.

Every time the Norwegians prepared one of these flights from their rocket range on Andöy Island off the northern coast they were careful to write to the Russians well in advance. They were fully aware of how sensitive letting off missiles so close to Moscow's territory could be. Accordingly, sometime in mid-December, the government dutifully informed the Russian Foreign Ministry via the embassy in Oslo that they were about to launch a rocket for scientific research. Because the actual launch time and date depended on the weather, they were not able to give a precise date, merely stating that it would take place after 5 A.M. some time between January 15 and February 5.

The Russians lost the message. Perhaps an idle official in the Foreign Ministry simply forgot to pass the letter on to the military and left it in a file or someone else in the Defense Ministry failed to tell the people who needed to know: the General Staff, the Strategic Rocket Forces or the missile attack warning center. That is why, when Black Brant finally blasted off soon after 9:24 Moscow time on the morning of January 25, the Russian nuclear command and control system started counting down.

As the rocket climbed toward a thousand miles above the earth's surface it was following a path that was of intense concern to the Russian war planners. In the view of the high command, still wedded to the view that a surprise U.S. nuclear attack was entirely possible, the northern Norwegian Sea would be a likely launch point for a submarine missile. It could arrive in twenty minutes or less and knock out the defense communications system with the electromagnetic pulse from a high-altitude nuclear burst.

Thus the high command was especially alert for any sign of a threat from this quarter. Unfortunately, its ability to interpret such a sign was deficient. By 1995, a gaping hole had appeared in the early-warning system. Early warning depends on long-range radars on the ground and orbiting satellites. Radars alone do not necessarily give accurate information about a missile attack. The standard Russian Malnya satellites follow elliptical orbits, swooping low over the United States and Chinese missile fields before swinging further out into space when they are over Russia itself—and nearby waters such as the Norwegian Sea. The high command has long hoped to introduce newer geostationary satellites that would remain permanently over Norway and watch for a sign of a sub launch. Once upon a time, in the days when the military was serviced by half the economy, they might have got their wish. But now the technology for the infrared sensors on such a satellite has proved beyond the resources of the military technicians. None are in orbit.

Instead, the frozen waters of the northern seas were scanned by aging "Hen House" long-range radars on the Arctic and Baltic coasts of Russia. The decades-old Baltic watching post is not even in Russia anymore, since it was originally built in Latvia when that country was a secure province of the Soviet Union. There was a more up-to-date early-warning radar in

Latvia, but the locals blew it up after they got their independence in 1991. In fact, much of the vital early-warning system
now finds itself in newly independent and not necessarily
friendly countries such as Azerbaijan, Ukraine and Kazakhstan
as well as Latvia.

It was to three of these antiquated monitors that Black
Brant first showed itself. No one, of course, had warned the
operators about the Norwegians' plans and they feared the
worst. If it were heading for Moscow it would get there in five
or six minutes. There was no time to reflect on whether it was
really likely that America had suddenly decided to obliterate
Russia. Just as if they were still in the darkest days of the cold
war, they flashed news of an incoming hostile missile to the
attack warning center on the edge of Moscow. Still watching
their screens, they noticed the booster stages dropping off the
strange missile as it shot ever higher into space. Nothing that
they saw looked any different from a military launch. Thanks
to the deficiencies of their equipment, they could not tell that
the missile was heading north, toward the pole.

At the missile warning center the speeding object was immediately classified as a threat. The duty officers switched on
the emergency communication system to alert the General
Staff command post deep underground near a small village just
outside Moscow. There, the general on duty had to make the
momentous decision to activate the Kazbek nuclear command
and control system. Lights flashed on the suitcases. It must
have been a terrible moment as the suitcase owners reached
for their keys. This had never happened before, not even in the
worst moments of the Cuban missile crisis. Out across Russia,
the missile operators went on high alert. They were fifteen minutes or less away from launching a massive nuclear strike at
the United States. One senior general later admitted that the
high command was "stressed."

The decisive vote on whether to launch or not belonged to
Yeltsin and his crony Pavel Grachev, the Minister of Defense at

the time, who the month before had assured the President that Grozny could be taken in a matter of hours. (Perhaps it was fortunate, given Yeltsin's well-known drinking habits, that the Norwegians like to launch their rockets early in the morning.) The two men talked anxiously with the Chief of the General Staff, General Mikhail Kolesnikov. He was the man who would send the final launch orders to the silo controls. It had been just four minutes since an unsuspecting Norwegian technician sent Black Brant on its way.

Of the three men, General Kolesnikov was the one who may have been most convinced that this really was the beginning of an enemy attack. The next day he was still maintaining that the innocent scientific rocket had in fact been "a new operational tactical missile." In those desperate minutes he may well have been urging Yeltsin to give permission to launch. Technically, he could have done it all on his own.

Finally, about seven minutes into the rocket's flight, it became patently clear that it was not headed for Russia. Twenty-four minutes after launch it finally crashed into its target, the Norwegian island of Spitsbergen, far out in the Arctic Ocean. The briefcases were shut and repossessed by the ever present *shuriks*. The nuclear forces went back to their normal alert status, ready to launch on warning.

On the other side of the world, this terrifying brush with nuclear disaster went almost unnoticed. A few scattered newspaper accounts gave it brief mention, reporting inaccurately that the Russians had shot the Norwegian missile down. The giant antennae of the National Security Agency picked up the frantic commands and discussions that flashed over the Kazbek network that morning, but such intelligence is considered so sensitive that very few people, even in the intelligence agencies, were allowed to see the "blue border" reports describing the Russian alert. SAFE, the main classified database at the CIA Intelligence Directorate, contained no mention of the affair.

This portent of disaster would have been serious enough in the days when "Arbat," the Defense Ministry and General Staff headquarters, still commanded and controlled a newly built and well-financed nuclear machine. But, as the performance of the radar systems watching the Norwegian Sea indicated, the system was beginning to break down. The nuclear weapons were passing out of control.

Two years after Black Brant's near-fatal flight, Igor Rodionov had had enough. In February 1997 he bluntly announced that "Russia might soon reach a threshold beyond which its rockets and nuclear systems cannot be controlled. [Even] today, no one can guarantee the reliability of our systems of control." Elaborating, he referred to the "increasing psychological weariness of the corps of officers" and pointed out that "owing to a shortage of satellites, there are several hours at a time when we are unable to carry out tracking work outside the Russian borders."

It was a dire statement, entirely contradicting the official position of both the U.S. government and the Kremlin. Boris Yeltsin derisively dismissed his defense chief's warning as "lamentations" concocted purely in order to extract more money from the treasury. Newspapers friendly to the Kremlin said that the minister was "hysterical" and should be fired. Rodionov's warning got no more serious attention in Washington, where administration officials dismissed the minister's warnings as simply a maneuver to increase his budget. Despite a state which was billions of dollars behind in paying wages and pensions, where even the workers in nuclear weapons plants were going on strike, where senior generals were doing billion-dollar arms deals or selling nerve gas technology to the highest bidder, the ultimate weapons of mass destruction were supposedly still under control.

There were people who knew better. "Rodionov is absolutely correct," wrote Colonel Robert Bykov, a veteran of the Strategic Rocket Forces and the General Staff, who had long served in the heart of Russia's nuclear war machine. "We could launch an accidental nuclear strike on the United States in the matter of seconds it takes you to read these lines."

Most of the communications equipment for the nuclear control system had been put in place back in the 1970s. The complex radio systems were crammed into poorly ventilated rooms in the command bunkers deep underground and left running for years at a time. A decade later, the components were starting to break down on a regular basis. In the early 1990s the breakdowns became more frequent. Now parts of the system would suddenly switch themselves into combat mode, as if a launch was imminent.

By 1997 the system was disintegrating on an hourly basis. The very complex mechanism that enabled the President and the high command to keep firm control of the strategic arsenal had originally been designed at a secret institute in St. Petersburg known as NPO Impulse. The scientists and technicians here were responsible not only for designing and building it but also for troubleshooting and maintenance. Originally, of course, a job at NPO had been one of the most prestigious and best-paid in the country, and the people who worked there were drawn from the technical elite of the vaunted Soviet educational system. Spending their entire careers at NPO, they preserved an institutional memory of the nuclear control system they served. Now, however, there is no more money for the institute and the workers are scattering to the four winds to make a living in the new Russia as best they can.

"They are nowhere to be found," Colonel Bykov grimly pointed out, yet the work they did long ago "continues to be the Strategic Rocket Forces' main command and control system."

Shelkovo, a suburb of Moscow, houses the main tracking facility for Russia's 156 early-warning satellites. Not far from the vital military center is a bustling market of the kind that have sprung up all over Russia in the last few years, with everything from cars to washing machines on sale. By 1996, the electronics stalls were getting some new customers, officers from the tracking facility up the road. They were shopping for parts to try to keep the early-warning satellite tracking system in operation. Even so, as Rodionov pointed out, there was no satellite coverage of North America for hours at a time. In a crisis, the commanders would have to make their best guess.

In a crisis, there might be other problems. On February 10, 1997, there was a wild party in the Kremlin guardroom to celebrate the victory in a parliamentary election that day of Alexander Korshakov, Yeltsin's sinister former chief bodyguard. Among those subsequently fired for being too drunk to carry out their duties was the Ninth General Staff Directorate officer in charge of the President's nuclear briefcase.

The system was designed so that only operators in the General Staff Central Command Post could order a launch on the direct order of the chief. But as things unravel, it becomes more and more possible that the decision to fire might be taken by someone else. Rodionov spoke of the increasing "psychological weariness of the officer corps." This was hardly surprising, given that even the officers in the Central Command had not been paid for months and were taking jobs on the side. The Strategic Rocket Forces, once an elite 300,000-man body comprised mostly of volunteers, has been cut by almost two-thirds to 114,000 men, 70,000 of whom are conscripts. In some intercontinental ballistic missile units officers are having to work up a hundred hours a week. Colonel Bykov told of the "smart aleck" in a missile regiment out in the field who figured out a way of launching on his own without using the necessary password. A command post duty officer had become mentally unstable as a result of inhaling poison fumes from a faulty air duct and been taken straight to the hospital.

In conveying the seriousness of the situation, the well-educated Colonel Bykov reached for a chilling classical allusion. In ancient times Herostratus burned down the great temple at Ephesus simply in order to perpetuate his name. "Officers manning control desks are also people," wrote the colonel. "We have no guarantee today that some Herostratus will not turn up in Russia's missile forces."

The Clinton administration does not share such dark forebodings. "The Pentagon, the State Department and the White House all agree, having looked at the question very carefully" said State Department spokesman Nicholas Burns in October 1996, "that the Russian government has control over its nuclear weapons force and over the nuclear material in the Russian stockpile."

The spokesman was making the statement because someone in the CIA, frustrated by official refusal to face facts, had just leaked an intelligence report that put things in a very different light. "The Russian nuclear command and control system is being subjected to stresses it was not designed to withstand as a result of wrenching social change, economic hardship, and malaise within the armed forces," wrote the authors of "Prospects for Unsanctioned Use of Russian Nuclear Weapons," classified top secret. "Despite official assurances, high-level Moscow officials are concerned about the security of their nuclear inventory." The report confirmed that local command posts below the level of the General Staff "have the technical ability to launch without authorization of political leaders or the General Staff."

The commander of the Strategic Rocket Forces, worried about what his own troops might do, had recently set up a special procedure for reporting unauthorized missile launches.

Even more worrying was the increasing loss of control over the 22,000 tactical nuclear weapons. "These appear to be the weapons most at risk,"stated the report, noting not only that nuclear torpedoes on submarines have locks that could easily be removed by the crews but that the KBU electromechanical blocking devices to prevent unauthorized use on other weapons were being turned off because they were too difficult and expensive to maintain. Given this situation, the CIA analysts somberly raised the possibility of "conspiracies within nuclear armed units" to commit nuclear blackmail. Russian officials themselves were particularly worried about nuclear units in the far eastern sectors, where "troop living conditions are particularly deplorable" and "where nuclear weapons might fall into the wrong hands."

Things were obviously changing at the CIA, at least at the working level. (What was judged fit at the upper levels to put in the National Intelligence Estimates that went to the President was a different story.) When Jessica Stern had first arrived at the National Security Council she could never quite understand why intelligence officials who worried about nuclear materials finding their way into the wrong hands were nonetheless adamant that there was little risk of actual nuclear warheads going astray. She always thought that this unshakable faith in Russian military nuclear security was "based on nothing."

Part of the reason for such complacency may have been the earnestly cooperative attitude of General Evgeni Maslin, the man in charge of the Twelfth Directorate of the General Staff, the custodians of the weapons stockpile. Unlike the obstreperous Minatom boss, Victor Mikhailov, prone to getting drunk and making passes at lady interpreters in the middle of meetings, Maslin always appeared ready to bond with American officials. The general rarely raised an objection to U.S. aid proferred under the "Cooperative Threat Reduction Program" sponsored by Senators Nunn and Lugar. He gave grateful thanks for security help like the upgraded railcars arranged years before by Bill Burns or Kevlar armored blankets for wrapping around warheads in transit.

While Mikhailov denied the possibility of anyone ever making off with material from a Minatom facility, despite abundant evidence to the contrary, the charming Maslin would concede that he always worried about security. U.S. officials, charmed by this sympathetic approach and impressed by the general's professionalism, went away convinced that whatever else was wrong with the Russian military, the nuclear custodians could still be relied on to carry out their duties. They trusted that he was telling the truth when he swore that he knew the location of every single nuclear warhead, large or small, in the Russian stockpile. They were impressed by the layers of security surrounding a nuclear weapons site—the Twelfth Department detachment that had custody of the warheads themselves, the special security troops of the General Staff who provided the immediate armed protection for the site, the Ministry of Interior troops who kept watch on the area, the men from the FSB counterintelligence service who watched the guardians and each other.

Now, however, undeniable evidence was piling up that the same military rot that had been so humiliatingly revealed in Chechnya had spread to the nuclear forces. It had always been an article of faith that while miserable conscripts like Mikhail Kubarsky might be left unpaid, even allowed to starve, troops who handled nuclear weapons and especially the handpicked officers who served in the Twelfth Department were properly taken care of. Even if their pay arrived late, it did come, as did the bonuses that went with their critical responsibilities.

But by the beginning of 1996, that was clearly beginning to change, intelligence reports confirmed that the public complaints of officers like Rodionov were all too true and that even the men of the Twelfth were going short.

Knowledgeable Russians took the dire state of affairs for granted, laughing at the very question of whether the men guarding the warheads were being paid. "Of course not. The commanders of ballistic missile submarines have not been paid in four months." If men who controlled not only nuclear warheads but the missiles that could deliver them halfway around the world were not being looked after, was it likely that anyone was bothering about the guardians of a nuclear storage bunker.

A professional intelligence service such as Iraq's, given the mission of getting its hands on a nuclear weapon, endowed with all the money it needed and with a network already in place in Russia, would find its opportunities increasing all the time. Six years after Greenpeace came so close to getting their hands on a Scud warhead in Germany, that warhead is almost certainly still sitting in the same storage site where it was dumped after being brought back to Russia. Just months before he was ejected from the Kremlin, Mikhail Gorbachev pledged to have half of all tactical bombs and warheads dismantled by 1996. The promise has been ignored. Three thousand tactical missile warheads, artillery shells and bombs are designated for future operational use, in line with the military's declared new policy of reaching promptly for the nuclear option in a war. The rest are stored in three huge depots in the heart of Russia, their safety locks decaying or switched off, guarded by unpaid and angry soldiers in a society where responsibility and morality are fast disappearing and thievery reigns supreme.

Despite the assurances of Maslin and others, Western intelligence agencies suspect that the high command does not know if all the weapons are present and accounted for, because they were never counted properly in the first place. In theory, they are inspected twice a year. No one checks to see if the weapon has not been exchanged for an identical-looking training dummy. Many of them, such as the Scud warheads, could be moved by just three men. The artillery shells, shorter-range missile warheads, small nuclear bombs, land mines, torpedo warheads and atomic demolition devices—"chemodan" or "suitcases"—are light enough to be lifted by just one man.

●

In 1996, for a brief period, General Alexandr Lebed was Secretary of Boris Yeltsin's National Security Council. As such he had unrestricted access to Russia's darkest defense secrets. He knew that there were supposed to be one hundred and thirty-two nuclear suitcases in the stockpile. Worried about their security, he ordered a check to make sure that all these mini-nukes were accounted for. Despite an intensive search, he could only locate forty-eight. Eighty-four were missing.

Revealing this terrifying news to a group of visitors in May the following year, the general conceded that the explosive yield of the suitcases was low (on the order of a few kilotons), but, he joked, they would make a "decent boom."

Eighty-four nuclear weapons, already neatly packaged in suitcases. No one knows where they are. No one knows how to stop them.

14

WILD ATOM

Collectively, the high-level group around the table had decades of experience at the upper levels of U.S. national security, but they had never faced a crisis like this. For over an hour, they discussed and argued about what they should recommend to the President. The news from the Americans locked up in the secret Russian nuclear city was potentially too serious to ignore. If the worst was true, then nuclear weapons were coming to the United States.

The CIA official watched intently from the shadows. The senior officials were playing his game.

Dan Wagner is an expert on nuclear smuggling. He was the emissary from CIA headquarters at Langley to Jessica's Nuclear Smuggling Working Group. Inevitably, like Jessica and others working on the issue, Wagner had asked himself the question "What if?" What if a worst-case scenario came true and the bomb-grade materials were stolen in really big quantities from a porous Russian storage site? What if they were bought by terrorists who knew how to make a bomb and bring it to the United States? What would the government do? Could it rely on getting the intelligence in time? Would the Russians help? Would the terrorists really know how to build a bomb? What would it look like? How would they smuggle it in and could it be detected before it was too late?

One day in December 1996, Jessica found herself walking through a door with a blazing red "secret" sign into a window-less warren underneath a golf course in southeastern Washington. She intended to help find the answer to these questions.

She had left the government the previous year. Despite what she had achieved, her tour as a visiting Council on Foreign Relations Fellow was up. Now she was spending her days delving more deeply into the implications of weapons of mass destruction becoming available to terrorists. Many of her friends and allies who had fought to get the government to give urgent attention to the control of Russian nuclear materials had also gone their separate ways. Frank von Hippel was back at Princeton and had recruited Ken Luongo to join him. Matt Bunn had joined John Holdren at Harvard to work on a project called "Managing the Atom." General Burns was investigating judicial corruption in Pennsylvania and had already locked up a number of judges. Ken Fairfax, who had taken over her job when she departed, had left the White House after a brilliant tour and was waiting to go overseas again. He was still plagued by the mysterious illness that first appeared when he was haunting nuclear sites in Russia.

Now, behind the door with the red sign, Jessica was back in the world of chaotic Russia and nuclear smuggling. There was the dapper Wagner, very much in control of things. She noticed Rich Galbraith, another alumnus of her old group, who had represented the U.S. Customs Service. Now he was in charge of training Russian and other Customs organizations on how to stop nuclear shipments. John "Jay" Stewart appeared, her old friend and ally from DOE Intelligence. His temerity in pushing the theme of "Russian Fission" and nuclear weapons on the loose had cost him his career in intelligence. He had taken a senior executive post with an energy company but he still stayed very much in touch with his old subject. There were other faces from her days at Livermore: Bert Weinstein, the head of Z Division, whom she had called the day Ken Fairfax's momentous cable arrived from Moscow, and John Immele, a brilliant weapons scientist. They were all there to play Wagner's game.

When Wagner called Jessica he was doing a tour at the National Defense University on the banks of the Potomac in southeastern Washington. The university lies within an army base, Fort McNair, where comfortable houses reserved for high-ranking generals line the smoothly paved driveways and manicured lawns at the water's edge. The men and women ensconced in the imposing neoclassical building are military officers, intelligence officials or anyone else whose job involves national security. Many of the students are in uniform, some of them foreign. Latin American generals wander the halls. Officials from the Vatican have been spotted there deep in military discussions. Even the Russian Army sends officers for courses. Pentagon generals officially designated as semi-retired and attached to the NDU might be spending much of their time in the Balkans riding herd on one of the warring factions there.

This is the graduate school for national security professionals. They spend much of their time below ground level in the War Gaming and Simulation Center, acting out battles, wars and crises waiting to happen with the help of simulated TV newscasts, intelligence briefs and other elaborate props.

It was here that Jessica found her old friends and colleagues, all gathered by Wagner to role-play U.S. government officials in Wild Atom, the ultimate "what if" game of nuclear theft.

Wagner had recruited an all-star cast. Jessica spotted James R. Schlesinger, who in his time had run the CIA, the Pentagon and the Department of Energy. He was going to take the role of President. Fred Iklé, for years a Teutonic-accented high-level adviser and official at the Pentagon would be Secretary of Defense. Doug McEachin, recently retired as head of the CIA's intelligence wing, was stepping in as Director of Central Intelligence. Former Chief of Staff of the Army Edward Meyer took on the role of Chairman of the Joint Chiefs. Jessica herself was playing Madeleine Albright, U.S. ambassador to the United Nations. She was the only woman in the senior "policy" group.

Other players were divided up into Interagency Working Groups as specialists on law enforcement, intelligence and weapons technology. For most of them, these were the real jobs that they worked at every day.

Wagner, in collaboration with the high-powered Center for Strategic and International Studies think tank, had devised an elaborate and coherent scenario. Plotting the complex series of events that would serve as the background for the game, he drew on what he and intelligence professionals like him thought might happen for real. Jessica and the other players would be told only fragments of the total picture. They were going to have to take action on the basis of confusing or ambiguous scraps of information, just as in the real world.

Arbitrarily, Wagner had picked a date for the crisis: mid-February 2001. Bill Clinton would have left office the previous month. This would be a new government, grappling with their first crisis.

The game began when the players were handed an intelligence report. Since 2 A.M. the previous day, the National Intelligence Agency had been picking up unusual activity on secure communications channels between the Kremlin, the General Staff, Minatom, the Ministry of the Interior and the FSB counterintelligence agency. The report did not say what was in the messages, but these centers were transmitting at three times the normal rate. Outside of Moscow, the main activity was in the southern Ural Mountains. Other intercepts indicated that patrols had been stepped up along the Chechen and Kazakh borders.

At 5:20 A.M., the NSA had issued a NOIWON telephonic alert, the crisis procedure for warning senior U.S. government officials of a possible nuclear emergency. Four hours later the President had called his Russian counterpart to ask what was going on. The Russian leader had been reassuring, insisting that nothing unusual had happened and there was no call for alarm.

Jessica was surprised at how ready some people in the room were to believe the Russians. It seemed clear that in a situation of this kind the United States would almost certainly have to rely on its own intelligence.

The next item of information fed to the game gave a possible clue to the reason for the report of unusual communications activity. The players learned that at 4 A.M. the next morning there had been an urgent call from a group of Americans visiting a "secret city" in the southern Urals. This was entirely believable. Since the days when Frank von Hippel had visited the nuclear processing plant at Mayak in the secret city of Chelyabinsk 65, the Russians had become more willing to accept American help in upgrading security. Thanks to the efforts of Ken Luongo, Ken Fairfax and others, this effort had gone into high gear, spearheaded by scientists from the American weapons laboratory at Los Alamos. With help from the U.S. Army Corps of Engineers, a secure storage site at Mayak is almost finished.

According to the scenario, a team from Los Alamos had just checked into the town's 1960-era hotel with the radiation counter over the front door, ready to begin work. Abruptly, without explanation, they had been sternly ordered to stay inside. From the windows of their rooms they were able to see a lot of military vehicles moving about the streets. Even though they were confined, the Los Alamos team had used their secure satellite phone to call home base and report what was happening.

The intelligence and weapons lab specialists in the game might have suggested at this point that the military activity in the city could be accounted for by an accident, such as had actually happened there in 1957, when the military had evacuated thousands of people. But Wagner had closed off that possibility.

The scientists, he revealed, had unpacked some of the monitoring equipment they had brought with them for use at the plant and switched it on to test local radiation levels in the atmosphere. As they explained over the phone, levels were normal. At least that ruled out an accidental release.

That left two other possibilities. It could be that the authorities had just discovered a major theft. On the other hand, it might be only a full-scale drill. For the intelligence analysts reviewing the facts in front of them, either assumption could be valid. They were informed that the "hotel staff" thought the army and police were out looking for "local mafia," but that was not conclusive. They had to find out more.

The intelligence team was asked to get more information. Didn't the CIA have an agent in the area? The answer was no.

"Why not?"

"My budget's been cut by forty percent. We don't have any humint down there," answered the CIA player, sticking rigorously to realism.

"How long will it take to find out?"

"Some time. I can't say how long."

Intelligence could not come up with instant answers, a fact of life that other players found hard to grasp.

Eventually it was decided that someone would have to be sent from Moscow to Chelyabinsk to find out more. Now Wagner threw in another fact of life—a bureaucratic turf battle between the FBI and the CIA.

In recent years, the FBI, supposedly restricted to domestic

law enforcement, has been expanding its overseas presence under the rubric of combating organized crime. FBI Director Louis Freeh's assertion of a role for the Bureau in dealing with possible thefts of nuclear weapons or materials from Russia had not gone down well at Langley. It was entirely in character for the CIA station and the FBI office in Moscow to assert their right to take the lead in investigating the Chelyabinsk incident. The FBI and CIA players politely argued the point, but by the end of the day they had still not reached an agreement.

Now the game controller fed in other scraps of intelligence that might put the Russian news in a different light.

The "U.S. Interests Section" attached to the Swiss embassy in Iran was reporting intense efforts by the Iranian government to find and recover a particular shipment of military supplies from Russia rumored to have been stolen the previous month. Over the same period the progovernment press had been carrying vehement denunciations of Hezbollah, the militant Lebanese Shiite group that had long been supported by Teheran.

There were, in addition, rumors that several Iranian officials known for their close ties with Hezbollah had been arrested on a charge of "theft of state property."

NSA had picked up electronic transfers, totaling millions of dollars, into a Zurich bank account that had in the past been used by a KGB front company now believed to have fallen into the hands of the mafia.

Finally, there was a CIA report from an "untested" source that the Hezbollah had acquired nuclear devices and planned to explode them in the United States and Europe as well as American bases in Saudi Arabia.

Looked at with a professional intelligence eye, and there were plenty of them in the game center, these reports might explain whatever was happening in Russia and Iran, or they might not. They were unconfirmed, raw intelligence. They would have been sifted from thousands of disparate items of intelligence "noise" that poured into Washington every day from around the world. Perhaps the whole Hezbollah theft story was an elaborate deception to cover Iran's own role and plans? Who had wired that money into the Zurich account and way? They had to find out more on all fronts. Perhaps the Pakistanis could help. It was particularly important to try to find out the truth about the relationship between Iran and Hezbollah. Could the President of Iran control Hezbollah if he wanted to? If Hezbollah was indeed acting totally independently, then that had a lot of implications for the sophistication of any weapon that might be built from the stolen material.

Among the players on the technical team the arguments were more firmly grounded. They already knew that Chelyabinsk 65 had tons of plutonium and tens of tons of highly enriched uranium 235 on hand. They also knew from experience that the Russians did not know how much they had stored, so Moscow would not be able to calculate precisely how much had been stolen. But it could be assumed that if there had been a large theft, the amount would be enough for at least one weapon.

Building weapons was something the technical players knew all about. Would the Iranians be able to build a uranium "gun-type" bomb? Yes. How powerful would it be? Between two and ten kilotons. Could a group like Hezbollah do it? With technical help, sure. On their own? Maybe.

What about a plutonium "implosion" bomb, always trickier because it involves using carefully arranged high explosives to squeeze the pit uniformly in a split second? Yes, the Iranians could do that. Possibly the Hezbollah could too, but only if they had help. That would be a more powerful weapon, depending on the sophistication of the design. Two kilotons if it was a crude IND (improvised nuclear device), twenty kilotons if they really knew what they were doing. Up to four square miles of complete destruction, perhaps half a million casualties.

On their own at least, Hezbollah would not be able to manage a plutonium implosion weapon. But they were certainly technically capable of putting together an RDD (radiation dispersal device) using the plutonium. There would be no nuclear detonation, but high explosives would spread billions of toxic plutonium particles far and wide. At the least, that would cause mass panic. An entire city would have to be evacuated. Cleaning up would cost billions.

How would any of these weapons be delivered? The Iranians had Scuds, which would be able to do the job if the target was a U.S. base in Saudi Arabia. Perhaps Hezbollah could get their hands on a Scud as well. Any variant of the weapons they had already discussed could be carried on a missile. Someone mentioned that Hezbollah could stow a weapon on a ship. They certainly had the money to buy one.

Left unanswered, assuming that there had just been a big theft in Russia and that either Hezbollah or Iran had obtained nuclear materials to build a bomb, was the question of how long it would take them to do it. How much time did the United States have to try to find the material before it was too late? No one could give a firm answer to that, maybe weeks.

These discussions had gone on in separate rooms in the game center. For the final session of the first day, everyone gathered in a small auditorium on tiers of red plush seats to watch the "principals"—the players representing the heads of agencies—have a high-level meeting with the National Security Adviser to tell him what to recommend to the President.

Interestingly enough, the high officials, active and retired, who were impersonating high officials in the game were for the most part strangely quiescent. Possibly they were intimidated by the National Security Adviser, since James Schlesinger was doubling in that role as well as that of President. They were all well aware that they were acting out events set in the first month of the post-Clinton administration. They were all therefore new to their jobs and this was the first time they had worked together as a team—a realistic touch, given that the players themselves were working together for the first time.

They behaved as if their performance in this crisis really would affect their standing and future job prospects in an administration. In any event, for the most part they confined themselves to reporting the conclusions of their teams without recommending action. Schlesinger provided the rhetoric.

The one area of dispute in the meeting concerned the vexed question of "public diplomacy." So far the ominous events under consideration were supposedly known only to a few people inside the government. What should the public be told in such a situation? What should the President tell Congress? Should he go on TV?

Schlesinger was adamant that he would recommend that the President talk to the nation. Energy Secretary Jay Stewart hotly opposed the notion, pointing out that so far most of what they knew came from "raw intelligence" reports similar to hundreds that poured into the intelligence agencies every year. "Do you know what you are doing?" he asked angrily.

The next morning Wagner changed the whole shape and pace of the game.

The players were greeted with the news that a U.S. satellite had detected the unmistakable flash of a nuclear explosion just outside Moscow. The Russian leader had already called the President.

Since their last talk, when "President Lebed" had been blandly reassuring, the Russian's tone had changed markedly. He had explained that he had been misleading the previous day because his own subordinates had not briefed him properly. He was now ready to give information. The blast had not come from a military weapon. It was a terrorist device, exploded accidentally while being transported by Chechen nationalists. They had not intended to set it off but were now claiming credit and threatening further bombs unless they got what they wanted. There had indeed been a theft from Chelyabinsk, a major one. He listed the approximate quantities of the various materials that had been stolen. The amounts were so large that even the famously inexact Russian nuclear accounting system had been able to tally the loss. The theft had happened two months earlier.

The Russian bomb did not directly affect the United States but the news changed the whole atmosphere. Now they were reacting to the fact that the unthinkable had happened and nuclear weapons were on the loose.

It took time for the significance of one crucial new piece of intelligence to dawn on the group. The theft had happened *two months* before. Up until now they had been assuming that there was plenty of time to find out more, to approach the Iranian government, to develop proper response measures. Allowing two weeks for the material to be smuggled from Russia to Iran, that left six weeks for whoever had it—perhaps Hezbollah—to build their bomb. If that early report from the "untested" CIA source in Teheran was accepted as true, a weapon could already be on its way to the United States. There was no more time to consider ambiguities. They had to find the bomb.

Now the emphasis in the game shifted from intelligence to preventing disaster. This put the focus on the law enforcement players. But the law enforcement team was having its own dissensions. The FBI players swiftly declared themselves the lead agency that would manage the law enforcement response. They were going to set up a "crisis management system" to coordinate matters. Other members of the team noted that despite the Bureau's massive budget and abundant manpower, they did not seem to have the necessary plans or skills to actually intercept a weapon.

"Fine," said Rick Galbraith, the Customs player, to the Bureau representative. "You set up your management system and talk to the press and we'll do the work."

Galbraith and others on his team were frustrated by the caution of the CIA team. There were urgent questions to be answered. What sort of bomb were they looking for? What would it look like? Could it be concealed in a bread box or was it as big as the room they were sitting in? The intelligence analysts would not venture to say. They explained that they did not have enough data.

The technical group were more confident. The experts did their calculations. Given the level of weapons engineering sophistication they were assuming the other side possessed, they were able to tell the group that would be looking for the bomb that they should search for a round metal object about three feet across. Of course, there was the possibility that the other side would have thought about shielding the device from radiation detectors. Further calculations. If they had added shielding, that would double the weight and size of the weapon, narrowing down the types of transport they could use. On the other hand, it would make it almost impossible to detect.

With this information as a basis, Galbraith and his colleagues thought about how they themselves would bring in a bomb. Given the weapon's size, a ship would probably be best. The scientists pointed out that they could not count on waiting to find it after it was unloaded. Simply exploding it on a ship in harbor would cause massive destruction.

Finding the ship would not necessarily be an insuperable problem if they were able to eliminate vessels on their way from low-risk countries like, say, Holland, and concentrate on likely prospects: ships from the Middle East, ships that made a sudden unscheduled request to dock for repairs, ships whose point of origin did not show up in Lloyd's Registry. But if the lethal cargo did not have to be unloaded before it was detonated, they would have to make the interception out at sea. That would mean setting up a picket line well off the coast to stop and search suspect ships. From the point of view of the coast guard player, this looked like a pretty formidable job.

Could NEST, the nuclear search and bomb disposal operation that had so dismally failed in the New Orleans Mirage Gold exercise, find the bomb before it left the Middle East? Someone floated a proposal that the Iranians should be tested with an offer to send a NEST team to Iran to look for Hezbollah's weapon and share intelligence. The U.S. ambassador to the United Nations could approach the Iranian ambassador to sound out the idea. There was also a proposal to use "information warfare" against Hezbollah, promoting the idea that NEST was all-seeing and could easily foil their plans.

Someone on the intelligence team suggested contacting Hezbollah and making an offer to buy the material back. Later on, after the crisis was defused, the United States could retaliate against Iran. The players, enclosed in the underground rooms of the center, were becoming more and more absorbed in the realistic fictions of the game. The stark possibility of a nuclear device making its way to an American city was concentrating their minds. Collectively, though some were reluctant to admit it, they were groping their way to an awful truth.

The controller fed in another intelligence update. The New York police had picked up an expatriate Iranian student behaving suspiciously in a restricted area. Some of the players reacted in character. The military saw no reason why he should not be locked up and the truth about his mission sweated out of him. The FBI agent delivering the news, formerly a member of New York's finest, announced proudly, "We took him down. We'll hold his butt.'

The Attorney General injected a note of lawyerly sobriety. "I need to know who arrested him, on what grounds and why specifically he is being held," he said. It was a reminder that civil liberties were not automatically suspended in a crisis. This was an attitude that the military players found hard to comprehend. Exchanges in the law enforcement group grew testy.

Nevertheless, the arrest of the Iranian was further confirmation that the device would be exploded on a ship after it had reached harbor with the aim of causing maximum casualties from blast and radiation.

Again, the nuclear wizards scratched calculations to estimate the likely number of casualties. No one could be confident about the yield of an amateur weapon. Maybe it would be as large as twenty kilotons, but the consensus fell between two and four kilotons, quite enough to cause a quarter of a million casualties. There was another possibility, almost as unpleasant to contemplate. Maybe the Hezbollah would not succeed in building an actual nuclear weapon, but would content themselves with putting together a radiation dispersal weapon. The experts concluded that with the wind blowing in the right direction, the toxic particles would scatter over an area between ten and sixty square miles. They thought that with timely evacuation the death list would not be very high—no one would drop dead immediately—the casualties would show up as a marginal increase in the cancer rate over the long term.

Nonetheless, the effects would be cataclysmic. The entire city would have to be evacuated. Ordinary people knew enough about plutonium to panic at the possibility that their families, their children, were breathing in this deadly poison. The city would have to remain empty while it was cleaned. The cost of that exercise beggared description.

Nuclear blast or RDD, everyone agreed that a detonation would be the greatest disaster in American history. The unpleasant truth was that, unless the picket line of ships making searches out in the Atlantic got lucky, there was little that the United States could do to stop it.

"President" Schlesinger was enjoying his role. Fully entering into the spirit of the game, he was every inch a chief executive. Wagner was delighted; the authority he projected was making the game seem real. Jessica was ready to vote for him to take the actual job. Jay Stewart thought that perhaps he was enjoying the part a little too much, especially in his eagerness to make a TV address to the nation. "How can you do it?" he argued. "The consequences of what you do will be different from anything else that any President has ever done. This wouldn't be like Roosevelt and Pearl Harbor, or Kennedy and

Cuba. This would be the biggest thing ever." Schlesinger was undeterred.

Few players were really ready to admit that they, in their make-believe roles and real-life professions, were ill prepared to deal with such a crisis. With current technology, even an unshielded weapon could not be detected from more than a few tens of feet away. The notion of helicopters cruising over a city in the hope of picking up radiation from a hidden weapon was completely out of the question.

If the weapon was coming by ship, the chances of finding and intercepting it off the coast were poor, though at least they were better than the odds on discovering it once it reached its target. Neither the navy nor the coast guard had enough equipment to do the job, assuming it was practical to get close enough to inspect every likely ship approaching the East Coast in any case. Once upon a time the navy had deployed sensors aboard some of its ships—in the Mediterranean—but that program had been discontinued in the early 1990s. Someone suggested stripping any sensors that might be in place in the harbors and putting them aboard ships. It was about all that could be done.

John Immele, who was playing Z Division in the game, had a rebuttal for these gloomy conclusions. The events they were discussing, he pointed out, were set five years hence, in 2001. Therefore a lot of "promising R&D" currently in the pipeline would have come to fruition. By then there would be sensors that could pick out neutron emissions from a weapon from airplanes flying overhead. All things would be possible. They just weren't ready yet.

Jay Stewart lacked Immele's technical credentials, but he was extremely skeptical that any kind of quick fix was just around the corner. He would believe airborne neutron detectors when he saw them. The discussion devolved into heated debate over arcane and very highly classified technology. The supervisors on hand from the War Gaming Center blenched.

There were people in the room whose clearances were not high enough to learn of such things.

Others thought the only way to spur action on the new technologies would be a genuine crisis. "It will take this [a real-life version of the game scenario] to get there by 2001," muttered one of the scientists. "We need our own nuclear World Trade Center."

No one ever knew what happened when the ship finally reached the East Coast. The coast guard and Customs were setting up their picket line. The Federal Emergency Management Agency was trying to work out a strategy for "consequence management." The FBI was still insisting that it was in charge. The Attorney General was considering whether it would be legally possible to lock up suspects without due process or to bring in the military for a domestic law enforcement operation. But time was up. The game was over. Jessica found it startling to emerge into the bright sunshine and well-tended lawns of Fort McNair on the banks of the placid Potomac after so many hours underground, peering into the future.

In a final session, all the players came together to assess the game. Inevitably, the make-believe and real worlds merged. The representative of the Joint Chiefs of Staff gave a ringing endorsement not only of the merit of the game itself but of the Pentagon's entire planning effort against the threat of nuclear terrorism. The FBI was similarly upbeat even though, as one participant sarcastically noted, "they seemed to think that the elimination of an American city would be just a crime like any other, where you track down and arrest a criminal and then turn him over to a U.S. Attorney for prosecution and conviction."

The CIA alone felt moved to confess inadequacy. "We don't have any way of dealing with this problem, now or in the future," said one player.

Fred Iklé, having enjoyed the experience of serving as "Secretary of Defense," said he thought that the exercise had been "a great success," demonstrating that the various agencies of the U.S. government could work together in developing a seamlessly coordinated plan to deal with the threat.

This was too much for Jay Stewart, who emphatically pointed out that if what they had been discussing ever became a reality, the low estimate of casualties would amount to more deaths than America suffered in World War II. He saw no sign that the U.S. government was thinking seriously about the question, preparing to deal with cities laid waste and millions of dead. There was no basis for believing that intelligence could be our first line of defense. The United States would have to proceed on the assumption that there would be no warning of any kind. There was no reason for anyone to congratulate themselves.

This was not a popular attitude among the other players, although Jessica was inclined to agree. There appeared to be a division between high-ranking officials used to barking orders into a phone, confident that they would be executed, and others who were suddenly faced with the reality of searching a hundred thousand square miles of ocean or some such task.

One well-qualified observer who had followed the game from start to finish summed up his conclusions more bluntly. "If this scenario ever happens," he confided privately, "we're up a creek without enough paddles."

•

In a cluttered office at Building 6 at the World Trade Center, the Customs House, there sits a man who has learned about smuggling in a more practical way. Like many of the players who sat with Jessica for those two days, this man works for the government. He too has had to act a part. But, unlike them, he has to put his life on the line when playing a role. He is a veteran Customs investigator who has gone undercover many times. When he impersonates an arms dealer or a weapons smuggler in order to infiltrate the relevant criminal circles, he has a strong incentive to play the part convincingly.

This makes him probably the closest thing to a professional smuggler on the government payroll. He does not think highly of the country's defenses against anyone seriously interested in moving a nuclear device across the border.

Among the many different methods a sophisticated smuggler might use to get a bomb into New York City, he suggests one that would take advantage of the bonded warehouse system.

Commerical shipments that come into a U.S. port or airport but are merely in transit to another country are kept in bonded warehouses. Goods in bond are not inspected by Customs. The only check is on the weight of the container or package, which must be the same going in and out.

Once upon a time all bonded warehouses were owned and controlled by the government. But some fifteen years ago the warehouses were privatized, sold to licensed private companies, and there are now no government personnel, no Customs officers, on duty in them. Tracking is done by computer. A smart smuggler would arrange to buy a bonded warehouse firm and also perhaps a bonded trucking company. The "goods," such as a nuclear weapon three feet in diameter, would arrive in transit consigned to another country—Mexico, for example.

"Take it to a bonded warehouse. No U.S. government people ever see it. Once it's in the warehouse, you get in there and manipulate the cargo." In other words, the weapon could be taken out and something else—it would not matter what so long as the weight matched—put in to replace it. The original container then duly goes off to Mexico and is thrown away. The real cargo can be easily moved into New York City, perhaps to the World Trade Center. He sees absolutely nothing standing in the way. "You could bring in the whole Russian Army in bond and then just let them out of the warehouse."

Smuggling nuclear weapons is not a new idea. In the foyer of the Department of Energy headquarters on Independence Avenue in Washington, D.C., there hangs a copy of the letter that started it all. Few of the busy officials who hurry past every day on their way to the elevator, their necks festooned with security passes, ever stop to read it.

Signed by Albert Einstein in August 1939, as Adolf Hitler prepared to invade Poland and ignite World War II, the letter is addressed to Franklin Roosevelt. Einstein informed the President that the success of recent experiments in nuclear research could lead to "a new and important source of energy in the near future" and the construction of "extremely powerful bombs." This historic warning presaged the Manhattan Project, the bombs dropped on Hiroshima and Nagasaki and the thermonuclear missile age. The great physicist did not foresee global nuclear arsenals or other refinements that eventually led to Minister Rodionov's briefcase, but he did predict that "a single bomb of this type, carried by boat or exploded in a port, might well destroy the whole port with some of the surrounding territory."

On September 20, 1945, while the ashes of Hiroshima and Nagasaki were still smoldering, a Pentagon official wrote a highly classified report warning that "the present bomb is composed of parts of such weight and size that a strong man can handle any of them alone. A quantity of these bombs could be distributed and assembled stealthily throughout the major cities of the United States." Preventing this "would require a regimentation of individual freedom of action to a degree which would be repugnant to the American people."

In 1957 a top secret study for the National Security Council warned of the danger of an attack on Strategic Air Command bases with smuggled weapons. Officials drew up plans to restrict all shipping from the Communist countries to isolated ports and expand the U.S. Coast Guard into a million-man defense force against nuclear smugglers. In order to test the ways that a nuclear warhead could be brought across the borders, Special Forces teams carrying simulated nuclear bombs made dozens of dummy runs using every conceivable means, including trucks, small planes and boats. None were intercepted.

Nothing happened. The dummy runs and plans for a million men patrolling the beaches were shelved. The potential problem was too enormous. The government took the other option and forgot about the whole issue. Occasionally, events raised the unpleasant possibility that nuclear weapons may not always stay safely in the hands of responsible governments, as when the Baader-Meinhof terrorists attacked Bill Burns's stockpile in Germany. But that incident was kept very secret. The nuclear weapons and materials discovered littered in the wreckage of the former Soviet Union made the possibility hard to ignore. News of desperate Russian officers stealing nuclear components, of unguarded troves of plutonium, of workers in nuclear weapons storage sites and factories going unpaid galvanized even the Oval Office, but only for a while. Some truths are too uncomfortable to live with.

●

A few months after Wild Atom, Jerry Dzakowic passed through Washington and called on Jessica. She took him for a walk in Rock Creek Park, a slice of natural wilderness carved into the heart of the city. There were signs of buds on the trees and a few early crocuses on the ground between lingering patches of a late winter snowfall. Jessica walked quickly and Jerry puffed a little on the uphill climbs. He was just back from a trip to the Urals, checking up on the bomb-grade uranium that the United States was buying from Victor Mikhailov.

Both were acutely aware that out beyond the trees, the commitment that Jessica and her friends had once generated in the government was waning. Nuclear theft and smuggling were out of the headlines and therefore attracting decreasing amounts of attention at the CIA. The NSC nuclear smuggling group was withering from neglect. Russia seemed closer to breaking apart than ever, with whole regions threatening to withhold taxes and behaving more and more like independent countries. The United States was still trying to decide what to do about the plutonium-laden blankets shimmering in the cooling pools at the Aktau breeder in Kazakhstan. All the while official spokesmen were insisting as fervently as ever that Russia's nuclear arsenal was under tight control.

It was dusk and the two friends were just walking out of the park when Jerry broke the most recent news about the nuclear situation in Russia, news that Jessica could not repeat to anyone. She did not sleep well that night.

ACKNOWLEDGMENTS

For the genesis of this book we must thank Graydon Carter and Henry Porter at *Vanity Fair*. It would, however, have never come to fruition without the tireless encouragement and timely support of Sarah Chalfant at the Wylie Agency and Rob McQuilkin at Anchor Books. Alan Samson at Little, Brown UK also gave us support at a crucial moment.

NOTES

Many people have helped us with the research for this book. Principal among them in generosity and patience has been Jessica Stern. We would also like to express our gratitude to Bruce Blair and John Sobko, and to those who have helped us in the United States, Europe and Russia and who, for understandable reasons, prefer to remain anonymous.

CHAPTER 1

Interviews with General William Burns, Pennsylvania, March 1996. Nuclear weapons effects: U.S. Army Field Manual 100-5, 1976. Baku: Interviews with former CIA and DIA officials, Paul Goble, Robert Gates, Mirza Michaeli. Bill Gertz and Rowan Scarborough: "Soviet Rebels Storm an A-Bomb Facility," *Washington Times*, February 19, 1990. *Black January in Azerbaidzhan*, Human Rights Watch/Helsinki, 1991.

CHAPTER 2

Interviews with Jerry Dzakowic, Livermore, California, February 1996; Washington, D.C., February 1997; and on telephone. Other interviews with officials in Livermore, Los Alamos and Moscow. Hugh Gusterson: *Nuclear Rites: A Weapons Laboratory at the End of the Cold War* (University of California Press, 1996).

CHAPTER 3

Interviews with General William Burns; former CIA and DIA officials; Victor Mikhailov, Moscow, April 1995. Dr. Graham Turbiville: *Mafia in Uniform* (U.S. Army Foreign Military Studies Office, Fort Leavenworth, Kansas). Stephen Handelman: *Comrade Criminal: The Theft of the Second Russian Revolution* (Yale University Press, 1997). Victor Yasmann and Mike Waller: "Russia's Great Criminal Revolution," *Journal of Contemporary Criminal Justice*, December 1995.

CHAPTER 4

Interviews with Jessica Stern. Interviews with former intelligence officials, Washington, D.C. "Russian Fission: The Nuclear Consequences of Political Disintegration (U.S. Department of Energy, 1993, unpublished). Bill Gertz and Rowan Scarborough: "Russian Program Killed for Doubting Yeltsin," *Washington Times*, July 27, 1995.

CHAPTER 5

Personal observation by authors in Murmansk, April 1995. Interview with Mikhail Kulik, April 1995. PIR Center: "Nuclear Materials Storage in the Northern Fleet" (Moscow, 1995). Reports on nuclear situation on the Kola Peninsula by the Norwegian Boolean environmental group. Oleg Bukharin and William Potter: *Bulletin of the Atomic Scientists*, April 1995.

CHAPTER 6

U.S. Department of Energy: "Mile Shakedown Series of Exercises" (Nevada Operations Office, Las Vegas, February 18, 1995). Federal Emergency Management Agency: "Exercise Mirage Gold" (Washington, D.C., April 1995). FBI After-Action

Report: "Mirage Gold," October 16–21, 1994. The Landshut and Prague cases are summarized in U.S. Senate Permanent Subcommitte on Investigations: "Illicit Trafficking in Nuclear Materials," March 22, 1996. Interviews with senior Czech intelligence officials, New York and Prague, February and April 1995.

CHAPTER 7

Interviews with former high-ranking U.S. administration and CIA officials, Washington, D.C.; Nordex corporate official, Vienna. Nordex corporate records. "Clinton's Shady Messenger," *Washington Times*, March 1, 1997. Federal Election Commission records. "The Russia Connection," *Time*, July 8, 1996. On beryllium case: "The Russian Connection," *U.S. News & World Report*, October 23, 1995; interviews with present and former intelligence officials. Descriptions of Nordex headquarters in Vienna and Lilienfeld mansion from personal observation by authors. Interviews with Ukrainian official and legal authorities. "Russian Trader Is a Mystery Man," *Central European Economic Review*, March 1995.

Most of all, anyone discussing Nordex has to pay tribute to the groundbreaking work of Hannes Reichmann, formerly with *Wirstchaftwoche* and now *Profil* magazine, a great journalist and helpful colleague.

CHAPTER 8

Interviews with Frank von Hippel, Princeton, February 1996; Ken Luongo, Washington, D.C., April 1996; Charles Curtis, April 1996; Matthew Bunn, Washington, D.C., February 1996. Center for Science and International Affairs: "Avoiding Nuclear Anarchy" (Cambridge, Mass., 1996). General Accounting Office: "Nuclear Nonproliferation" (Washington, D.C., 1996).

CHAPTER 9

Interviews with Elwood Gift, Alex Riedy and numerous other members of the Sapphire team, May 1996. William C. Potter: "The 'Sapphire' File: Lessons for International Nonproliferation Cooperation," *Transition*, November 17, 1995. John A. Tirpak "Project Sapphire," *Air Force Magazine*, August 1995.

CHAPTER 10

Interviews with Ken Fairfax, Jessica Stern, Alexei Yablokov, Victor Mikhailov and others in Moscow. Alexei Yablokov: "All of Russia Will Have to Pay," *Izvestia*, March 12, 1995. Michael Dobbs: "Russia Promised to Sell Centrifuge Plant to Iran," *Washington Post*, May 29, 1995.

CHAPTER 11

Interviews with Matthew Bunn, Jessica Stern and others who attended the Oval Office meeting. Subcommittee on European Affairs of the Senate Committee on Foreign Relations: "Loose Nukes, Nuclear Smuggling and the Fissile Material Problem in Russia and the NIS," testimony by John Holdren and John Gibbons, August 22 and 23, 1995. John Holdren: "Reducing the Threat of Nuclear Theft in the Former Soviet Union," *Arms Control Today*, March 1996.

CHAPTER 12

Interviews with David Kay, Washington, D.C., June 1996, and Ambassador Rolf Ekeus, April and May 1997. Khidir Abdul Abas Hamza's disappearance in Athens was covered by Jon Swain, London Sunday *Times*, April 1, 1995. Saudi involvement in the Iraqi bomb project was reported by the authors in "Royal Mess," *The New Yorker*, November 28, 1994. For the

BND chief's statement, see Jessica Stern in *The Nonprolifera-tion Review*, Winter 1996.

CHAPTER 13

Interviews with General Sergei Zelentsov, Twelfth Department of the General Staff, and with a former officer in the Twelfth Department, Moscow, April 1995. Interviews with Bruce Blair, Washington, D.C., March 1996 and April 1997. Aleksandr Budberg: "Igor Rodionov: I Am Bogged Down in the Struggle for Survival," *Moskovskiye Komsomolets*, April 12, 1997. Bruce Blair: *Global Zero Alert for Nuclear Forces* (Brookings Institution, 1995). Bruce Blair: "Where Would All the Missiles Go?" *Washington Post*, October 15, 1996. For a masterful account of the Norwegian missile incident, see Peter Pry: *War Scare* (Turner Publishing, forthcoming). "CIA Rates 'Low' the Risk of Unauthorized Use of Russian Nuclear Warheads," *Washington Post*, October 23, 1996. Colonel Robert Bykov: "We Could Launch an Accidental Nuclear Strike at the Enemy," *Komso-molskaya Pravda*, March 15, 1997. John B. Stewart, Jr.: "Re-thinking the Unthinkable: Russia's Evolving Nuclear Weapons Threat" (George C. Marshall Institute, Washington, D.C., 1996). Also the Jamestown Foundation's daily "Monitor" is use-ful for tracking the disintegration of the Russian military.

CHAPTER 14

Interviews with Dan Wagner and numerous players and others attending the Wild Atom game at the NDU, December 1996.

In addition we owe thanks to those who work full-time to alert the public to these issues, including William Potter and his col-leagues at the Monterey Institute of International Studies, Leo-nard Spector at the Carnegie Endowment for International

Peace, Tom Cochran and Stan Norris at the National Resources Defense Council and Graham Allison's team at the Center for Science and International Affairs at Harvard. Their material and assistance have been invaluable.

INDEX